Extreme Wine

Extreme Wine

Searching the World for the Best,
the Worst, the Outrageously Cheap,
the Insanely Overpriced,
and the Undiscovered

MIKE VESETH

ROWMAN & LITTLEFIELD
Lanham • Boulder • New York • Toronto • Plymouth, UK

Published by Rowman & Littlefield
4501 Forbes Boulevard, Suite 200, Lanham, Maryland 20706
www.rowman.com

10 Thornbury Road, Plymouth PL6 7PP, United Kingdom

Distributed by National Book Network

British Library Cataloguing in Publication Information Available

Library of Congress Cataloging-in-Publication Data

Veseth, Michael.
  Extreme wine : searching the world for the best, the worst, the outrageously cheap, the insanely overpriced, and the undiscovered / Mike Veseth.
     p. cm.
  Includes bibliographical references and index.
  ISBN 978-1-4422-1922-9 (cloth : alk. paper) — ISBN 978-1-4422-1924-3 (electronic)
  1. Wine and wine making. 2. Wine industry. I. Title.
  TP548.V46 2013
  663'.2—dc23

                                                                          2013006779

∞™ The paper used in this publication meets the minimum requirements of American National Standard for Information Sciences—Permanence of Paper for Printed Library Materials, ANSI/NISO Z39.48-1992.

Printed in the United States of America

Contents

World Distribution Of Vineyards*

(*including those producing table and drying grapes)

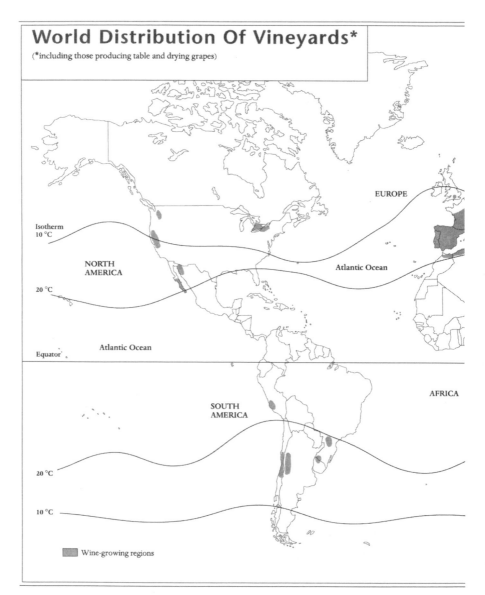

Wine-growing regions

The Wine Belt, where most of the world's quality wine grapes are grown, circles the globe from approximately 30 to 50 degrees of latitude in the northern and southern hemispheres. This map shows a more precise representation of the Wine Belt by identifying the zones where average growing season temperatures are between 10 and 20 degrees Celsius. Other factors also impact the location wine growing regions.

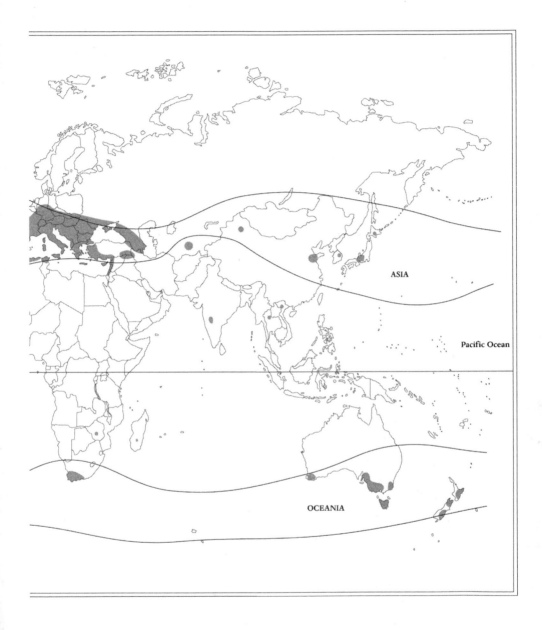

ASIA

Pacific Ocean

OCEANIA

X-Wines

In Vino Veritas?

Wine lovers do some extremely weird things in pursuit of their liquid passion. They sniff, swirl, and slurp to try to tease out all of the aroma and flavor notes. They spit out expensive wines (at fancy tastings) and then gulp down cheaper stuff at parties and receptions. They buy "cellar-worthy" wines in order not to drink them (at least right now). They invest, if that's the right word, in all sorts of wine-related paraphernalia, including specialized refrigerators and climate-controlled cellars, variety-specific crystal glasses (Riedel makes a special one for Pinot Noir from Oregon), high-tech rabbit-eared corkscrews, and mystical double-venturi aerator filter gadgets that make a vaguely obscene sound as the wine that is poured through them is transformed into a softer, more fully developed beverage.

The rituals of wine are complicated, esoteric, and, for newcomers, quite intimidating—no wonder so many people drink beer instead! One of the most peculiar is the habit wine people have of tilting their glasses at an angle and staring intently at the way the color of the wine changes from the center of the glass to the edge.

Here's how it's done. Fill your wineglass about one-third full and tilt it at a forty-five-degree angle over a white surface. (Personal confession: I sometimes wear long-sleeved white shirts to tastings so that I can be sure to have a clear background for inspecting the wine. Talk about weird behavior!) Look at the color at the center of the bowl and how it changes (if it does) toward the rim. Check the "telltale intensity" of the wine right at the edge. For red wines especially, the more intense (as opposed to watery) that extreme edge, the better the wine is likely to be, according to one expert.[1]

Tilt the glass "sideways"—that's what they say. It must look like a lot of silly navel-gazing to uninitiated spectators who may wonder why we don't just drink the damn stuff and get it over with. Tilting, swirling, sniffing—even spitting—searching for clues to the endlessly fascinating mystery of wine.

I like the idea that you can learn what is happening in the center of your wineglass by studying its extreme edge, and I decided to apply the same technique to the study of wine more generally. Writing for my blog, *The Wine Economist* (WineEconomist.com), I began to look for Extreme Wines (or X-Wines for short), figuring that I could learn something about how the world of wine is changing by looking closely at the outer edges, where the process of change will first become visible to the naked eye. The result of this experiment in sideways logic is the book you hold (probably at a forty-five-degree angle—sideways) in your hands right now.

X-WINE AND THE X GAMES

A lot of interesting things are revealed when you push something out to the limit. And I'm not just talking about wine. Sometimes you don't know what's really going on until you go to extremes. Take sports, for example, and the X Games in particular.

For many people the Olympic Games define the true essence of sport. The X Games, on the other hand, are sort of an extreme version of the Olympic Games. The Olympic Games were first organized in their present form in 1896 and were inspired by a philosophy captured in the Olympic Creed, which tells us that the most important thing is not to win, but to struggle. The Olympic motto, *Citius, Altius, Fortius* (Faster, Higher, Stronger), is about striving; it's not win, baby, win.

Now anyone who likes wine knows that it is good to struggle; aren't we always told that the best wines come from grapevines that are "stressed" in some way? But as soon as points are awarded and medal counts commence—and especially once media attention and corporate sponsorship are involved—all that noble struggle stuff (or a lot of it, anyway) disappears, and the pressure to win starts to build.

Enter the X Games. The X Games were not invented by philosophers or politicians; ESPN (the global television sports network) conceived of them as a purely commercial product and launched them in 1997. The X Games push everything to extremes. No "soft sports" like synchronized swimming or ice dancing, no matter how physically demanding they might be. X Games competition includes sports like motocross, BMX, and snowmobile racing; rally car competitions; and skateboard and snowboard tricks. The action is fast, the crashes frequent, and the noise, well, it sometimes rises to earsplitting levels—and that's just the crowd at the skateboard park.

Summer and Winter X Games feature fewer sports than the Olympic Games because they are intentionally made for television. No need to waste airtime on low-interest events like the biathlon (a wickedly difficult and demanding winter sport that combines cross-country skiing and rifle shooting). If the biathlon were an X Games event, it would probably involve surfers, not skiers, and they would be armed with AK-47s, not target rifles. And, of course, they would be shooting at each other. Bam!

The sports are chosen for their viewer appeal, pure and simple, and although I think the target audience is pretty young, I must admit that the excitement of some of the events transcends generational boundaries. X Games are held every year (forget about that four-year Olympic cycle), winter and summer, with regional competition franchises in Europe and Asia as well as the United States.

Olympic athletes compete for honor and a bronze, silver, or gold medal (plus fame and endorsement fortune, of course). X Games athletes get prize money in additional to the medals, with no effort made to disguise the economic incentive. Dollars are easier to add up than bronze, silver, and gold, so keeping score is a snap.

At this point, I think you should grab your smartphone (because if you are an X Games fan you probably have one) and check out some X Games video clips from ESPN.com. And then . . . well, you might want to ask why a wine book is telling you about over-the-top skateboarder or snowboarder tricks.

It's that extreme thing. Don't you see that the X Games are the edgy part of sport, just like the color at the rim of your sideways wineglass is the edgy part of the wine? The fact that they are so intense tells you that there is a lot going on, especially when the media and commercial elements are considered.

Look deeper and you will see the power of the X Games all the way through sports. It's not just the X Games anymore, it's all games. And it's not really a game, it's a business.

Once you've thought about it this way, you no longer see the X Games as an extreme version of other sports. Rather, you see all the other sports as tamer versions of the X Games. And those few sports that are completely different, that have retained the essence of their original values—I dunno, maybe the biathlon is one of them—they are the *real* extremes.

This is the method to my madness. I believe that studying the extremes on the outer edges of the world of wine will help us understand what is really going on at the center and reveal where the real extremes lie.

GEOGRAPHICAL EXTREMES: THE WINE BELT AND BEYOND

There are two bands that circle the globe at about latitudes 30 degrees to 50 degrees north and south that I call the Wine Belt. These broad bands are wine's historical and traditional homes. The northern band stretches across Europe and includes Italy, France, and Spain (which together account for more than half of all global wine production) as well as Germany, Austria, and Hungary. The United States, now the world's largest market for wine, sits comfortably in the northern belt, along with countries that may not immediately spring to mind but that are also key wine sources: Bulgaria, Moldova, Georgia, Lebanon, Israel, and China. (China is the world's sixth-largest wine producer as this is written and may someday overtake the US as the top wine market).

The southern Wine Belt covers much of the generally accepted New World of wine—South Africa, Australia, and New Zealand; Uruguay, Brazil, Chile, and Argentina. The list of countries is short, much shorter than the list of those in the northern band, because in the Southern Hemisphere these latitudes are mainly ocean—the landmasses are mainly farther north or south (Antarctica).

Generally speaking the Wine Belts are the areas where climatic conditions are favorable for growing *vitis vinifera*, the grape most commonly associated with wine. These belts are the customary boundaries of the wine world in terms of both production and consumption. Growing grapes and making wine anywhere else is an extreme activity, and there, of course, is where I think we should go.

There are lots of potential ports of call on our extreme wine tour. The index of *The Oxford Companion to Wine* lists forty-five countries, ranging from Afghanistan (A) through Zimbabwe (Z), in its "Rest of the World" wine region category.[2] Most of them are countries that we just don't associate with wine (Japan, for example, or Iran), but that lie within the Wine Belt. Others are at the physical extremes: Kenya and Ecuador are two countries that lie dead on the equator, for example—as unfriendly a latitude as you can imagine for viticulture. Or Bhutan and Nepal, both high in the Himalaya Mountains. And yet all manage somehow to grow grapes and make wine. It is incredible the extremes that people will go to for wine. Let me tell you about three examples.

ICEWINE: POLAR EXTREMES

Canada is known for a lot of great things: maple syrup, world-class hockey, Tim Hortons donuts, and the Royal Canadian Mounted Police. But it doesn't very often come up in discussions about wine. Canada, according to our collective imagination, is the great frozen north—they might drink a lot of wine (and they do), especially in French-speaking Montreal (oui, oui!), but they could never be a wine-producing country. What would they make—Tundra Red and Tundra White?

This extreme view of Canadian wine is a bit over the top, of course. Growing wine grapes up north in the Yukon is problematic, but viticulture is possible down south, near the US border. In fact, there are productive wine regions in both British Columbia and Ontario, where large bodies of water temper the harsh climate so that tree fruits and wine grapes both prosper. Canadian wine can be excellent, but it is Canada's remarkable extreme wine that has made it famous: icewine.

Icewine is a very particular product. The grapes for icewines are left on the vine long after regular grapes have been picked. By law, natural icewine in Canada can only be made from grapes that have been frozen to -7 degrees Celsius (17 degrees Fahrenheit) and harvested at minimum 35 degrees Brix. The juice, what is left of it, is highly concentrated, so each grape yields just a drop or so. Picking is done by hand, of course, since many clusters will have experienced mold or bird damage or fallen prey to disease.

Vidal Blanc is the grape of choice for Canadian icewine—its tough skin can stand up to harsh weather—along with lesser amounts of Riesling and other varieties. Most of Canada's icewine is produced in Ontario, where winemakers can pretty much count on frightfully low temperatures early in the winter season. But the first icewines came from out west in British Columbia. North America's first commercial icewine was made in 1978 by German-born Walter Hainle and his son Tilman of Hainle Vineyards Estate Winery in warm-sounding Peachland, British Columbia.

Canada didn't invent icewine (credit Austria with that) but it is the world's largest producer of this chilly elixir, making nearly a million liters in a good year, according to John Schreiner's authoritative *The Wines of Canada.*[3] Tiny bottles of icewine bring enormous prices—fifty dollars, one hundred dollars, even five hundred dollars and more for a half bottle at retail. Who pays these spectacular prices? Japan and other Asian countries are the largest export market. Icewine is the quintessential high-end gift wine—attractively sweet, beautifully packaged, and luxuriously expensive. Tourists snap up bottles at duty-free to take home to Asia.

I've heard that so much icewine is bought by Tokyo-bound travelers that some Canadian duty-free stores have special bonded facilities in Japan to make purchases more convenient. Pay at the airport in Canada, and pick up your icewine at baggage claim in Japan. Sweet! Icewines are so expensive and sought after in Asia that counterfeiting is a serious problem. Some experts believe that as much as 50 percent of the icewine sold in Taiwan is bogus—sweet wines from Canada and elsewhere that are doctored up and repackaged. The situation in China may be even worse.

Icewine clearly pushes the limits of wine making, both in the vineyard and in the cellar, and it depends of course upon natural conditions that threaten the vines themselves. It marks one boundary of the extreme wine world.

ETV: EXTREME-TERRAIN VITICULTURE

Intense cold is dangerous to all but the most rugged vines. In some cold climates (China, for example), they actually bury the vines in the fall, covering them with a thick insulating layer of soil, and dig them out each spring. This is just one of the extremes people go to for wine.

If cold is a threat, then obviously altitude is an enemy. Standard meteorological tables indicate that on average, temperature drops about 3.4 degrees Fahrenheit per one thousand feet of elevation gain (or 6.5 degrees Celsius per one thousand meters).[4] But sometimes altitude can compensate for latitude. This is one explanation for high-altitude vineyards in Nepal, for example, and for those in Salta, Argentina, up north near the Bolivian border, which are probably the highest in the world.

Bodega Colomé (now part of the Hess Family Estates group of wineries owned by Swiss financier and wine mogul Donald Hess) was the first winery in Argentina, founded in 1831 and constructed at an astounding 7,500 feet of altitude.[5] Colomé's Altura Maxima vineyard is perhaps the highest in the world, at more than ten thousand feet of elevation. Maximum temperatures are lower at this altitude extreme, of course, but sunlight is very intense (don't forget your sunscreen lotion if you visit) and the diurnal variation (difference between maximum and minimum daily temperature during the growing season) is very large. The grapes heat up during the day, developing sugar and flavors, then chill down at night, allowing acidity to remain high. This combination produces some quite exceptional grapes and distinctive wines. The landscape of these high desert vineyards is one definition of "extreme."

The opposite extreme? Vineyards on the moon! Well, not literally the moon, but it might as well be. It sure looks like the moon, and most of the references I've consulted somewhere make mention of the "lunar-like landscape." The photos do not disagree.

The moon in this case is an island about sixty miles off the coast of Africa.[6] It's called Lanzarote, and it is one of the Canary Islands. The environment is very unsuitable. The soil—well, there almost isn't any, because the island was created by repeated volcanic eruptions and the black rubble or grit doesn't seem like it would support much life. Rainfall is scarce, too, and hot winds that blow off the Sahara Desert somehow manage to reach here, making plant life of any kind pretty scarce. Grapevines in the wild like to grow where trees rise up so they can use them as trellises to reach up toward the sun. There are precious few trees on Lanzarote for wild grapes to climb.

And yet there are vines on Lanzarote, and wine is made here. Large conical depressions are dug into the black *picon* volcanic ash, with one to three vines planted at the bottom, where they are sheltered a bit from the harsh winds and can benefit from whatever rainwater runs into the crater. Low crescent stone walls offer further protection on the windward side. These vineyards look nothing at all like any I have seen elsewhere. They really do look like vines on the moon.

"Heroic viticulture," Jacques Fanet calls it, and I think he is right. But the hard work and determination of the Lanzarote vignerons would go unrewarded were it not for *picon*'s special trick. A heat pump, we all know, can pull warmth out of even the coldest winter's day's air. *Picon* pulls water out of hot, dry wind. It possesses the hydrostatic ability to condense what moisture there is in the dry air and fix it to the layers below, where the vines' roots search it out. It's magic. If there are vineyards on Prospero's unnamed island where Shakespeare's play *The Tempest* is set, I think they must look and work like this.

EXTREME WINE REFLECTIONS

And so our first extreme wine tour has taken us north to Canada, up to the heights of the Andes mountains, and down into volcanic craters. What do these extremes tell us about wine? Here's my take. Following wine to its physical extremes highlights the fact that, despite all the hoopla and hype, wine is still basically an agricultural product, not just another manufactured good. I say "not just" because we must accept that even the most "natural" wines are necessarily manipulated or manufactured to some extent. But with many or most of the products that we use every day, that manufactured aspect seems to dominate and, since manufacturing is seldom truly place-specific, the sense of somewhereness that wine lovers call *terroir* is easily missed. Wine, on the other hand, more than just about anything else, is (or can be) a somewhere thing.[7]

Perhaps the most important thing to take away from this first set of extreme wine cases is simple. Wine must be a very special thing for people to go to all the trouble (and expense) to produce it under such extreme circumstances. If wine were simply the sum of its constituent parts—water, acid, flavorings, and some alcohol—it wouldn't generate such a determined, dedicated response. Wine must speak to us in powerful ways to cause us to care so much about it. The fact that you've decided to spend time and maybe also money on this book already suggests that you have an unusually strong interest in wine. Perhaps this book will help you take it to extremes yourself.

A TALE OF CURSES, MIRACLES, AND REVENGE

One reason that I am interested in extreme wine is that I have spent so much time studying its opposite—the solid center of the wine world, the *vitis vinifera* equivalent of the traditional Olympic Games. Everyday ordinary wines— what you might call supermarket wines in some contexts—those are the kind of wine that I write about most often on *The Wine Economist*. That's my focus because these are the wines that people drink (as oppose to collect or invest in), and this is the part of the world of wine that affects the most people.

I wrote about the three big forces that have shaped this part of the wine world in my 2011 book *Wine Wars: The Curse of the Blue Nun, the Miracle of Two Buck Chuck, and the Revenge of the Terroirists.*[8] The book's subtitle is long and unwieldy, but I think it draws you into my story, which is all about curses, miracles, and revenge.

The Curse of the Blue Nun is globalization and the diabolical dilemma it creates. Globalization has pushed wine production and consumption to far corners of the earth, bringing aboard new consumers and new wine-making regions. The bounty of choices we have today in wine shops and supermarkets is one consequence of this process. The pressure to make simplified wines to satisfy a least-common-denominator global market is another.

That's where the curse part comes in. Blue Nun wine from Germany was originally a product of startlingly fine quality. It became the world's first global wine brand because of its quality and of course because of its effective brand identity—the Blue Nun label was and is enormously easier to understand than the complex descriptions found on typical German wines. So the Blue Nun flew around the world. The curse? Well, the opportunity to supply the bigger market pushed Blue Nun and other German producers to dilute the very quality that originally defined their wine. Globalization created Blue Nun and then destroyed it. (Blue Nun has returned as a quality wine again as global standards have risen.)

More choices are great . . . up to a point. There are so many wine choices available today that deciding what to buy is a real problem. Some confused consumers walk away in frustration—they end up with beer, soda, or water instead. Others go for bottles with cute animals on the label (we call them "critter wines"). The most common strategy is to use price as a guide. If it costs more, it must be better (alas, this is often not the case).

This is the Miracle of Two Buck Chuck. Two Buck Chuck (a.k.a. Charles Shaw wine) has been sold in the United States by Trader Joe's stores for as little as $1.99 per bottle. Consumers who wouldn't touch such cheap wine in other stores (if it's *that* cheap it must be *swill*) take it home by the case at Trader Joe's. Why? Because of the miracle: the trust that they have in Trader Joe's store brands. They trust Trader Joe's even more than price as a guarantor of quality.

Wine in the global age has become a confidence game—money and power flow to those who can give consumers the confidence they need to buy the wine they love in the face of an overwhelmingly confusing set of choices. Wine companies like Gallo in California or Möet Hennessy in France play the game by developing strong wine brands that buyers recognize and trust. Wine critics like Robert Parker and Jancis Robinson and wine publications like *Decanter* and *Wine Spectator* are influential as both players in this global game and referees. The current champions of the confidence game are probably the three retail chains that occupy the world wine-selling podium. The bronze medal goes to Aldi, the hard-discount retailer that sells the most wine in Germany. Costco, the number-one wine retailer in the US, gets the silver medal. And Tesco takes home the gold. Britain-based Tesco is the biggest wine retailer in the world, much of its sales from house-brand wines that trade on Tesco's reputation for quality.

The Miracle gives consumers more confidence, which is one reason why the world of wine is expanding so rapidly (except, paradoxically, in the traditional wine cultures of Europe, where wine drinking is in steep decline), but the Curse hasn't gone away. In fact, some would argue, the Miracle may magnify the Curse by putting pressure on winemakers to dumb down their wines or focus on particular features (to make "Parker wines," for example, designed to suit famous wine critic Robert Parker's palate).

That's why the Revenge of the Terroirists is so important. Terroirists are champions of terroir—that untranslatable French word that refers to a sense of time and place and is thrown about with gleeful abandon by wine enthusiasts (add that to the list of peculiar things we do). Terroirists resist the Curse and try to undermine the Miracle in order to protect and preserve wine's unique qualities.

There's more to *Wine Wars* than the simple story I have told here, of course. That's why I had to write a book. But these are the basic elements, and at the end of the book I reach an optimistic conclusion—our collective wineglass is at least half full. Globalization and the confidence game have both positive and negative effects on the wine world. Really, it could go either way—a world of great wine choices for every palate or a dreadful dark sea of despicable McWine. The key, I argued, are the terroirists. I hope they get their revenge, because it is necessary to balance the curses and miracles of modern wine. Vive les terroirists!

But I recognize that this belief is a matter of faith, and I need go beyond that. *In vino veritas*, it is said, in wine there is truth, and I think the truth will be revealed through the wine itself. The extremes of wine will tell us the truth about the rest.

GOING TO EXTREMES: THE PLAN OF THIS BOOK

What sort of extremes shall we explore? Space may be the final frontier in *Star Trek* reruns, but it was the first extreme we explored here, charting some of the wine world's edges and ending with a lunar landscape of vines. Time is another dimension that we could explore, looking at the oldest and newest wines. Archeological discoveries reported in 2011 indicate that surprisingly large-scale wine production was taking place in Armenia 6,100 years ago (no, they didn't find any unopened bottles or flasks, so we don't have any six-thousand-year-old tasting notes).[9] The find is important, researchers say, because it shows that wine was so important as to justify construction of a dedicated production facility. This comes as a surprise, I guess, because no one thought that ancient peoples would go to such extremes to provide a reliable source of wine.

The extremes of time and space are very interesting, but I want to dig deeper. I'm interested in extremes that are a bit edgier (extreme extremes, I guess) and subject to heated debate. So which extremes did I choose?

My list of extreme wines is partly inspired by Google, or by Google's users, in any case. WordPress, the company that hosts *The Wine Economist* blog along with thousands of other web pages, routinely reports a bounty of harmless data it has gathered from visitors to its websites. Among the thousands of bits of information collected is a list of search terms that prompted user visits. I can't find out who was looking for what (a good thing, I think, on the day that I posted an essay called "The Trouble with Wine Porn"), but I can see what questions brought the most wine enthusiasts to my door, and they have inspired many of the extremes that I explore in this book.

A lot of *The Wine Economist*'s readers are searching for the wine world's outer limits. "What is the best wine?" they ask. The best wine value? The best wine brand? The best wine magazine? (A few, according to the data, are searching for "world's best economist," and the fact that they end up at a wine blog suggests certain weaknesses in Google's algorithms!) Implicit in these queries, I think, is a certain anxiety. There are lots of wines out there and consumers are worried that they are choosing poorly, paying too much, or getting advice from biased or incompetent wine gurus. The search for the best is often motivated by fear of the worst.

So we will begin with the best and worst wines. Since there are many ways to think about what wines, wine styles, and wine regions might fit into this category (and there are differences of opinion within each one), this will certainly give us a number of dimensions to push to the extreme.

It is difficult to avoid money's (or media's) impact in the modern world. If you don't believe me, just pick up a major newspaper (or download one if, as is likely, you are reading this on some sort of electronic device) and compare the culture, sports, and business sections. Some days I find that the sports and culture pages are more intensely focused on business than the business pages themselves. So it is no surprise that I will want to examine the economic edges of the wine world, searching for the cheapest, most expensive, and most overpriced wines.

Media's influence points the way to other extremes that should be explored. Most famous (and forgotten)? Most infamous? And the sensationalist extremes of rarest (and most ubiquitous) and unique. Along the way we will explore extreme wine tourism, extreme wine people, extreme wine booms and busts, and of course, since we live in the age of celebrity, the predictable phenomenon of celebrity wine. The list of extreme questions that we can ask about wine is nearly endless, and there's nothing simple about the answers, especially if we go a bit deeper and ask why—what forces have pushed these wines to the edge? And how do these extreme forces reflect (or not) something deeper that is driving the wine world's deep currents?

I fear that I have exploited my *Wine Economist* readers rather ruthlessly in writing this book. I not only used their search queries as inspiration, I also mined their comments for insights as I tested out ideas and themes on the blog. Many of these experimental essays made their way into this book, much improved by the feedback, so thanks to my readers for their help. A few topics didn't survive critical scrutiny—extra special thanks to my readers for that! In the end I found myself with so many ideas to explore that I'm afraid I sometimes abruptly jump from one extreme to another. Try to stay with me when this happens—I think you'll enjoy the journey, however bumpy it sometimes gets.

Let me warn you that the news that we will gather on this journey will not always be good. It is impossible to look at wine (or anything else) through the lens of extremes like the *Lifestyles of the Rich and Famous* and come away entirely confident about its future. Sorry . . . it's only business. But you'll thank me for it when we are done.

IN VINO VERITAS

So what will we learn by gathering together all these wineglasses and tilting them at different angles and then arguing about what we see or don't see? Well, we will learn that wine lovers do silly things . . . but we already knew that, I guess. I also think we will learn that X-Wines are a lot like the X Games. What we see at the extreme is just a more intense reflection of what's happening everywhere. And what is really extreme will surprise you.

2

The Best and the Worst

My friend John used to travel a lot, and he liked to bring home little mementos to help him remember his experiences. Pretty soon he had a large collection, with corresponding pressure to add to it creatively on each travel occasion. The problem was choosing the right one—the best possible souvenir. There were always lots of possible choices, and it was never easy to choose. Sometimes, in fact, he came home empty-handed because he just couldn't decide which one was the perfect choice. (Wine enthusiasts may identify with the story so far, since choosing the right wine from among all the selections available in this global age is often equally challenging—and frustrating.)

Then John had one of those "aha!" moments. Instead of the *best* souvenir, he would look for the *worst* one—the cheapest (usually), tackiest (often), and most tasteless (nearly always) trinket for sale. Sometimes, but not always, John's choice had a thermometer embedded in it somewhere. (Worst thermometer souvenir—that would be an interesting specialty collection.) And it was almost always imported from some far-distant land and not a product of the country or region being visited. There were generally a number of good candidates for "worst souvenir," John told me, but somehow there was always one that stood out from the rest.

Best and worst are the inevitable extremes of our experience with wine, vacation souvenirs, and other types of consumer goods and, although they seem like extreme opposites, John's case shows that they are sometimes related in unexpected ways. For John it was best or worst—nothing in the middle held any interest at all.

I've been fortunate to taste a lot of good wine in my time, and I really can't decide which was the best. "Best" is very complicated and depends on many factors. But I have no trouble remembering my worst wine experience. Somehow Sue and I were appointed to the judging panel of a local amateur wine-making club event. We had to taste all the wines (about a dozen each red and white wines if memory serves) and then come up with a pair of winners.

The wines varied considerably in quality and style, as you might expect from nonprofessional efforts, and it wasn't easy to make sense of them or pick winners. Our choice for the top white wine, in fact, turned out not to be made of grapes at all! It was a pretty tasty sweet fig wine (which shows how confused the judges were). I think the red winner was a Zinfandel.

Somewhere in the group, however, was a bad, very bad wine. I know that because later that night all of the judges were violently ill. One of the wines must have had a bacteria problem that gave us all the typical symptoms of food poisoning. I won't go into any more details, but let's just say that it wasn't the long "finish" we were looking for. Worst wine ever!

THE WORST WINE: BOTTOM-FEEDER BLANC?

Fortunately for you, the reader, this book isn't all about my own worst-case-scenario wine experiences. The question is, "what are the worst wines in the world?" and I think it is appropriate to organize our search according to the method of police captain Louis Renault, played by Claude Rains in the 1942 film *Casablanca*. Let's round up all the "usual suspects" and look for a guilty party.

So where do you go looking for bad wines? That's easy: look down! Everyone knows that you shouldn't judge a book by its cover, but a surprising number of otherwise well-informed folks seem to judge a wine by its price. Maybe that's because you can't peek inside a bottle of wine and "read" a few pages before you buy it (something that is possible in online book sales today). So most wines are mysteries until we get them home and pull the cork. The one piece of data that is hard to dispute is the price, and it is an easy next step to the conclusion that if a wine is expensive it has to be good and, well, how can it be any good if it's so cheap?

There is a relationship between wine price and quality, but it is a very broad connection having to do with the quality and cost of the inputs. On a bottle-by-bottle level, however, there is often no relationship between price and perceived quality at all.

But let's embrace the prejudice for the moment and go with it. Where do you look for the cheapest wines (if you assume they are the worst)? Here's where the "look down" advice comes in. As I explained in my previous book *Wine Wars*, a common (but not universal) marketing strategy in a wine shop or supermarket aisle is to put the most expensive wines on the top shelf and the least expensive wines at the bottom. Thus the physical act of reaching up for the more expensive product is uplifting, while bending down to pick up the bargain brand feels like, well, like you are stooping, slumming, or otherwise humbling yourself. Bottom-shelf wine? Must be bottom-feeding rotgut!

Line up the usual suspects that come ashore when you throw out this net and you will find many familiar names. Here in the US, expect to find suspects with names like Charles Shaw (a.k.a. Trader Joe's stores' Two Buck Chuck), Carlo Rossi (Gallo), and Franzia (made by the Wine Group), among others. They all look guilty, based on the circumstantial evidence of low price, but like the usual suspects in *Casablanca*, they are all really innocent. You might not think that these wines are especially distinctive or have even a weak sense of terroir, but they are far from being the worst wines possible. In fact, they are surprisingly good!

Inexpensive wines were often quite horrible in the "bad old days" just a couple of decades ago, which is perhaps when the prejudice against them developed, but more expensive wines were frequently quite bad then, too. Jim Lapsley's history of wine making in Napa Valley, *Bottled Poetry*, makes it pretty clear how much the science and craft of wine making have improved in just a few years.[1] Although the importance of improved wine-making techniques may be most noticeable at the bottom of the wine wall, Benjamin Lewin's book *Wine Myths and Realities* argues effectively that they have been a powerful force throughout the world of wine.[2]

The bad wines of yesterday have become pretty good because the state of the art of wine making is constantly improving and the "trickle down" to the bottom shelf is really a raging cascade. Why? Economic incentives! As Jamie Goode and Sam Harrop explain in their excellent book *Authentic Wine*, small-scale wine producers may sometimes take chances with their wines in the quest for a personal style or other objectives, but the large-volume wineries that are responsible for most of the low-price wine available to us cannot afford the risk.[3] They need quality and consistency. "There isn't any market for funky or strangely flavoured wines in the commercial end of the marketplace," they write.[4]

Famous British wine critic Hugh Johnson noted this fact back in 1970 when he made his first visit to California.[5] He was particularly drawn to a wine that came from one of the state's leaders in wine research. With its labs and experiments, this winemaker was able to craft an inexpensive wine that was, Johnson thought, head and shoulders above the everyday wines that people drank back in the Old World. The wine that was so unexpectedly good (for its price)? Gallo Chablis poured from a half-gallon jug.

Competition is the other big factor to consider. Competition at the bottom of the wine wall is fierce, and because these are branded products, reputations are at stake. Bad wine can exact a high long-run cost. But good wine can do miracles. When the Trader Joe's chain began selling the Charles Shaw wine made by Bronco Wine Company, it unleashed a quality chain reaction. Other inexpensive wines had to raise their game, and so did the wines selling just above them on the shelf. Why pay five dollars when you can get wine just as good for two dollars or three dollars? And when five-dollar wines improved, that put the pressure on the seven-dollar price point, and so on.

Two Buck Chuck isn't the only source of competition, however. Globalization brings a world of wines to your doorstep. Many countries erected barriers to keep international wines away in the bad old days, which encouraged sloppy domestic wine making. Now that the global competition is there at all levels of the wine market, no volume producer of wine can make a mistake. My terroirist friends think I'm crazy when I say it, but cheap wines today are far from the worst thing you can buy here in the United States. Next suspect!

WORST WINE: WHAT'S THE WORD? THUNDERBIRD!

If the worst wine isn't on the bottom shelf, where is it? Imagine that you are standing in a wine shop or supermarket wine aisle and look around you for a likely target. Maybe the bag-in-box products or Tetra Pak wines that look like supersized juice boxes? You might be suspicious of the alternative packaging of these wines, but bags and boxes are perfectly good containers for wine that will be consumed within a year or so of release (don't even think about aging these wines). The wine in these containers is perfectly sound and not always even cheap anymore, as even bag-in-box wines have moved upscale in terms of both price and quality.

Okay, how about cheap fortified wines like Thunderbird, Wild Irish Rose, MD 20/20, and Night Train? Well, maybe you are onto something here, so let's take a closer look.

Extra alcohol is added to these wines to "fortify" them and their users. They can be a cheap and convenient escape and are often associated with alcoholism among the poor and homeless. Several US cities have actually imposed bans on the sale of these items (and high-alcohol malt-liquor products, too) in certain designated zones in an attempt to discourage public drunkenness.

If fortified wines are candidates for the "worst wine" award, it must be said that they are also in the running for "best wine." Vintage Port wines and fine Sherries are some of the most exquisite liquids in the world. The purpose of the alcohol isn't to give you a buzz, however. The brandy that is added to Port stops fermentation (by killing the yeast), leaving a wonderful sweet wine that is very stable and safe to ship. The alcohol acts as a preservative. Alcohol is added when Sherry is produced because "flor," the cap of fermentation yeasts that accounts for many of Sherry's distinctive flavors, can only survive within a fairly narrow range of 14.5 to 16.0 percent alcohol.

Just adding alcohol to wine (or making the wine so that alcohol is quite prominent) doesn't make it bad, but it doesn't necessarily make it good, either. Sometimes it has nothing to do with the wine, really, and is just a way to skirt government regulations. For many (post-Prohibition) years here in Washington State taverns were forbidden to serve spirits. Weak beer and wine were all that was allowed, although, for some reason, the wine could legally contain up to 18 percent alcohol by volume, much more than the beer could legally contain, which made wine an attractive option for pub patrons looking for a jolt. It did not take very long for the local wine industry to supply the demand for sweet high-alcohol grape drinks that were wine in a technical but not an aesthetic sense. It *did* take a long time, alas, for the industry to rediscover its quality-wine roots. I tell this story not because Washington's bad experience with wines of this sort is so unusual but rather because it is so typical of similar times around the world.

Several of the most successful early national wine brands were fortified wines. Richards Wild Irish Rose, for example, was the very profitable foundation of the company that evolved into Constellation Brands—the largest wine company in the world until it sold off its Australian wine portfolio in 2011 and yielded the top spot to E&J Gallo.

Gallo is famous for its own fortified product, Thunderbird, which was inspired by a 1950s salesman's visit to a liquor store, where he saw packets of lemon-lime Kool-Aid attached with rubber bands to big bottles of inexpensive Gallo White Port. The do-it-yourself market for a high-test lemon-flavored sweet wine was there even before the finished product. Thunderbird was a marketing success for many reasons—the wine itself was technically sound even if it might not have been your personal choice; the name (the same as a popular Ford sports sedan), the packaging, and even the radio jingle were all appealing. "What's the word? Thunderbird. / How's it sold? Good and cold. / What's the jive? Bird's alive. / What's the price? Thirty twice." Who could resist?

But wines like Thunderbird and "Mad Dog" MD 20/20 (which originally signified 20 percent alcohol by volume in a twenty-ounce bottle) are far from the world's worst fortified wines. For my money (poor choice of words—I don't think I'm ready to buy any of these wines), the worst-in-class prize goes to a wine made in England from a 130-year-old recipe that originated with Benedictine monks. Yes, I'm talking about Buckfast Tonic Wine.

Buckfast (for Buckfast Abbey, where the monks hold forth) is the modern incarnation of a traditional wine style. Tonics, fortified with alcohol or other substances, were once very popular (guess what the stimulant was in the original version of Coca-Cola!). Buckfast is syrupy sweet, fairly alcoholic (15 percent), and laced with caffeine at a higher concentration than Red Bull. I think it might be carbonated, but it is such a thick syrup that it's hard to tell. Consumed in large quantities (the recommended technique is to drink directly from the bottle, perhaps to avoid the distinctive aroma), it has been singled out by police in Ireland and Scotland as an enabling factor in a wide range of serious and violent crimes, some of which are committed using the Buckfast bottle itself as a weapon.

The Buckfast Abbey monks began making their tonic wine in the 1880s, importing base wine from France, adding their own ingredients, and selling it directly to consumers who sought its medicinal benefits. The wine was transformed into its current state by the unintended consequences of government policies. Direct sales were forbidden starting in the 1920s, so a private company contracted with the monks to market and sell the product. The limited output of the original quaint facilities was transformed by the profit motive into the alleged danger to public safety we see today. Claims of health benefits have long ago disappeared.

Inexpensive fortified wines . . . and even Buckfast Tonic Wine . . . can be very bad, but are they the worst wines on your supermarket or wine-shop shelves? Incredibly, the answer is no! These wines might not taste very good (a matter of personal preference, I suppose), and I'm sure they aren't very good for you, either, especially when consumed in ill-advisedly large quantities. But there are worse-tasting and potentially more dangerous wines out there disguised as quality products.

WORST WINE? AND THE WINNER IS . . .

So I have bad news for you. The worst wines are scattered everywhere, hidden, disguised, and ready to strike you. They are actually less likely to be found among the cheapest wines or fortified wines because wine-making technology and high alcohol content respectively generally protect these wines from the sort of wine faults that can ruin your wine experience and sometimes make you downright sick.

I had the opportunity to understand what really bad wine is like when I attended a professional wine faults workshop organized and taught by Amy Mumma, who was then director of the World Wine Program at Central Washington University. Amy's background is in biochemistry, and this gives her an unusual ability to detect and analyze wine flaws and advise wineries (something that the legendary Émile Peynaud was famous for). To steal a line from *Ghostbusters*, Amy is the answer to the question "Who ya gonna call?" when something goes badly wrong with your wine.

Amy led my group of about fifty wine professionals through a tasting of twelve wines that illustrated different fundamental flaws, ranging from what was probably a simple shipping problem (the wine "cooked" when its shipping container got too hot) to a palate-destroying example of a badly corked wine. When retailers are suspicious that a wine on their shelves may be faulty, they call Amy and, if the problem is bad enough, she buys the bottles for use in her classes. All of the flawed wines we sampled were purchased through normal retail channels. No telling how many similarly flawed wines consumers took home before Amy was called in to make her diagnosis. No telling how many of them you and I might have purchased, either.

One wine really got my attention. A white wine, it had a foul nose and looked a little cloudy. Don't drink it, Amy said, but look very closely at the wine. What do you see? Silky black strands? Strands of bacteria that poor technical wine-making practices allowed to happen. No, they probably won't kill you, she said, but they could make you feel very sick. I don't think anyone felt lucky enough to risk taking a sip.

The worst wine we sampled was a real dog (no offense to canines intended). It was a Merlot plagued by the thankfully rare "perfect storm" combination of reduction, oxidation, and Brettanomyces. It looked bad, smelled bad, and tasted (gasp!) horrible. Certainly one of the worst wines I've ever tried. Drawing upon her science background, Amy was able to explain to us how this awful combination of defects occurred, but the question of why anyone would try to sell it remains. Ignorance? Incompetence? Arrogance? Cash-flow demands? Hard to say. Some wine flaws (like the "cooked" wine) can happen after wine leaves the maker's control, but many of the flawed wines on retail shelves were already in bad shape when they left the warehouse. No excuse for this. Reputation is critically important in the wine business, and it is established (or destroyed) one bottle at a time.

Are cheap wines more likely to have flaws like this? No, Amy said, the high-volume wines get too much quality-control attention for a seriously flawed wine to get out, although cork taint can happen to anyone. Very expensive wines, such as a high-end Burgundy she had set aside for class use, can be ruined, too. Disappointingly, she said, some of the most badly flawed wines come from the sort of small producers that terroirists like me are predisposed to support.

Amy's class was great—she's a wonderful teacher—and gave us a lot of useful tools for detecting and understanding wine flaws and for dealing with related trade and consumer issues. Amy answered all our questions but one: who made these awful wines? She kept the makers secret, so I can't report them here, but the fact is that your personal worst wine could be almost anywhere on the wine shelf just waiting for you to pull its cork.

What's the worst wine you've ever tasted? I asked Amy. You may not want to know her answer. The worst wine Amy ever sampled smelled and tasted like somebody urinated in a tin can of clams, she said. Seriously. Absolutely disgusting. The smell was the result of a process of putrification caused by high levels of bacteria, and the wine was discovered on the shelf, retail-price, in wine shops. "I think some of the worst have been high levels of mercaptans or those with excessive ethyl acetate that you can't even get near your face without your eyes watering," she said.

That's my selection for the World's Worst Wine, and I am glad I didn't have to taste it. In fact, I suppose that the good news about the worst wine category is that the standard of quality in the global wine market is so high that really, really foul wines are rare, even if they are not quite rare enough for comfort. So what's the opposite—the best wine? Well, as they say on Facebook, it's complicated.

THE BEST WINE BY THE NUMBERS

Wine critics taste thousands of different wines each year and often travel the world to seek out hard-to-find gems, so their ratings are a logical place to look in search of the best wine. What are the critics' favorite wines as indicated by their published reviews? Apparently I am not the first person to ask this question, because the editors at the very useful website Wine-Searcher.com have collected data on the top scores given by several critics.[6] Here's my analysis of this treasure trove of data.

Stephen Tanzer is apparently the toughest "grader" of the four sets of ratings I consulted on the Wine-Searcher.com listings: as of this writing he has only given one wine—a 2010 Egon Muller-Scharzhof Scharzhofberger Riesling Trockenbeerenauslese from the Mosel, Germany—a "perfect" score, which would be one hundred out of one hundred using the grade scale he employs. As of February 2011, however, he had given fourteen wines his highest score of ninety-nine points. None of them were famous first-growth Bordeaux. In fact, none of them were Bordeaux wines at all, and only three were even from France—a 2003 Domaine Jean-Louis Chave Hermitage Cuvée Cathelin, a 1996 Krug Brut Vintage Champagne, and a 1978 Guigal Côte-Rôtie La Mouline. (Tanzer recently gave very high ninety-seven to one hundred estimated scores to barrel samples of the top Bordeaux wines of the 2009 vintage.)

Interestingly, all eleven of the other wines on the Tanzer ninety-nine list are from Germany or Austria and are, like his sole one-hundred-pointer, made in the style known as Trockenbeerenauslese (thankfully abbreviated in most wine conversations as TBA). TBAs (usually but not always made from Riesling grapes) are precious works of art made from individually selected late-harvest grapes that have been infected by the "noble rot" of botrytis, which gives the sweet but balanced wines exceptional depth of flavor. For Tanzer it seems the best TBA wines must be transcendental, while everything else (or nearly everything) is just wine, however great it might be.

PARKER'S PERFECT PICKS AND ROBINSON'S 20/20S

Robert Parker, like Tanzer, is an American and so perhaps unsurprisingly also uses the one-hundred-point scale popular in American schools (Parker is generally credited with inventing or at least popularizing the one-hundred-point wine-rating system). But Parker does give one-hundred-point "perfect scores" to wine. Indeed, he has given a lot of them over the years, so either he tastes more wines than Tanzer, or maybe he tastes better wines, or perhaps he is just an easy grader. Hard to know. A printout of the list of one-hundred-point Parker wines goes on for more than five pages.

What is especially noteworthy about Parker's ratings is the fact that he has been able to taste many vintages of these wines, usually in the course of annual regional tasting trips, but sometimes at special events when wines that are almost literally impossible to find are brought out. I wish I was there the night they opened the one-hundred-point bottles of Château d'Yquem from the 1811 and 1847 vintages. Imagine a wine that is two hundred years old and still first class. What an amazing experience that must have been.

Parker's treasure trove of reviews gives us a different way of thinking about the best wine. Of all the wines he has tasted, which wines earned the most one-hundred-point scores? Château d'Yquem did it three times, for example, 1811, 1847, and 2003. That's pretty good, but not as good as Château Pétrus. Pétrus has had seven one-hundred-point Parker vintages (1921, 1929, 1947, 1961, 1989, 1990, and 2000). Guigal Côte-Rôtie La Landonne ties Pétrus with seven one-hundred-point years. But the winner is Guigal Côte-Rôtie La Mouline with nine! This wine is a dry Syrah from the northern Rhône Valley. Parker said that it "offers a stunning perfume of espresso roast, licorice, pepper, blackberries, and black cherries intermixed with hints of chocolate and spring flowers."[7] Taken together, the three top Guigal wines (from three different vineyards) have received the one-hundred-point rating an astounding twenty-one times.

Rhône and Rhône-style wines figure prominently at the top of the Parker table, but Trockenbeerenauslese wines do not, an indication that even at the top end among those with the best-trained palates, wine is still a matter of personal taste. (To be fair, I must note that Parker has given one-hundred-point scores to several wines that are very much like TBAs, including three vintages of a Donnhoff Riesling Eiswein from Germany's Nahe Valley.)

Jancis Robinson is British, and perhaps that explains why she uses the twenty-point rating scale (half points allowed) that is also used by *Decanter* magazine and is also the choice of wine gurus at the University of California at Davis. Robinson is not so stingy as Tanzer nor so generous as Parker. Unlike Tanzer she does give "perfect" 20/20 scores, but not so many perfect scores as Robert Parker. Several wines earned the 20/20 score more than once and, judging as we did with Parker, her top wine would be Château d'Yquem, which received the perfect score for seven different vintages (1811, 1831, 1847, 1921, 1945, 1983, and 1990, if you are keeping track). Clearly with great wines like d'Yquem, the number of high marks you give depends on how many different opportunities you have to sample it, if you are lucky enough to taste these rare wines at all.

Château Cheval Blanc comes second, with five top-ranked vintages. Guigal Côte-Rôtie La Mouline was third, with four 20/20 scores on the day I checked, followed by the Domaine de la Romanée-Conti and Spain's Vega Sicilia Unico, with three each. I had an opportunity to ask Jancis Robinson to reveal her favorite wines, and she said that particular bottles (at particular moments) stood out. One was a magnum of 1947 Cheval Blanc that was the best red-wine tasting experience of her life. A bottle of 1978 Domaine de la Romanée-Conti Montrachet (which does not appear on the 20/20 list—perhaps the rating wasn't published) stood out as the best white wine.

THE PEOPLE'S CHOICE?

If you want to know what wine drinkers and collectors (and not just wine critics) think about wine, go to www.CellarTracker.com. Founded in 2004 by Eric LeVine (voted Wine Person of the Decade by the readers of the *Dr. Vino* blog), CellarTracker is the most important "social media" wine resource on the web. It is, first of all, a wine-cellar management tool (hence the "cellar tracker" title) where more than 230,000 users keep track of their collections. As of December 2012 their combined cellars held more than thirty-seven million bottles of wine.

If CellarTracker were just a database program to log wine in and out and keep track of its value, it would be pretty useful but perhaps not exceptional. What sets CellarTracker apart are the reviews.

CellarTracker is the people's wine critic mother ship. Members post their own ratings (one-hundred-point scale) and tasting notes that can be viewed, reviewed, and compared by anyone with an Internet connection or a smartphone link.[8] The depth and quality of the reviews varies, of course. Some CellarTracker users are clearly masters of particular wine types and regions, providing real expert opinions, while others appear to be enthusiastic amateurs, so CellarTracker ratings must be taken with a grain of salt (like all wine ratings). Still, it is interesting to see what wines were rated the best of the best by this broad group of consumers and collectors.

The list of top-rated wines for 2010 (published by Wine-Searcher.com) is instructive. No wine received a one-hundred-point average rating, but a 2005 Syrah with the audacious name The 17th Nail in My Cranium from cult California producer Sine Qua Non managed an incredible 98.9 mean score. A 2002 Syrah called Heart Chorea from the same maker came in fourth on the list with a 98.3 average rating. Number two with 98.8 points was a 1982 first-growth Bordeaux from Château Latour. A 1990 Krug vintage Champagne Clos du Mesnil earned third place with 98.6 points. The 2001 vintage of Château d'Yquem placed joint fifth alongside a Châteauneuf-du-Pape and a Napa Valley Cabernet.

I don't have the raw data from the ratings, so I can't tell you if there is a statistically significant difference between the average scores of the top wines. All of these are very limited-production wines, so I do not expect that there were hundreds of reviews for each one of them. Perhaps, therefore, it is appropriate to lump these wines (along with others at the top of the table) as collective "best wines."

As long as I'm on the subject of "people's choice" best wines I might as well lay my own cards on the table. I am not an expert wine taster and I do not rate or review wines, but I do have opinions and I think the best wines I have ever tasted were the ones that were served at the Riesling Rendezvous conferences organized by Château Ste. Michelle and Ernest Loosen, Riesling makers from Washington State and Germany respectively. Three dry Rieslings from Nikolaihof (Wachau, Austria) and three Spätlese Rieslings from Dönnhoff (Nahe

Valley, Germany) that were served in a session organized by Riesling expert Terry Theise stand out in my memory.

BEST AND WORST: NOTES FROM THE EDGE

What can we learn from this examination of the best and worst in wine? Some conclusions come quickly. It is easy to think that the best wines are the most expensive and the worst ones the cheapest, and this turns out to be untrue. Although none of the wines included in on the "best" lists here fall into the Two Buck Chuck category, some at least can be purchased without taking out a second mortgage on your home—the Rieslings in particular, although the Riesling Eisweins and Trokenbeerenausleses can cost a pretty penny.

More concretely, the cheapest wines are not the worst. They may be high-volume, mass-produced wines that aim for homogeneous quality rather than distinctive character, but they rarely suffer the repulsive faults of the worst wines, simply because they are so carefully monitored during production. When these wines go bad, it is because they fall victim to disasters than can strike any wine, cheap or dear: tainted corks, for example, or being left too long in an overheated railcar or delivery truck. Corked or cooked they may be, but not inherently awful.

The worst wines are the result of wine making that is often careless but sometimes simply extreme, as when deeply committed "natural wine" advocates try to produce completely "sulfite-free" wines. The risk of allowing wine faults to creep in may be justified by the reward of making a wine that flirts with perfection in some way—in this case as perfectly natural as can be.[9] But not everyone will agree that the reward is worth the risk.

Sometimes the best and the worst are separated by tiny margins. Château Beaucastel, for example, is a Rhône Valley maker of some of the most highly rated wines in the world (wines that appear on many of the lists discussed here). They are, according to some, also frequently plagued by the wine fault Brettanomyces ("Brett" in the industry). Brett is a yeast that produces compounds that can be seen as positive wine features in small quantities (smoke, bacon, or spice, for example) or as negative (Band-Aids, barnyard, sweaty saddle), depending upon the particular compounds in the wine and the sensory threshold of the wine drinker. Pushing certain wines to the edge to gain the positives risks falling over the edge.

The best wines on the lists we've seen here also go to extremes. The top Syrah wines from the Rhône and California on our lists go to extremes in many respects, including aging wines in new French oak barrels for over three years. The TBAs that Tanzer treasures push the extremes in another way, hanging on the vine weeks and weeks after the usual harvest. Quantities are necessarily limited for wines that go to such extremes, but I guess it's the qualities that count.

Best and worst? It's a subjective judgment, of course, and we can agree to disagree on that basis. But it seems to me that it's the extreme wines that push the envelope at both ends!

3

The Fame Game

MOST FAMOUS, MOST FORGOTTEN, AND MOST INFAMOUS

Fifteen minutes of fame. Back in 1968 artist Andy Warhol predicted that, in the future, everyone would be famous for fifteen minutes. Fame, in other words, would become a devalued commodity, bestowed for fairly trivial accomplishments and, perhaps for that reason, soon withdrawn. The public's attention span and the half-life of celebrity would both be very short.

The future is now, I suppose, and Warhol's forecast does not seem far from the mark. Reality television creates and destroys fame at a rate not far behind Warhol's four-per-hour production rate. Many celebrities, it seems, are famous for being famous rather than for some notable accomplish or newsworthy act.

These social forces have naturally affected the world of wine, too. Winemakers do not just make wine, they are "rock star" celebrities. Wine competitions have proliferated so that gold medals abound, giving each winner that momentary glow. Wine critics and writers release scores of lists each year naming the top wines in dozens of categories, ranging from *Wine Spectator*'s tidy Top 100 to *Decanter*'s massive World Wine Awards to more modest and focused ratings, like the ten best-value rosé wines for summer sipping on a sunny deck. Each list focuses a spotlight on the top wines, giving them a momentary lift that lasts until the next list appears.

Under these circumstances it seems like one should either embrace celebrity in all its jaded glory or reject it completely. Halfway "guilty pleasure" measures (like surreptitiously reading *People* magazine in the dentist's office waiting room) are undignified. And anyway, someone is bound to catch you in the act. If fleeting fame is the norm, in wine as in all else these days, then we need to push to the extremes: the most famous wines, the most *infamous*, and finally the wines that have fallen the furthest on the celebrity scale, the most forgotten. Let's see what we can learn about wine today by probing these famous extremes.

THE NIGHT THEY (THE BRITISH) INVENTED CHAMPAGNE!

Although nothing about fame and fortune is uncontroversial, I am fairly confident that the world's most famous (or at least most recognized and aspired to) type of wine is Champagne. Even people who cannot tell Burgundy from Bordeaux without an atlas (or with one, for that matter) can tell you something about Champagne. It's the bubbles, I suppose, and the way they tickle your nose. No, on second thought, it's really something else.

Champagne is of course the sparkling wine that comes from the eponymous Champagne region of France and is fermented in the bottle using the traditional *méthode champenoise*. It is also incorrectly a term generally applied to sparkling wines made elsewhere using a variety of production methods, a fact that has led to all manner of international negotiations and lawsuits instigated by the French producers, who are keen to protect their valuable intellectual property. Here in the United States, Champagne can only come from Champagne, except for several brands of sparkling wine whose names were grandfathered into a trade agreement specifying the legal use of regional designations. Thus can you find cheap and cheerful Cook's California Champagne, which has nothing in common with its French namesake except the name, in the same general supermarket region with authentic products costing five or ten times as much.

The key to appreciating Champagne, in my opinion, is not so much the bubbles but the irony. Although Champagne is France's best-known wine, it is certainly not made from the best wines of France. The Champagne region itself is viticulturally marginal—its wines tend to be acidic and thin, not full and robust. The wines of Champagne would be unlikely candidates for global distribution in their base form, by which I mean made using the same fermentation techniques generally employed elsewhere. But sparkling wines are subject to additional processing, and acidic wines like those of Champagne, made from only marginally ripe grapes, are just the thing to use as a base for the secondary fermentation that produces the bubbles and effectively creates Champagne.

A second irony is that the magical process that is responsible for Champagne's effervescence was invented by the British and not the French—one of many fascinating facts to be found in the 2010 book *Wine Myths and Realities* by Benjamin Lewin, MW.[1] The Royal Society in London published a paper on the production of sparkling wine in 1662, according to Lewin, predating the first known production of bubbly in Champagne in 1695. British glass was stronger and could withstand the greater stress of pressurized bottles, giving them an unexploited technological "first mover" advantage. Apparently the story that Champagne was invented by the cellar-master monk Dom Pérignon is just that—a story. If anything, Lewin suggests, Dom Pérignon probably worked to get bubbles *out of* his wine to prevent the bottles from exploding. Apparently, cold winters in the region stopped fermentation prematurely, only for it to resume in the spring after the wine was in bottles. What a mess!

It is a final irony that famous Champagne is so characteristically unlike most of the wines in the world and is thus in a way an unreliable representative, especially for people who pretty much only experience wine through ritual Champagne toasts. For wine enthusiasts the ideal wine is one that captures a particular time and place—a wine that is "made in the vineyard" as we like to say, that reflects local terroir and vintage variation. If the wine is as natural as possible, that is an added bonus. Significantly, most Champagne that is drunk in the world is none of these things. Champagne is made in the cellar, not the vineyard. The manipulation that converts the thin base wines into festive sparklers happens behind the scenes and often literally underground. The best-selling Champagnes are manufactured to match a uniform "house style" standard year in and year out. They are thus blends of base wines from many different parts of the Champagne region and from several different years. The goal is generally *not* to make the best wine possible from the grapes from this year's harvest, but rather to make this year's wine indistinguishable from last year's or next year's so as not to undermine in any way a buyer's loyalty to "the brand." Vintage Champagnes exist, of course, and "grower

Champagnes" that reflect local terroir also exist, but they are the exception to the rule; they are not the wines that made Champagne famous.

The most famous wine is not much like wine at all, when you think about it. In fact, I have observed that most people don't even taste it when they drink it. They simply enjoy the way it makes them feel and the experience it creates. When I organized a formal sparkling wine tasting for my university students, they were surprised to discover the actual flavors of Champagne, especially when they spit!

IT'S ALL IN HOW YOU SELL IT, DEAR

The key to Champagne's glory is marketing. In fact, from an economic stand-point, you might say that Champagne isn't made in the vineyard or the cellar but rather at the advertising agency. Champagne is the most heavily promoted wine on earth. This is one reason it is so expensive. The economic breakdown of a typical bottle of Champagne, according to Lewin, looks like this:

Wine grapes ($10) + production cost ($3) + promotion ($16) + producer profits ($5) + retail margin ($15–25) = retail price ($49–59).[2]

Even though production costs are high (high land prices in the Champagne region are to blame as well as costly cellar manipulation), Champagne is even more expensive to promote than it is to make. The focus on marketing is nothing new. Champagne producers have always sought to associate them-selves and their products with celebrities, first and perhaps most famously with the French royal court and then with royalty and elites everywhere. Then as now, celebrity placement is invaluable. In recent years, for example, hip-hop artists have been very influential in promoting Champagne to a new generation of consumers. Louis Roderer's ultraexpensive Cristal Champagne, originally created in 1876 for the Czar Alexander II, has benefited from its association with artists like Puff Daddy and Jay-Z, who made reference to the brand in their music in addition to notorious public displays of conspicuous consumption. (Jay-Z has subsequently disassociated himself from the brand.)

Significantly, from the standpoint of fame, Champagne is not promoted as an independent luxury good but rather as a critical element in a luxury lifestyle that includes many other extreme goods, services, and experiences, such as watches and jewelry, designer fashion, leather goods, cosmetics, and so forth. If you want to see how all these pieces fit together into a bubble-friendly luxury lifestyle (but you don't have time to go where the beautiful

people hang out in your part of the world) just aim your web browser at www
.lvmh.com, which is the website for Möet Hennessy Louis Vuitton, the king of
the hill when it comes to the global luxury-goods business. The firm, always
spelled out Möet Hennessy Louis Vuitton but always abbreviated LVMH, is
the result of the merger of luxury drinks company Möet Hennessy and luxury
luggage, bag, and accessory maker Louis Vuitton. Here is a partial list of the
multinational conglomerate's famous brands:

- Fashion: Louis Vuitton, Givenchy, Céline, Emilio Pucci, Thomas Pink,
  Marc Jacobs, Donna Karan, Fendi
- Watches and jewelry: TAG Heuer, Zenith, Bulgari, DeBeers
- Perfumes and cosmetics: Christian Dior, Guerlain, Parfums Givenchy,
  Acqua di Parma
- Retailing: DFS, Sephora, Le Bon Marché Rive Gauche, La Samaritaine
- Wine and spirits: Möet & Chandon, Dom Pérignon, Veuve Clicquot,
  Krug, Mercier, Château d'Yquem, Hennessy, Belvedere (Poland), Glen-
  morangie (Scotland), plus many international sparkling wine and
  superpremium wine brands, including Domaine Chandon (US), Cape
  Mentelle (Australia), and Cloudy Bay (New Zealand)
- Other activities: Group Les Echoes (a media group specializing in busi-
  ness, finance, art, and culture) and Royal Van Lent (world leader in the
  construction of luxury superyachts).

Möet Hennessy Louis Vuitton is thus best seen *not* as a Champagne and
handbag company but as a firm that specializes in creating and marketing the
bits and pieces of a comprehensive luxury lifestyle to global elites with substantial discretionary income (or deep lines of credit). Any one of these products gets the company's foot in the door, and the rest just follow naturally.

Champagne is famous, therefore, in part because it isn't really just wine.
It is really fame (and luxury) itself. That's why even people who don't know
what Champagne tastes like will nonetheless enjoy the way it makes them feel.
And although other Champagne houses are perhaps not so transparently devoted to the fame game as LVMH, they play the game and take the winnings.

Since this is a book about extreme wine, I must report that there is a race
underway to create the most extreme expression of Champagne. This super-
cuvée frenzy is a manifestation of what Robert H. Frank has called luxury

fever.[3] Luxury goods are often also positional goods. Their inherent qualities are only part of what makes them desirable. The fact that others can't or don't have them adds to the allure, completing the package. It is kind of an arms race, I suppose, because the players all want to have the rarest, most exclusive, most expensive Champagne, and once one of them has it, everyone else feels the need to top it. Like a real arms race, being ahead of the pack matters even if, as with a real arms race, at some point getting further ahead doesn't really do you any good and might actually bankrupt you. Luxury wines are only one example of luxury fever—and probably not even the best one—but I'm sure you see how the luxury arms race works.

Dom Pérignon is the most famous of the luxury cuvées, if you don't count Cristal's recent rise to hip-hop celebrity. It is to ordinary Champagne as Champagne is to an inexpensive Spanish Cava (as good as that can be) in terms of its ability to impress or create a memorable moment. Dom Pérignon is a vintage Champagne, which makes it more exclusive than the basic non-vintage bubbles—plus it has that cool bottle and years and years of promotion behind it. But once all your friends are drinking Dom, you need to step up a cuvée notch or fall behind. Dom Pérignon Oenothèque was created to quench this desperate thirst. Oenothèque wines are drawn from the maker's reserves (its wine library, hence the name). So whereas your friends are probably drinking the ordinary 2002 vintage Dom they bought down at the big-box discount store (or maybe the 2002 Dom Rosé, which is more exclusive and costs about twice as much), you can double down them both with your bottle of übercool 1999 Oenothèque. It's a winner every time—at least until something even more expensive and difficult to obtain comes around.

As you can see, Champagne's fame is no accident—it is carefully calculated at every step along the way. No wonder it is the most famous type or style of wine in the world. But what about the most famous particular wines? Well, that's easy—the list was made more than 150 years ago and, unlike almost everything else from that era, it's still current today.

THE GANG OF FOUR (PLUS ONE)

I call the most famous group of wines in the world the Gang of Four (plus One). They are the *grand vins* made by Château Haut-Brion, Château Lafite Rothschild, Château Latour, and Château Margaux (plus Château Mouton-Rothschild). If you are a wine enthusiast, you probably already know that these are the famous first-growth wines of the Classification of 1855. If not, then you might be scratching your head wondering what the fuss is all about. Either way, the story is worth telling.

The Great Exhibition of 1851, held at the glittering new Crystal Palace in Hyde Park, London, was more than just what we would call today a World's Fair—it was a demonstration of British industrial might and political hegemony. It was (or was seen by the leaders of other countries as) a sort of in-your-face statement that was all the more powerful because of its universal popularity. More than six million visitors passed through the gates, spending enough money to generate a budget surplus.

Inspired by the Great Exhibition (or perhaps provoked by it), Emperor Napoleon III of France organized his own fair, the Exposition Universelle, which was held on the Champs-Élyseés in Paris in 1855.[4] The organizers sought to show off the best of French art, culture, and industry, so how could they ignore wine, which combines all three? Obviously they did not, or our story would end here. A stunning tableau was produced to highlight the wines of Bordeaux. A ranking of the best wines of the region was produced, which placed the Gang of Four at the peak of Bordeaux wine (and by implication French wine and hence world wine), with the one, Château Mouton (not yet owned by the Rothschilds), in the second tier.

This was the famous Classification of 1855, which enshrined a few French wines as the world's very best. How were the top wines selected? Well, you might imagine that they were chosen through a rigorous regimen of competitive blind tastings. That's how it might be done today—you could make a reality television series out of the competition. But all that fuss and show wasn't necessary because the organizers turned the job of making up the Bordeaux wine league table to the brokers whose job it was to sell the wine. They already knew which ones were best. The best wines were the ones that commanded the highest prices. Case closed!

Bordeaux wine brokers had for decades kept lists of wine prices.[5] The gap in prices between the Gang of Four and the rest was huge. Lewin calculates that, if you take the average 1855-era price of the top four wines to equal one hundred, the price of the next-most-expensive wine (Château Léoville) was just sixty-two, and the price of Château Brane-Mouton was less than fifty-five. The very best (which was actually Haut-Brion at 111) were head and shoulders above the rest in terms of market price.

PLUS ÇA CHANGE, PLUS C'EST LA MÊME CHOSE

The Classification of 1855 exists today with only one change in the top tier. Brane-Mouton, which was purchased by Nathaniel de Rothschild in 1853 and subsequently renamed Mouton-Rothschild, ascended from second to first in 1973 after decades of effort, both viticultural and political, by Baron Philippe de Rothschild. Thus today's Gang of Four (plus One) was established. The stability of this list is remarkable. There are not many other 150-year-old lists that would still be valid today. The stability of the Bordeaux economic hierarchy, especially at the top, is stunning, especially when you consider how much the wines and even these châteaux have changed.

Wine geeks like me find it interesting that the famous classification was made according to wine producers, not vineyards, but this is natural, I suppose, since the ranking was given by Bordeaux brokers who bought and sold wine "brands," rather than Burgundy merchants, who might have given priority to terroir. This matters because it makes the stability of the top-flight rankings more surprising. Although the top producers all have excellent vineyard sites, it is a fact that the actual footprints of many of the châteaux have changed over the many years since 1855, with some expanding significantly. The vineyards are different now, and so are the wines. The Bordeaux *grand vins* of the nineteenth century were pale pink and only mildly tannic, according to Lewin, and only gradually acquired the color, aroma, and taste that we associate with Bordeaux today. And of course the ownership of most of the properties has changed as well.

So what accounts for the unexpected stability of fame and fortune in Bordeaux? Much of it is due to the quality of the wine itself. Even Adam Smith, writing in *The Wealth of Nations*, noted that the wines of certain French producers were obviously superior to the rest, and the diarist Samuel Pepys especially praised Ho Bryan (Haut-Brion). Some of it is due to a virtuous cycle that Lewin comments upon. If a wine is thought to be the best and is priced accordingly, its production naturally receives extraordinary attention that in turn ensures that it is the best. High ratings thus produce wines worthy of high ratings, while a vicious cycle haunts wines that received lower ratings in the past and were therefore neglected and continue to make poor wines today. There are exceptions to this rule (even in Bordeaux), owners who have rested on their laurels while the wines (and eventually their reputation) have declined.

Lewin argues that the Classification of 1855 must be regarded as a brilliant "marketing ploy" that brought such intense attention to the wines of the Médoc that the distant flame of their fame back then burns even more brightly today. And it continues to pay dividends, too, in wine shops and auction houses around the world.

MOST INFAMOUS: AUSTRIAN ANTIFREEZE

Infamy is the dark side of fame, and wine has its share. Certainly one of the most infamous cases is the Austrian antifreeze vintage of 1985. This scandal damaged Austria's reputation for a generation and certainly rates a mention in this chapter. Although it is common to think of wine as a pure and natural product, most of us know that many chemicals and additives are often used, the most common probably being various forms of sulfur used since the times of the Romans to discourage bacterial growth.

Jamie Goode and Sam Harrop devote an entire chapter to wine additives in their fine book *Authentic Wine.*[6] The list begins with sulfur dioxide, since it is both the most common additive and the most controversial because of differences in opinion about its health effects, and moves on to sugar (added where legal to compensate for underripe grapes), acid (added where legal to compensate for overripe grapes that have lost their natural acidity), yeasts (added in addition to or instead of native yeasts to ensure fermentation), and fining agents like egg whites, isinglass, and polyvinylpolypyrrolidone (PVPP), used to remove unwanted tannins and proteins.

Various kinds of nutrients are sometimes also added to fermenting wines to keep the yeast happy and doing its job. Water is sometimes added, too, in order to bring down sugar concentration and therefore alcohol levels in fermenting wine. This is illegal almost everywhere but a common practice nonetheless, perhaps because it is so easy to do and so difficult to detect. A winemaker friend calls the added water "Jesus units" because the water is instantly transformed into wine.

You might not think of the oak that you smell and taste in a glass of Chilean Cabernet Sauvignon as an additive, since wine is traditionally aged in oak barrels, but if sulfur dioxide is an additive, then the complex chemical elements associated with oak aging are, too. And oak effects can be added in many ways—barrels, staves, oak chips, and even powders. Oxygen is another additive that is both natural and artificial. Corks and barrels allow for some natural oxygen transfers that help wine age. Microoxygenation, which is exactly what it sounds like, is a technical treatment that can soften wines during the production process. Tiny amounts of oxygen are streamed through the wine. Wine enthusiasts who use aerators to help young wines "breathe" are doing something similar, I suppose. Other common wine additives include ascorbic acid and sorbate and copper.

Winemakers are not required to reveal additives and ingredients to their customers here in the United States, apart from a sulfite warning for wines when this is used, which is almost always. What would the label look like if wine was held to the same standard of transparency as yogurt or breakfast cereal? Goode and Harrop provide two examples. Randall Grahm has sometimes listed ingredients on his Bonny Doon wines. Here is an example: "Ingredients: grapes, tartaric acid, sulfur dioxide. In the wine-making process the following were utilized: untoasted wood chips, French oak barrels, cultured yeast, yeast nutrients, malolactic culture, copper sulfate."

An even more comprehensive account of additives is provided by a wine produced for the British supermarket chain Co-Op: "Grapes (Sauvignon Blanc), acidity regulator (potassium bicarbonate), preservative (potassium metabisulphate), copper sulphate. Made using antioxidants (carbon dioxide, nitrogen), yeast, yeast nutrient (diammonium phosphate). Cleared using bentonite, filtration, pectinolytic enzymes."[7]

Most people have no idea that their glass of wine holds all of these chemical additives, and apparently most don't care. Perhaps they are better off for it because, as I have said, most of these additives are part of the package of traditional wine-making practices and only a few of them are potential health concerns, and then for only a very small part of the population. A 2012 *New York Times* article highlighted the lack of interest in Randall Grahm's revealing wine labels. "I imagined it would have an impact," Grahm told the *Times* reporter, "I wasn't sure if there would be a backlash, or they would be freaked out, but most people haven't really noticed. In a perfect outcome, I would have liked to see interest, and gradually the start of a drumbeat about transparency."[8]

Ignorance may be bliss most of the time when it comes to wine additives, but what would you think if I told you that your glass of imported Riesling was filled with antifreeze? I'm quite sure that you would spit, dump, and run as visions of the skull-and-crossbones poison logo flashed through your

mind. This was the effect of the Austrian scandal of 1985. Some wine producers, seeking to add the impression of sweetness and improve the body of
wines from a poor vintage, took the illegal step of adding diethylene glycol,
a harmless chemical that is also used as an additive in auto antifreeze blends.

The antifreeze association was a killer even if the additive itself was not
(the urban myth of thousands of deaths due to the adulterated wine is apparently just that). But the revelation did great damage to the Austrian wine
industry, which saw its exports fall by four-fifths in the year after the scandal. *The Oxford Companion to Wine* reports that Austrian wine regulations
are now some of the most demanding, so this infamous episode is unlikely
to be repeated.

REAL BOTTLES, FAKE WINE

A whole wing of the Wine Infamy Hall of Fame is reserved for fake wines—
wines that are intentionally concocted to fool buyers or investors. We need
a whole wing—or maybe an entire building—because this practice is so
completely commonplace. Fakery can take place in many ways. The United
States banned the importation of Italy's Brunello di Montalcino wine a few
years ago, for example, because of fakery. Several producers were found to be
using grapes that were not authorized for the high-priced Brunello (but were
apparently legal for the less expensive Rosso di Montalcino). In essence they
were passing off a less valuable wine for a costlier one. You would think that it
would be easy to detect the fakery simply by tasting the wines, but apparently
this isn't always the case (a fact that makes you wonder if people are paying
more for the wine itself or for the prestige attached to the label).

A scam that Lewin calls the Scandal of the Century took place in the early
1970s in Bordeaux when a merchant named Pierre Bert perpetrated an "inge-
nious fraud."[9] Bert illegally arbitraged bulk-market price differentials between
AOC (appellation d'origine contrôlée)–designated wines and less expensive
vin de table wines. AOC wines earned higher prices, whether red or white, but
the gap between ordinary and AOC was higher for red wines than for whites.
Bert bought large quantities of AOC white wines and fraudulently transferred
the AOC certificate to an equal quantity of ordinary red wine. Shifting the
AOC designation made the red wine very much more valuable and the un-
designated white wine only a little less costly. The rather large profit on the
"upgraded" red more than offset the loss on the downgraded white.

Once again, you would think that buyers would taste the difference, but apparently it is not as simple as it appears. Indeed, Bert defended himself at his trial by asserting that not only was the practice widespread, but he had never received any complaints from his customers. As in Austria, new regulations make a repeat scandal less likely, although probably not impossible.

It may be no surprise to learn that China is famous for its fake wine—travelers in Asia report being offered all sort of fake merchandise, so why should wine be any different? The Chinese government busted one winery in the coastal city of Qinhuangdao that was said to be selling wine that in fact contained only 20 percent fermented grape juice. The rest was a cocktail of additives, including sugar water mixed with coloring agents, flavorings, and other chemicals.

The most infamous fakes are copycat versions of the great Bordeaux wines, especially older vintages. Authentic empty bottles of vintage Bordeaux wine are in high demand among fraudsters, who refill them with lesser wines of various sorts and sell them at great profit to collectors who may never open them or, if they do, may be unable to taste any difference. I was surprised to discover that the most valuable wine in my small collection is an empty bottle—worth more to a Chinese faker than any full bottle I own. It is an empty jeroboam (double magnum) of 1994 Château Pétrus that was given to me (empty) by a friend. As originally filled, this bottle of the world's most famous Merlot was worth hundreds, perhaps thousands, of dollars. Empty, it was worth as much as five hundred dollars to a Chinese faker—so long as it was authentic. "No fakes," a Chinese professional wine counterfeiter was reported to say. Real fakes only, I guess. No fake fakes, please.

MR. JEFFERSON, I PRESUME

The top nominee for the title of Most Infamous Wine at the time of this writing is a cache of wine bottles that has become immortalized, first in a book and then in a major motion picture, as the Billionaire's Vinegar.[10] The case is so infamous that I am afraid you probably already know the story, but I will give a brief account of the facts.

Thomas Jefferson developed an apparently sophisticated taste for wine during his term as US Minister to France between 1785 and 1789. He drank wine, purchased wine, and even visited the main wine-growing regions. Back in the US, he planted vineyards at Monticello and was known for his cellar, which held the great French wines, especially Bordeaux.

Fast-forward to a French cellar nearly two centuries later. According to the story, a brick wall is being demolished to make way for renovation and, lo and behold, a hidden room is revealed, containing about one hundred dusty old bottles. Some of them have symbols etched: "1787, Lafite" and "Th J." Are these bottles of Château Lafite 1787? Were they intended for Thomas Jefferson, but for some reason were diverted to this unlikely place? If "yes" is the answer to both questions, then surely these must be the rarest, most valuable wines in the world!

They certainly were the most valuable wines of their day. An American billionaire's son purchased some of them in a 1985 Christie's of London auction for a then-world-record price of £105,000. Some of these wines later passed to another American billionaire, Bill Koch, who became suspicious of the authenticity of the wines, which he traced back to a Munich entrepreneur and wine trader named Hardy Rodenstock. The suspicions turned to lawsuits when the engraving on the Jefferson bottles was found to have been made with modern equipment.

Investigations and lawsuits involving Koch, Rodenstock, and others drew world attention to these particular wines and to the millions of dollars that are spent each year on rare old bottles that are difficult but apparently not impossible to fake. When billionaires and even some mere millionaires now gaze upon their cellars, they do so with some combination of fear, denial, and resignation. The Jefferson bottles were probably just the tip of the iceberg. Who knows how many other faked bottles sit quietly collecting dust?

Scandals provoke reform—this was true for the Austrian antifreeze and the Fraud of the Century, and so reform has come to the wine auction business, too. In 2012 Château Lafite announced that all its wines would henceforth be shipped with a special tamper-proof tag that would ensure authenticity. Much more attention is now paid in wine-collecting circles to the provenance of older vintages—the paper trail of ownership that is the best assurance that bottle, label, and wine are all the same. If bottles can be faked and wine, too, it seems that paper cannot be far behind. Who knows when the Billionaire's Vinegar will be topped by another even more infamous wine?

MOST FORGOTTEN: SWEET MEMORIES

What is the opposite of most famous? Not most infamous, although that is certainly a revealing extreme. Most forgotten, of course! But how should I proceed?

I have spoken about wine to dozens of audiences in recent years, and I find that they save a warm spot in their hearts for the nearly forgotten wines of their youth—the wines they shared and sometimes chugged down surreptitiously when they had just barely reached the legal drinking age (or maybe a little before that). For baby boomers here in the United States, names like Blue Nun, Mateus Rosé, Boone's Farm, Annie Green Springs, and perhaps especially Thunderbird and Ripple all inspire nostalgic feelings. The memory of these wines and the youthful indiscretion they represent is sweet and perhaps more pleasant in the end than the wines were themselves. Liquid memories!

I know that there are many wines that are forgotten because they long ago disappeared. There are hundreds of wine-grape varieties, and while new ones appear every year in the form of hybrids, I am sure that others fade away as the last small vineyard patches are cleared to make way for other vines or other crops or perhaps a housing development or shopping mall. Gone and soon forgotten, I think. The dinosaurs disappeared, too, but not a few at a time. Scientists believe that they died out in a big bang. Wine grapes suffered an equivalent mass extinction in the nineteenth century: the phylloxera epidemic that destroyed vineyards across Europe and then around the world. The world of wine came back from the brink when scientists learned that they could overcome the root-sucking aphid by grafting European *vitis vinifera* vines to phylloxera-resistant American grape rootstock.

Grafting saved the vineyards, but it didn't save all the grapes of the vines. It was natural that hard choices were made when replanting took place. Carménère, now emerging as Chile's signature grape variety, was once a fixture in Bordeaux, but it was phased out after phylloxera because it was susceptible to a yield-reducing vine disease called coulure. So forgotten did Carménère become that the Chileans did not realize that they had large quantities of it until 1994, when it was scientifically established that some of their Merlot was really the lost Bordeaux variety. Chile's phylloxera-free isolation saved Carménère, but I suspect many other grape varieties were not so lucky, becoming extinct or hanging on in tiny plots in a few out-of-the-way places (many of the incredible 1,368 wine grape varieties surveyed in Jancis Robinson's magisterial 2012 book *Wine Grapes* fall into the latter category).[11]

So there are many forgotten wines, but which ones are *most* forgotten? To fill this category I nominate three wines—Tokaji, Cotnari, and Constantia—that were once the most famous and sought-after wines in the world. Their great fall from the pinnacle of world wine attention makes them candidates for the most forgotten award even if, as you will see, they have not really receded entirely into pure memory.

WE THREE KINGS

We live in a world where dry wines are revered and sweet wines, with a few exceptions (think Trockenbeerenauslese?), are unjustly disrespected because of their association with immature, unrefined tastes. But this was not always so. In a world where sugar, corn syrup, and artificial sweeteners were not so ubiquitous as they are today, sweet wines were king. Only about a hundred years ago the sweet Rieslings of the Mosel earned higher prices than dry Burgundy and Bordeaux! The most expensive Champagnes were the sweet ones—far sweeter, I'm told, than the sweetest sparkling wine you are likely to find today.

Constania's main claim to fame today is a celebrity association: Napoleon demanded it during his exile on the island of Saint Helena. But its unlikely fame went beyond the fallen emperor. Constantia was a sweet aromatic wine made from shriveled, late-harvest Muscat grapes at the Groot Constantia farm outside Cape Town, South Africa. The farm was founded in 1685 by Dutch governor Simon van der Stel, and the wine's fame reached its peak in Napoleon's day but eventually suffered the natural, economic, and political problems that came to plague South Africa and its wine industry generally. The old farm has been revived in recent years, however, and a new wine called Vin de Constance offers a lucky few a taste of the glorious past.

Grasă de Cotnari is named for the rustic part of Romanian Moldavia where it was made and was popular in Parisian salons in the last decades of the nineteenth century. The wine's quality came from the blend of indigenous grapes used—Grasă, Tămâioasă Românească, Frâncușă, and Fetească Albă—and the presence of botrytis, a.k.a. the Noble Rot. Like Hungary's Tokaji, the third king, Cotnari fell from its high throne over the last sixty years as world demand turned away from sweet wines and the country's Communist-era government turned away from quality wine.

Tokaji also shared the titles of King of Wine and Wine of Kings. *The Oxford Companion to Wine* gives a long list of reasons for its decline from its nineteenth-century heyday. Its association with the Austro-Hungarian Empire was a disadvantage after World War I, for example. The proliferation of lesser wines with similar names (Tokay here in the US, for example) was another problem. Even the recovery from phylloxera was slower than in other places, perhaps understandably because of the region's instability, and then the Communists came in and wine quality suffered. The wines returned to quality if not the same fame in the post-Communist era, the result in part of foreign investment.

The Three Kings may be almost forgotten (at least compared to their earlier fame), but they are not gone, and as I was revising this chapter I was presented with the opportunity to taste contemporary versions of these historic wines. A bottle of Alana-Tokaj arrived unexpectedly (a gift from the winery's owners, who are *Wine Wars* fans) just as I was preparing to leave to give a lecture. I savored the aroma, flavor, and texture of this wine, whose makers seek literally to go "back to the future" of high-quality Hungarian wine. A small glass of Klein Constantia's Vin de Constance was the perfect accompaniment to an elaborate foie gras dish a few days later at a festive dinner in Cape Town. Sublime! Only the Grasă de Cotnari was disappointing. I gasped when I found a bottle at an international wine shop in Seattle, but I knew from the price—less than ten dollars—that it couldn't possibly rise to the heights of the other famous bottles. And it didn't, alas. Interesting, but not memorable in the same intense way as the Alana-Tokaj and Vin de Constance. But maybe Grasă de Cotnari will rise like a phoenix from the ashes just as the other wines have done.

THE FAME GAME

What do these extremely famous, infamous, and forgotten wines tell us about the world of wine? Andy Warhol predicted that fame would become ubiquitous—flavor of the month transformed into flavor of the moment. A world distracted by shiny things and cursed with attention deficit disorder.

Wine—at least in the extreme forms examined here—tells a different story. While I am sure that there are many "fifteen-minute wines" that soar for a moment based on an important critic's favorable review or a grassroots "viral" Internet surge of interest, my extreme wine list unintentionally emphasizes the durability of fame and infamy when it comes to wine. Does this mean that Warhol was right—that enduring fame really has become exceptional, extreme? Or—and this is the direction in which I'm leaning—does it mean that wine itself is an outlier?

Is wine somehow different because of its deeper attachment to the earth, to history, to things that really count? And, if so, how long can wine exceptionalism persist in the face of money, media, and globalization? Maybe we can answer these questions by probing a few more extremes.

4

The Invisible Wine

RAREST, MOST UNEXPECTED, AND MOST UBIQUITOUS

What is the Big Mac of the world of wine? Big Macs, as you undoubtedly know, are the signature menu item of the McDonald's fast food chain. Mc-Donald's has over thirty-three thousand restaurants in 119 countries where 1.7 million employees crank out literally billions of meals each year. I suspect that just about every one of these restaurants serves Big Macs or a close substitute, like the Maharaja Mac (a vegetarian version of the Big Mac found in India).

If the Big Mac is not the most ubiquitous food on earth, it is surely one of the most common and instantly recognizable. Globe-trotting tourists may be shocked by many sights as they travel the highways and byways, but spotting a McDonald's serving Big Macs is probably by now no surprise at all.[1]

So what is the wine world's equivalent of the Big Mac—a brand-name product that can be found in the same basic form pretty much everywhere you might expect (and some places you wouldn't)—so ubiquitous that it's almost invisible? This question came up a couple of years ago in a conversation with Richard Hemmings, a creative wine writer who is a regular contributor to Jancis Robinson's website.[2] Richard was working on a research project about international wine prices, and he needed to know what wine would come closest to Ronald McDonald's favorite food.

BURGERNOMICS VERSUS VINONOMICS

Richard's project was inspired by the *Economist* magazine's famous Big Mac exchange-rate index. The *Economist* is interested in how exchange rates distort international trade. When a currency is overvalued on the global markets, its inflated foreign exchange value encourages imports but makes it difficult to export. If, on the other hand, a currency is undervalued internationally, its depressed value on the foreign exchange markets means people naturally prefer home-grown products to imports because of their lower cost. This also distorts the pattern of trade, but in the opposite direction.

Now, actually measuring whether a currency is overvalued or undervalued or at the equilibrium (which is called purchasing power parity) is a devilishly complicated technical matter that requires adjustments for all sorts of things. There had to be an easier and more convenient way to get some idea of what the currency markets were saying, and so someone hit upon using the ubiquitous Big Mac.

Although you and I might think of the Big Mac as just a sandwich, the analysts at the *Economist* realized that it is really a "bite" of the national marketplace. The price of a Big Mac in any country reflects the particular labor costs, real-estate values, transport conditions, raw material prices, taxes, and living standards there. Although it is by no means a perfect indicator of economic conditions, the price of a Big Mac does say something about the purchasing power of money. That general and imperfect relationship was all the *Economist* needed to get Burgernomics started.

The Big Mac index is released twice a year, and it compares the price of a Big Mac in the United States with local burger costs, converted to dollars using market exchange rates, from a host of foreign countries and draws conclusions from the comparison. In January 2012, for example, the *Economist*'s staff found that the average price of a Big Mac at several US McDonald's stores was $4.20. (Yes, yes, I know. They could have saved money buying an Extra Value Meal!) A similar Big Mac in Switzerland sold for $6.81 when the local Swiss franc price was converted to US dollars. This high price means that the Swiss franc was vastly overvalued. A Swiss citizen who lived by hamburgers alone (and had plenty of airline frequent-flier miles) would be much better off exchanging her francs for dollars and feasting in the United States. This overvalued currency (a side effect of the euro crisis at that time) hampered the Swiss economy's attempts to export and encouraged an import binge.

Norway was in almost as bad a situation. The dollar cost of the Big Mac was $6.69, a result of both high Norwegian taxes and an overvalued krone.

India was at the other Burgernomics extreme in January 2012. A Maharaja Mac sold for just the equivalent of $1.62, suggesting an undervalued rupee that encouraged exports but rendered foreign products uncompetitively expensive. China's currency was also undervalued using the Big Mac Index—a Big Mac cost just $2.44 there.

WHAT DOES WINE HAVE TO DO WITH HAMBURGERS?

At this point you are probably wondering what all of this has to do with wine. Well, Richard Hemmings got the crazy idea back in 2010 to try to do for wine what the *Economist* has done for hamburgers—use them as a way to measure international price differences, both of wine and perhaps more generally. To do this, however, he needed to know the wine equivalent of a Big Mac—a particular wine that is very widely sold at easily discoverable retail prices. And so our conversation began.

My first thought was Champagne—probably one of the big brands like Moët & Chandon Impérial (a.k.a. The Living Legend, according to Moët marketing copy). This entry-level wine, formerly sold under the Moët White Star label, may well be the most widely distributed Champagne in the world. My guess is that there is a stash of Moët on hand for the personal and sometimes official use of elites in every country on every continent in the world. How ironic, don't you think, that a luxury product would be so ubiquitous?

But even if you consider a Big Mac the Champagne of fast-food sandwiches, you can't really think that Champagne is the Big Mac of wines. It's just too expensive. Richard was looking for wine with mass-market appeal. So I suggested Jacob's Creek—the best-selling wine brand in Great Britain at the time. Jacob's Creek Shiraz, I thought, would fill the needs very well.

Jacob's Creek is not quite as popular here in the United States as it is in Britain, but it is very widely available. First released in 1976, Jacob's Creek is made by Orlando Wines, which was founded in the 1850s, the oldest winery in the Barossa Valley of Australia. Orlando is now part of the French drinks multinational Pernod Ricard, and it flows through that company's vast pipeline to the four corners of the world. I think you can probably find Jacob's Creek just about everywhere, and it probably would have made a very good basis for Richard's study. But he had a better idea. Since the French are so important in the global wine business, why not focus on France's most successful export brand, Mouton Cadet?

Mouton Cadet is an ordinary wine made by an extraordinary producer and is therefore able to ride that maker's reputation around the world. The producer is of course Château Mouton Rothschild, the only wine to break through the glass ceiling of the Classification of 1855 to achieve top-flight status. But it isn't the Mouton estate's *grand vin*. That wine sells for hundreds of dollars per bottle, and this one goes for a whole lot less.

Baron Philippe de Rothschild responded to a dismal 1927 vintage by releasing only a "second wine" rather than undermining the reputation of his premier bottling. It was not a great success, apparently, but it provoked the baron to create a popular brand, Mouton Cadet, beginning with the 1930 vintage. Cadet means youngest son (which Philippe was), and I tend to think of it as Mouton Jr. The price starts at about seven dollars here in the United States, according to a Google search of online merchants, with the 1.5-liter bottle going for about thirteen dollars. If Château Mouton Rothschild is a wine for the 1 percent, then Mouton Cadet is for the 50 percent at least, but probably not for the 99 percent of Two Buck Chuck.

Mouton and Mouton Cadet could not be more different, even if they both carry the baron's name. They are both Bordeaux wines, of course, but Cadet is a blend of many grape varieties sourced from many parts of the wine-making region. If Mouton is made to reflect a particular place and time—a terroir wine in wino terms—Cadet is more of a branded product, where vintage variations are suppressed to produce a consistent quality product that can be reliably purchased year after year.

This is what makes Mouton Cadet like a Big Mac. There are, I suppose, terroir hamburgers made by small local shops, and these probably vary a good deal, being both good and bad. The Big Mac, on the other hand, is always the same, or is meant to be. At one point Mouton Cadet, which now comes in Blanc and Rosé as well as the original Rouge, was one of the most popular wines in the world, selling more than a million cases in 2002, and it is sold today in 150 countries—more than the Big Mac! Mouton Cadet sales have declined in recent years as international competition has grown, but the ubiquitous nature of its existence is apparently timeless.

WHAT MOUTON CADET REVEALS

By 2011, Hemmings, with the help of JancisRobinson.com readers, had managed to assemble retail price data for Mouton Cadet in forty-two countries—the first large-scale international price comparison of this kind that I have ever seen, even if Hemmings's goal of getting data for all 150 countries wasn't achieved. The study revealed that where you buy Cadet and in what currency matters quite a lot, which was also a Burgernomics lesson. Let's take France as a baseline market. Hemmings reports that in early 2011 Mouton Cadet sold for €11.20 on a representative French online retailer's website. That was equivalent to $15.32 in US currency at the then-prevailing exchange rates.

The cheapest Cadet was found in . . . the United States! It sold for $7.99 or the equivalent of €5.84. That is a huge discount relative to the home market price, although I suspect that prices vary a good deal within the US and that many buyers paid more. The most expensive Cadet was found in Korea, with a price of 40,000 Korean won, which was equivalent at the time to $35.55 or €25.99. Brazil, Bulgaria, and Turkey also reported prices above thirty dollars for the wine while prices below twelve dollars were cited for Denmark, Panama, Jersey, and Tortola (in the British Virgin Islands).

There are many explanations for the huge international wine price differences, including international tariffs, domestic taxes, distribution costs, domestic competition, transportation costs, and so on. There are fewer explanations for price gaps within the European Union and especially within the Eurozone, that group of countries that share not just a common market but also a common currency. Nonetheless that €11.20 bottle of Mouton Cadet that Hemmings found in France sold for €24 in Bulgaria, €18 in Italy, €14.51 in Austria, and €12.99 in Ireland. But you could get it for just €10.79 in Germany. Those are very large price differences, and even if some of them might shrink if we looked at brick-and-mortar-store prices rather than the Internet-vendor rates that Hemmings used in many cases, they still reflect a large gap in what wine costs in different places.

Think global, drink local—this seems like good advice based upon the Mouton Cadet index. If you are going to drink the global product (Cadet), then you certainly need to think local, because local market conditions seem to matter so much in terms of the price of the wine.

THE SILENT MAJORITY OF WINE

While McDonald's is probably the most recognized restaurant chain on earth, American-style hamburger restaurants are certainly *not* the most common dining establishments. We might think they are because they are brightly decorated with golden arches and other trademarked logos, but in most cities McDonald's restaurants in particular and even fast food palaces in general are not so dominant as we might believe. There are probably more pizza restaurants in your town than there are McDonald's, for example. And probably more Chinese restaurants, too. But because they are not all identified by a single brand name, their culinary influence tends to fade into the background. They are the "silent majority" of the food world.

Cooperatives are the silent majority of wine. It is likely that nearly a third of all the wine produced in the world is made by cooperative cellars that serve the needs of dozens or even hundreds of winegrowers who choose to make wine in this way rather than sell grapes to private firms. You have heard of a few of these cooperatives, but the vast majority work in nearly anonymous circumstances. Let's stand back and appreciate the extreme scale of the cooperative wine phenomenon.

According to *The Oxford Companion to Wine*, more than half of all the vineyards in France belong to cooperative winery members and more than half of all the wine produced comes from *caves cooperatives. Cantina sociale* are even more important in Italy, where they are responsible for more than 60 percent of wine production. The figures are about the same for Spain and Portugal but lower in Germany, where cooperatives provide only about a third of the wine. When you think of Old World wine you may think Champagne this or Château that, but the truth is that the anonymous and almost invisible wines of grower cooperatives are what fill Europe's glass.

Most cooperatives got their start in times of trouble, when winegrowers found themselves vulnerable to adverse market conditions. An unusually large harvest, for example, tends to fill up winery capacity so that additional grapes bring very low prices or cannot be sold at all. In times like these, winegrowers became ad hoc winemakers, making their own wine rather than selling the grapes for a loss or not selling them at all. But grower wine-making facilities were seldom state of the art, and there was little incentive to invest in better equipment (or advanced wine-making training) since by definition the facilities were only used in emergencies and when prices were unprofitably low.

The cooperative movement addressed these problems, especially in France, where cooperatives were given preferential access to credit. By pooling their resources, cooperative members could achieve scale economies, adopt modern technologies, hire trained enologists, and at least sometimes also invest in the marketing functions needed to get the best prices for their wines.

Although many cooperatives are still quite small, serving the vineyards surrounding a rural village, some are enormous. Caviro, for example, is not just the largest cooperative in Italy, with forty-one wineries and more than twenty thousand winegrower members, it is the largest wine producer in Italy. Period. You may know one of its brands: Riunite, the wine made famous here in the United States by a 1980s advertising campaign that promised "Riunite on Ice / So Nice!" Another co-op, Gruppo Coltiva, is number two in Italy with eight thousand members and twenty-six wineries in many wine regions of Italy. Cavit is another large Italian winery that produces in the range of 70 percent of all wine from the Trentino region.

Cooperatives are active in the New World, too. FeCoVitA, a federation of cooperatives, is the second-largest producer in Argentina. Its Vino Toro box wines are very popular in the domestic market. Cooperative Vinícola Aurora is Brazil's largest wine producer. Many of the cooperatives in both Argentina and Brazil were founded by immigrants from the north of Italy who, finding the same market problems they experienced back home, adopted the same collective solution. Cooperatives have been important in South Africa, Australia, and California as well, where United Vintners was at one time said to be the largest grower cooperative in the world. It was acquired by Heublein, Inc., which was then in turn acquired by R. J. Reynolds Tobacco Company. Reynolds's wine business was sold to Grand Metropolitan, which merged with Guinness to create Diageo. Thus did a major wine cooperative become a footnote in corporate history.

Cooperatives are all collectively owned but are otherwise quite diverse. Some produce terrible wine while others are responsible for some of the best wine in the world. The difference, apart from geology, geography, and wine-making skill, is due to business organization.

Some cooperatives are a sort of "buyer of last resort." Growers are allowed to sell their grapes elsewhere or to make their own wines, and the cooperative exists to purchase anything that is leftover. Naturally only the poorest-quality grapes arrive at the cooperative cellar, so the wines are necessarily inferior, find little in the way of a market, and earn very little for their members. Not much incentive to invest in quality under these circumstances. Although they have not completely disappeared, I think there are fewer and fewer "last resort" co-ops left. Most of them have been put out of business except where government subsidies exist to keep them going to stabilize local incomes.

At the opposite extreme are cooperatives like the Cantina Sociale Produttori di Barbaresco in Piemonte, Italy. Their famous wines, made with the indigenous Nebbiolo grape, are ranked as some of Italy's finest, along with Brunello and Barolo. The cooperatives in Alto Adige, up near the Austrian border, are said to make some of Italy's best white wines. The co-op managers I spoke with there (including Peter Baumgartner of the Cantina Produttori Valle Isarco in Chiusi) told the same story. They were not "buyers of last resort." Rather, cooperative members were required to sell all of their grapes to the collective, and they had to agree to be paid according to quality, too. The emphasis was entirely on quality, and the result was obvious in the glass.

It is not quite accurate to say that the wines of the cooperatives cover the earth, but it isn't entirely wrong, either. Although you may not have pulled a cork or twisted a screw cap on a bottle of wine made by one of the cooperatives listed here, bear in mind that there are thousands more. In some particular parts of Europe, cooperatives are responsible for almost all wine production, and much of it is sold on the bulk market, to be bottled with house-brand labels or blended into a corporate product. Cooperatives may get little attention, but their wines are everywhere.

THE RAREST WINES

After what I said about the Billionaire's Vinegar in the last chapter, it probably follows that the rarest wine in the world is likely to be an irrefutably authentic 1787 Château Lafite from Thomas Jefferson's personal stash. Given all of the publicity that this famous fraud has generated, you would have to count yourself very smart or very fortunate if you came into possession of the real deal. Ironically, I think that wine fraud has made the rarest wines in the world both more common and even harder to find. They are more common, obviously, because there are more of them than ever before. Indeed, some fraudsters have faked wines that never actually existed so that the fakes are the only ones that can be found! This is what happens when you fake bottles and labels without reading carefully exactly when the first vintage of a famous wine was released. This has happened often enough to create a special class of famous fakes.

But fakery also, as with the Jefferson Lafite, has the effect of shrinking the supply of rare old wines because all of them necessarily come under suspicion and are subject to grave doubt unless provenance can be indisputably established. Thus the number of authenticated bottles may be less than the number of true bottles if some cannot prove their heritage.

Old bottles are probably the rarest, of course. The oldest wine that I had ever sipped before I started work on this book was served to me on two occasions at the Herbfarm Restaurant near Seattle. The Herbfarm specializes in seasonally themed multicourse wine dinners, and Ron Zimmerman, who runs the place with his wife Carrie Van Dyck, likes to serve an older wine from their vast cellar at the end of the meal. In my case that wine was an 1875 Barbeito Malvasia Madeira, which was memorable indeed. Zimmerman tells me that those old Madeiras were out of fashion until relatively recently and so he was able to scoop them up at what seem today to be bargain prices. Now the word is out, he says, and their price reflects a scarcity premium.

The Herbfarm has (as of 2012) the distinction of serving the oldest wine in the world that you can purchase by the sip or glass (as opposed to by the bottle), which I guess makes it the oldest wine that most people will ever have the opportunity to taste. It is a 1795 Terrantez Madeira that can be served along with the cheese course at one of the Herbfarm's incredible meals. The price? Well, remember that this is a rare wine—only about a dozen bottles are known to exist. You will have to pay $150 for a one-third-ounce "sip," $365 for a one-ounce pour, or $10,000 for the whole bottle. Pricey, I know, but remember that Jefferson was alive when this wine was made, and he might even have had a glass himself, so popular was Madeira in the new United States. And the wine is not vinegar, according to Zimmerman, who describes it as "one of the most profound wines" he's ever tasted. Yes, that would be a rare experience!

If we set aside the almost impossibly rare old wines (and the really impossibly old fakes), this leaves us with two categories of rare wines to consider here: the twenty-dollar-bill wines and the invisible wines.

RARE WINES: TWENTY-DOLLAR BILLS AND INVISIBLE WINES

Twenty-dollar-bill wines don't really cost twenty dollars, so you can put your wallet away. The name comes from a joke that is popular among economists and therefore essentially unknown to the rest of the world. The joke goes like this.

A noneconomist walks into a bar and says excitedly to the bartender (who is an economist). "Wow, this is my lucky day! I just found a twenty-dollar bill on the sidewalk in front of your bar!" The bartender takes a long look at the fellow, who is waving the bill in the air. "No, you didn't," he says. "Yes, I did!" replies the customer. "See, it's right here!" "Can't be—you're wrong," the economist-bartender coolly replies. "You're ignoring rational economic theory. If there *had been* a twenty-dollar bill on the sidewalk, someone would have already picked it up. So it is logically impossible that you could have found one." "But look—here it is!" the customer exclaims. "Look, buddy," the bartender says, turning away, "What do you think I'm going to believe—*your* bill or *my* theory?"

The joke of course (sorry, but economists always explain jokes, even the obvious ones) is that economists tend to believe their theories even when they can clearly see refuting evidence with their own eyes. You would think that this makes economists different from regular folks, but in the case of rare wines, we are all pretty much the same.

There are many "cult" wines that are famous for being impossible to buy. They are so scarce, the story goes, that they are all invisibly absorbed by the lucky few folks who years ago gained access to the wine-club distribution list. No one else ever gets a shot. They are as rare as rare can be. I call these the twenty-dollar-bill wines because if you saw one (at a wine shop or on a restaurant wine list), you would probably rub your eyes. Impossible! How could that be? Must be a mistake (or maybe a fake!). If they really had that wine for sale, they would already have sold it.

Now the dirty little secret of these wines is that they are sometimes quite reasonably available, but the myth of impossible scarcity is maintained because that's how myths work and because no one can believe their eyes. This was especially true during the Great Recession that began in 2008. Many impossible-to-find wines showed up in the marketplace as wine-club members resold their allocations and restaurants offloaded their new shipments, and some of their reserve wines were put on the market, too. You could pick up these wines on the sidewalk (well, not exactly . . .), yet the myth that they were impossible to find prevailed.

Opus One is an example that illustrates the twenty-dollar-bill concept at work, although I admit that it is not a perfect example. Opus One is a cult

Napa Valley winery founded in 1979 as a partnership between California legend Robert Mondavi and Bordeaux legend Baroness Philippine de Rothschild of Château Mouton Rothschild and of course Mouton Cadet. Opus One is a red Bordeaux blend made from grapes sourced from Mondavi's (also legendary) To Kalon vineyard. The website offers the opportunity to purchase a single bottle of the 2008 vintage of Opus One (no more!) for $225. It's not impossible to purchase, apparently, but it is very limited.

Objectively, however, Opus One and many other cult wines are relatively easy to find. I have read that Opus One produces thirty thousand cases (or 360,000 bottles) of its first wine, for example, which is a very considerable amount of wine given its selling price. It is rare, I admit, and I would be surprised to see it at a sidewalk sale, but its scarcity is as much the result of rational theory as concrete fact.

The real rarities, in my mind, are wines made in small quantities for local consumption from indigenous grapes—I call them the "invisible wines" because they are rarely seen outside their traditional homes. They have no large economic interests behind them and are frequently ignored or simply overlooked by wine media. Often they are produced in tiny quantities and can be found within a very small geographic neighborhood. They are wines to be savored if you are lucky enough to find them. Our last trip to Italy yielded three of these small treasures: Pignoletto, Lacrima di Morro d'Alba, and Ruché.

Pignoletto is a dry white wine grown only in the hills outside Bologna. "Lively, crisp, aromatic" is how Jancis Robinson describes it in her *Guide to Wine Grapes*.[3] Pignoletto is distinctly Bolognese—grown there, made there, and I think that every last drop of it is consumed there, too, since it goes so well with the rich local cuisine (almost as if they evolved together . . . which I guess they did). It would be hard to beat the simple meal of salumi, cheese, and bread that we had with a bottle of Pignoletto frizzante at Tamburini's wine bar in the Bologna central market.

Lacrima di Morro d'Alba is a distinctive red wine from the Marche region. Robinson describes it as "fast maturing, strangely scented." Burton Anderson says that it is a "purple-crimson wine with . . . foxy berry-like odor and ripe plum flavor."[4] Apparently it fades very quickly, but it is distinctive and intense while it lasts. It sure stood up to the very rich cuisine of Ferrara when we visited our friends in that city. We were fortunate that the restaurant owner guided us to this wine from the Mario Lucchetti estate.

Ruché comes from the Piemonte, and we stumbled upon it by accident (which I guess is how we usually stumble . . .). We were attending the annual regional culinary fair in Moncalvo, a hill town half an hour north of Asti. Thirteen "pro loco" civic groups from throughout the region set up food and wine booths in the central square and sold their distinctly local wares to a hungry luncheon crowd.

I had never heard of Ruché and honestly didn't know what it might be until I happened upon the stand of the Castagnole Monferrato group. They were cooking with Ruché, marinating fruit in Ruché, and selling it by the glass— they were obviously very proud of their local wine. I had to try it and it was great. Suddenly I saw Ruché everywhere (a common experience with a new discovery) and enjoyed a bottle at dinner in Asti that night. "Like Nebbiolo," Jancis Robinson writes, "the wine is headily scented and its tannins imbue it with an almost bitter aftertaste." An interesting wine and a memorable if unexpected discovery.

Wines like these are diamonds in the rough (sometimes they can taste a bit rough, too, but that's another story). So much attention is focused on famous names and international wine-grape varieties that we overlook the really rare, sometimes fragile wines.

A RARE VISION: THE ONE TRUE MALBEC?

This is the story of an attempt to create a truly original wine. It takes place in Argentina. The Biondolillo family has been in the wine-growing business in Mendoza for more than one hundred years. This means that they have lived through booms and crises, both in the wine industry and in the Argentinean economy more generally. Aldo Biondolillo, who holds a PhD in economics from the University of Minnesota, is the third generation to make a living this way. His sons Leonardo and Mariano are in the family business, too, and there is a very young fifth generation in the wings. Theirs is the kind of business that necessarily looks to the long run.

When Aldo began the Tempus Alba project in the 1990s, he was looking for a way for his family to continue the wine-growing tradition well into the future. He knew that they couldn't live on grape sales alone, and becoming a bulk wine producer would be a dead-end road. Commodity pricing—of grapes or bulk wine—often puts an emphasis on cost more than quality, and there is always someone who will charge less. Economic theory teaches that product differentiation is key to escaping the commodity trap. But how?

Aldo's project is ambitious: to create not just another good Malbec, but a different *idea* of Malbec. His method is to isolate the purest or perhaps just the best Malbec vines in the region from among the many different clones that have been planted here over the years. The goal is to identify the truest clones and, in the long run, to make them available to other wineries that could join a circle of producers making unique wines—unique in terms of the particular grape clones and then unique once again as expressions of their respective terroir.

And so Aldo and family began, planting eight thousand different Malbec cuttings in the mother block. The eight thousand vines were narrowed in stages to 589 vines and then finally to sixteen by teams of experts. After ten years of hard work, the project's first commercial Malbec was made in 2007.

It is called Vero Malbec (*vero* is Italian for truth, although the letters are also the initials of Aldo's grandchildren). The Biondolillos do not claim that it is the original Malbec brought over from France or The One True Malbec. It is their version of the truth, seen from their family's particular one-hundred-year perspective.

Everyone knows that I don't rate wines or give tasting notes, but I found the Biondolillos' version of the truth very appealing (as have a number of wine critics). It will be interesting to see how this wine develops over several vintages. It will be even more interesting if Aldo's dream of a wine-making circle evolves, so that a group of Mendoza winemakers adopt the Tempus Alba clones and produce their own unique wines, perhaps along the lines of the Coro Mendocino project in California.

Our visit to Tempus Alba's beautiful winery in Maipú was informative in several respects. First, it was interesting to see a project that is at once so scientifically ambitious (the labs and the clones) and, through the winemakers' circle idea, so socially progressive. Although there is a lot of plant science employed here, the work on narrowing down the cuttings was done using nose and palate, not by sequencing grape DNA.

I accused Aldo of being an empiricist in his search for true Malbec, and someone in the group said, "Well, of course . . . he's an economist." Aldo and I reacted in the same instant: "No, no, no!" we said in unison, shaking our fingers. We know that most economists are more comfortable with theories than with facts. (It is an old saying in economics, for example, that a theory cannot be refuted by facts—only a more appealing theory will do the job.) It's that twenty-dollar-bill thing. I was also fascinated by the visitors to Tempus Alba. The other wineries we visited in Mendoza were fairly remote and sometimes difficult to find; most had guarded gates meant to restrict entry to those with prearranged tours. Tempus Alba's winery is in the Maipú Valley, an area with a good many backpacker hostels. The courtyard was filled with the rental bikes of the twentysomethings who travel from winery to winery as long as they can manage to stay upright. The action in the restaurant and on the deck overlooking the vineyard was young, lively, and fun.

I'm not sure the one-hundred-plus per day biking visitors (a big wine tourist number by Mendoza standards) buy much wine, but they appear to have a great wine experience—almost a unique one, it seems to me. The self-guided tour shows them the winery, teaches some viticultural science, and even exposes them to the family's "dogma" or guiding principles. Then it is up to the sunny deck to taste the wines and have a bite to eat. Many will be untouched and just enjoy the good wine, food, and company, but some will stop and think, and that seems to be the idea behind Tempus Alba's whole approach. Is Tempus Alba's Vero Malbec really unique? I won't judge the wine, but certainly the idea is completely different and a potentially important addition to the rich mosaic of Mendoza wine.

WINE IN THE SHADOWS

Some wines are so extreme that they are practically invisible, which is an extreme extreme in a world that is so focused on fame (see the last chapter), driven by money (that's what's coming next), and defined by global media attention. What makes the invisible extreme interesting is that it comes in so many forms.

Some wines, like Mouton Cadet, are invisible because of their ubiquity— we simply take them for granted. Others, like the "silent majority" of wines made by cooperatives, hide below the money and media radar. Other wines are invisible because they are so famously scarce that you never see them (the twenty-dollar-bill wines) until you do, so associated with one particular place that they seldom get out (my new friend Ruché), or the fruit of one person's extreme vision (Aldo's Vero Malbec).

Most of the world's wines are invisible in one sense or another, when you start to add up the categories, which reminds us that despite all the hype, wine remains far more local than global and very much an ordinary everyday phenomenon. Fame is a strong force in wine, as in almost everything else today, but it seems that wine's simple pleasures—the ones we take for granted until they are unexpectedly revealed—may be its most powerful attractions and may be (?) its most extreme characteristics.

5

Money Wine

CHEAPEST, MOST EXPENSIVE, AND MOST OVERPRICED

I assigned my economics class to go to a typical local supermarket and survey the economic geography of the wine department there.[1] They came back with a slew of interesting statistics. Number of different wines? About eight hundred, they reported, from more than a dozen regions including California, Washington, Oregon, Idaho, Canada (Icewine), Portugal (Port), Spain (Sherry), France, Italy, Germany, Australia, New Zealand, and South Africa. They also classified the different wine-grape varieties represented (Merlot, Chardonnay, and so forth) as well as the many wines identified by geographical designation, such as Chablis and Chianti.

Most people are surprised at numbers like these because, while they know at some level that supermarket wine departments are enormously diverse, it doesn't really sink in until you do the math. Eight hundred wines. Wow, that's a lot!

I wrote about the student research on *The Wine Economist* blog and, well, I'm not really sure what happened next, but I think the store manager might have read the blog. If she did, I think her reaction must have been "Eight hundred wines? That's not nearly enough!" And that's true. The upscale supermarket down the street had more than twice as many different wines and the farm store a few miles away had twice as many as that. It's true, eight hundred wines wasn't nearly enough, and the next time I stopped in I saw workers putting up shelves for another four hundred different wines.

The number of different wines we have to choose from is an impressive wine statistic, but this chapter is about price, and that's where you find the most dramatic differences. The lowest price my students reported was just a little over two dollars per bottle equivalent. It was a five-liter box of Franzia wine that was on sale, with an extra discount if you had a shopper loyalty card, which every one of my bargain-seeking students was able to present. The most expensive wine? It was a bottle of Louis Roederer Cristal Rosé Champagne (rapper Jay-Z's former favorite) with a list price of more than $300, although the shopper-card discount brought it down to about $230. I can't say for sure, but I suspect that it was the most expensive single item of the ten-thousand-plus products in the store.

From two dollars to two hundred dollars—that's a hundredfold difference between the cheapest wine and the most expensive one. I am confident that that is the largest bottom to top price differential in the supermarket. This extreme ratio of high to low is one of wine's distinctive characteristics—something that makes it different from other everyday items—and it is also a barrier to the growth of the wine market. It is understandably difficult for new consumers to appreciate why a beverage that is basically fermented fruit juice can be worth both two dollars for this and two hundred dollars for that. What could possibly justify the cost difference? How could the two-dollar product be that bad and the two-hundred-dollar bottle that good? Outrageous!

EXTREME WINE PRICES

The fact that even "grocery-store wines" can be both affordably cheap and outrageously dear provokes this chapter, which offers my reflections on extreme wine prices. I'll tell you a little about wines that are very cheap, very high priced, and maybe even overpriced, and then I'll try to explain what I think the whole extreme wine price phenomenon means.

What is the most expensive wine in the world? I think it is impossible to give a definitive answer to this question because you can't pin down a moving target for very long. The most sought-after wines earn their high prices because of their scarcity, of course, but also because they are not just wine—for one reason or another they simply transcend the wine category.

Eleven bottles of Champagne sold for a total of $156,000 at an auction in Finland in June 2012—not the highest price ever but a good way to illustrate my argument. The wine, which was still drinkable if quite sweet by contemporary tastes, had spent the previous 170 years in the perfect undisturbed temperature-controlled storage location—in an undiscovered shipwreck at the bottom of the Baltic Sea. It was a mixed case (minus one): four bottles were Veuve Clicquot, one Heidsieck, and six from a maker that ceased production in 1829, Juglar. We know what the wine tastes like because the diver who discovered them impulsively popped a cork as soon as they were on the boat—the most expensive mouthful of sparkling wine in marine-salvage history!

Some of the wine from the wrecked schooner was sold at an earlier auction in Paris, where a Veuve Cliquot fetched $37,443. What made these wines worth so much? It would certainly be a once-in-a-lifetime experience to taste them, if any of the rest are opened. But no, it's not about the wine. It's about the history and of course the fact that these are trophies. Wines like these are looked at far more often than they are consumed (I call this conspicuous nonconsumption), and they are frequently a source of revenue for charities. Rare bottles are often donated to charity auctions and spend their lives being passed from cellar to cellar, raising money for good causes each time they change hands.

Trophy wines thus have more in common with fine art than with beverages. People collect them because they want to have them, and they are sometimes able to do some good in the process. Some people "invest" rather than "collect," and this can produce high prices, too. *Decanter*, the British wine magazine, publishes tables of auction results in each issue. The July 2012 issue reported that the highest price so far for a case of 1982 Château Lafite was £27,943—a very high price but still less than the £32,686 that was paid for a case of 1961 Château Latour. Famous wines from famous vintages earn the highest auction bids, but the prices decline pretty quickly when you move away in one direction or another. The highest price ever paid for a case of 1966 Lafite, according to *Decanter*, was a mere £5,113. Château Margaux's maximum price for that year was £920, so you can see how much difference a celebrated vintage makes in this world (and 1966 was not a bad year, just not as great as 1961 or 1982).

A small decrease in status also makes a big difference in price. The Classification of 1855 wines often trade at higher prices on the basis of their long-established reputation. Thus that 1982 Lafite (£27,943) earns a large premium over other famous wines from 1982, such as Château Cheval Blanc (£6,071) or second-growth Léoville-Barton (£1,200).

MOST EXPENSIVE VINTAGE: BORDEAUX 2009

Famous older vintages of Bordeaux wines are among the most expensive in the world, but some of their value comes from their age. How about newly released wine? Here again Bordeaux is a focus, and 2009 was by most accounts the most expensive Bordeaux vintage on record (although a few 2010 wines earned even higher prices). Quite an achievement during a global economic slowdown! Here are some of the amazing prices paid for the *en primeur* wines: Le Pin €1,050; Ausone €800; Cheval Blanc €700; Haut-Brion and Latour €600; Lafite, Margaux, and Mouton €550; and Yquem €540.

These prices are per bottle—except that no real bottles existed when the purchases were made. The 2009 vintage was still in barrels and would stay there for many more months. Since Bordeaux wines are almost always varietal blends—and since the blending doesn't take place until the wine is bottled—it is fair to say that the people who paid these big prices couldn't be completely sure what they were buying. They based their purchases on . . . on what? On faith (in the winemakers), on trust (in the critics' judgments), and, of course, on speculation, since much of the action at this stage is to lock up hot wines for profitable resale later.

John Maynard Keynes once compared speculators to people who bet on the results of the "people's choice" beauty contests that were popular in Depression-era Sunday newspapers. The trick wasn't to pick out the most beautiful entrant from among a set of published portraits, but rather to choose the "people's choice"—the one that *other people* would vote for in the greatest numbers. So making the bet was a matter of guessing what *other people* would think *other people* would do and playing the odds. That's Bordeaux en primeur in a nutshell. How did prices rise so high with the world economy in such a fragile state? There are many theories. Here are four.

The first theory is quite simple. 2009 was an extraordinary year and the wines are (or will be) spectacular. Wine enthusiasts would forever regret it if they didn't purchase this vintage, even at high en primeur prices. This theory was supported by the rave reviews of many wine critics. Perhaps it really was the vintage of the century in Bordeaux, although it must be said that vintages of the century seem to come around pretty frequently these days—their schedule is more like that of the World Cup than Halley's Comet.

A second theory was that the high prices of these wines reflected the full emergence of Asia as a market for fine wine. I'm not sure what to make of all the chatter I heard during the en primeur tasting circus, but the scuttlebutt was that American buyers failed to show up in the usual numbers, but they were not missed because of the demand from China, both direct purchases and London houses buying for eventual Hong Kong resale. One fact that supports this theory is the huge gap in prices between the top trophy wines and the rest of the Bordeaux market. It is said that Asian buyers want to purchase only the best, most famous wines (rather than looking for bargains or good value further down the list). I don't know if this stereotype is true, but the stratification in price indicates a disproportionate demand for the top wines, which is consistent with the China theory.

An article by Jancis Robinson suggests that the Bordeaux winemakers and their agents were using strategic techniques to try to boost prices, dividing them into tranches, for example, a popular practice in financial markets.[2] *Tranche* is French for a slice, and it is a word that moved from financial jargon to everyday use during the economic crisis, when we all learned how collateralized debt obligations (CDOs) were sold off in "slices" that allowed people to convince themselves that their subprime mortgage investments were safer than they turned out to be. Bordeaux wine is sold in tranches, too, with the price of the first slice used to set the standard for the second. In 2009, Robinson reports, the first tranche was ridiculously small, leaving excess demand and therefore forcing more buyers to weigh in for the second tranche (or risk not getting any wine), which was priced at €100 per bottle more than slice number one in some cases. Cost-conscious wine drinkers can only hope that the Bordeaux merchants do not start reading the technical economics literature on auction theory, where they would likely find other ways to manipulate the market to squeeze out higher prices.

A final theory is really no theory at all. It holds that the idea that Bordeaux 2009 or even 2010 (broadly defined) was the most expensive Bordeaux vintage ever is a misconception. There are about eight thousand Bordeaux producers according to reports I've read recently, and only about four hundred of them take part in the en primeur market. The total production of "first wines" by these makers is surprisingly small. I think it is fair to say that 90 percent of the market's recent attention is focused on less than 10 percent (by volume) of the wine produced in Bordeaux.

The prices of the top wines went through the roof, but what about the prices in the region as a whole? You don't have to have a theory to appreciate the fact that the makers of ordinary Bordeaux wines do not share the status or benefits of the trophy wines and are probably feeling the pain of hard times like so many winemakers around the world.

Bordeaux 2009 might be extreme in two ways: most expensive and biggest gap between top and bottom! Things have evened up a bit in the years since 2009–2010. Prices softened because they were unsustainably high. The dirty little secret of the en primeur market is that it only works if the wineries leave a lot of "meat on the bone" in the form of potential future profits to compensate buyers for the risk and time value of their early payments. But the higher selling price undermined this implicit bargain. Many of the 2009s and 2010s were worth less in 2012 than their original en primeur selling price—a sure way to undermine market support. Is the only choice to trim back asking price? Maybe, but maybe not! Château Lafite announced in 2012 that it would abandon the en primeur market in future years and sell its wines when ready rather than when expedient. The short-term cost is the loss of cash flow for several years while each vintage ages away awaiting its market moment. The long-term gain is greater control over the market but also potentially higher prices. Maybe the most expensive vintages are still to come?

MOST OVERPRICED WINE?

If there is one thing (maybe the only thing?) that wine enthusiasts have in common, it is their frustration with wine in restaurants. The list of complaints starts with price (too high!) and goes on to include selection (sometimes too narrow, other times too encyclopedic), age (generally too young), vintage (sometimes not the one shown on the wine card), serving temperature (whites too cold, reds too warm), type of glassware (can you bring out the good glasses, please?), and on and on. Seriously! Sometimes it seems like there is no end to a wine geek's tale of restaurant woe.

I was reminded of this fact as I read Lettie Teague's *Wall Street Journal* rant (or maybe she was venting and not ranting) about wine by the glass in restaurants.³ Teague can't decide which is worse in restaurant wine-by-the-glass programs: the price or the quality. The rule of thumb is that restaurants charge as much per glass of wine as they actually paid for the whole bottle (and sometimes even more). This makes her feel ripped off. At the same time, the wine has perhaps been sitting around open for who knows how long, losing some or all of its freshness. Fancy wine-storage systems can help with this, but still it's difficult to order a glass of wine (sometimes for twenty-five dollars or more) with much confidence.

Over at the *Financial Times*, Nicholas Lander approaches the issue from the business side and looks for a solution in cooperative arrangements between wine collectors (who are willing to sell off some of their stash at market prices) and restaurants who offer these wines to their customers at reduced markups.⁴ The collectors get a fair price on their investment, the restaurants get a middle-man return without big up-front costs, and customers get access to special wines at lower prices. A great idea, but perhaps hard to scale up.

Restaurant wine is like a double-sided jigsaw puzzle. The same pieces have to fit together to form two different appealing pictures—one for the customers and another for the business. If any of the pieces are upside down or missing, the whole experience is ruined.

The fact that a restaurant charges a semimonopoly price (hard to get a competitive bid once you've been seated) makes the situation more frustrating. One solution is to loosen the monopoly hold on price, which some restaurants are doing by reducing or eliminating corkage fees. Bring your own wine (purchased at normal retail prices) and enjoy dinner and a wine experience. Since wine is typically the highest-priced item on a restaurant bill (more expensive than the entree, for example), reducing the wine cost removes a disincentive to dine out. I don't think many customers take up the "no corkage fee" offer, but some do, and if treated well they are likely to return to dine again. If there are conditions on free corkage (the wine cannot be on our list, for example, or free corkage on one bottle if you purchase a bottle from us), they need to be clearly stated to avoid misunderstanding and hard feelings.

I found more good advice in an earlier *Wall Street Journal* column written by Dorothy J. Gaiter and John Brecher called "10 Ways to Save Money Ordering Wine at Restaurants."⁵ All their advice was as timely then as it probably is now: avoid wine by the glass (huge markup), ignore the conventional wisdom that it's smart to order the second-cheapest wine on the list (it's a trap), don't ignore house wines—but rule 6 really caught my eye: "*6. Never order Santa Margherita Pino Grigio.* We don't mean to pick on Santa Margherita. We know many people like it and that's fine. But because so many people like it, it is routinely one of the most outrageously priced wines on the list."

Nothing personal, Dottie and John said, it's just supply and demand plus a certain bandwagon effect that seems to afflict wine drinkers when confronted with a complicated and uncertain set of choices.

> We note it here only as a classic example of this: If you stay within your comfort zone, ordering only wines you already know, you will be punished for it, price-wise. In addition, no wine is going to seem like a good value to you when you know you could buy it at a local store for half the price or less. That's why it's so important to focus on labels or kinds of wines that you wouldn't otherwise see. . . . Remember: There is value in tasting something new.

Sensible advice and in line with rule 5—don't pay the "Chardonnay tax"—that is based on the same logic. But it's not always easy advice to follow in practice, given the high cost of restaurant wine. Everyone wants to find that delightful unexpected bargain, but no one really likes paying the bill for a wine experiment that disappoints. So restaurants and wine consumers alike seem to find themselves drawn to a small set of "usual suspects." Maybe we should break this habit by experimenting with extreme-value wines.

EXTREME-VALUE WINE

Our friend Jerry doesn't seem like the kind of guy who would go digging around in the closeout bin or shopping for wine at Aldi—too classy for that—but there he was at Joyce and Barry's house on Friday showing off his latest finds: cheap wine from a Grocery Outlet store. The wine wasn't so much good or bad as simply intriguing—is it really possible for a sophisticated wine enthusiast like Jerry to be satisfied shopping for wine at an "extreme-value" store? Only one way to find out, so we got in the car the next day and headed for the strip mall.

Headquartered in Berkeley, California, Grocery Outlet bargain market is America's largest extreme-value grocery chain, with more than 185 independently owned stores in seven states. It has been in business since 1946. Prices are low, low, low. Grocery Outlet stores are supermarket-sized spaces filled with off-brand and closeout products along with a wide enough selection of fresh goods to allow families to do all their grocery shopping in one place. The ones I have visited are nice if not especially fancy stores. I can see why budget-minded families shop there. I suspect that they keep the decor pretty basic so that people feel like they are getting bargains—and they do. The wine corner at the nearest store was large and well stocked. Many of the brands were "no-name" mysteries (one was even named "Mystery," as in "Mystery Creek" or something like that), although a few products from recognized mass-market makers were available. Mainly, I think, these were leftover wines closed out by distributors to raise cash or make room for incoming shipments, along with no-name brands "dumped" under a bogus label.

The wines came from all over—California, naturally, Australia, France, Italy, Chile. There was even a $3.99 "Champagne" from Argentina. Honest— it said "Champagne." Prices were suitably low—most of the wines sold for $2.99 to $5.99. It isn't hard to make money selling extreme-value wine when you can buy up surplus bulk wine for just pennies a liter and package it up for quick sale. Extreme-value retailers are the perfect distribution channel for wines like these. I walked out with three bottles of wine for a total of $13.97 plus tax. According to the sales receipt, "By shopping with us you saved $28.00," an average of 67 percent off the retail price.

I wasn't really surprised at what I saw as I surveyed the wine wall. Then, slowly, a different kind of wine mystery began to unfold. Sue must have sharp eyes because she picked out the first surprise. Sam's Creek Marlborough Sauvignon Blanc for $3.99. That's awfully cheap for a New Zealand wine here in the US. New Zealand is a high-cost wine producer that has succeeded in charging a premium price for its wine. Indeed, New Zealand has for many years earned the highest average export price of any country in the world, despite surging production that threatens to create unmarketable surpluses. Everyone worries that one day the export limit will be hit and prices will start to tumble from twelve to twenty dollars down to, well, $3.99. Is that what this Sam's Creek wine really means? The end of NZ wine's premium price?

Frighteningly, Sam's Creek isn't a no-name closeout wine. The label says that it is made and bottled by Babich Wines, one of the famous names in New Zealand wine, and the Internet tells me that Waitrose sold it for about ten dollars in Britain. I wonder if the unsold British inventory has somehow made its way here?

Two more bottles raised more questions about New Zealand wines. I paid $5.99 for a Isabel Estate Marlborough Sauvignon Blanc. I almost overlooked it, but the label caught my eye. Isabel Estate is a Marlborough quality producer, exceedingly well-known in Great Britain where this wine sells for about ten pounds (more than twice what I paid), but not so widely distributed here in the US, I think. How did it get here, and who among the Grocery Outlet clientele would recognize its quality sitting there surrounded by cheap and cheerful closeouts? The third wine makes the puzzle more complicated. It is a Te Awa Merlot from the Gimblett Gravels of Hawke's Bay. Te Awa Farm is another famous Kiwi producer, and while this wine—an estate product from a distinguished producer in a famous region—might have been slightly past its prime and therefore a typical closeout risk, it is still very surprising to see it sold at a place like Grocery Outlet for $3.99 rather than the $16–20 retail price.

These three New Zealand wines may be random surplus wines found in the sort of place where random wines go to be sold. Or they may be indicators of important changes in the world of wine. Kinda makes you wonder, doesn't it?

UNCORKING THE EXTREME WINE PHENOMENON

Studies have repeatedly shown that wine drinkers are influenced by price— but not in the way you learned in Econ 101. A lower price does not always produce more sales because insecure buyers infer quality from price. They assume that higher price means better wine. In a blind tasting of two identical wines, buyers will often rate one above the other if they are told it costs more. So why are many wine drinkers now stooping down and buying cheaper (sometimes very cheap) wines—and shopping at stores like Grocery Outlet—when in the past they have been programmed to consider these products inferior? I think there are three forces at work.

The first factor is what you might call the Two Buck Chuck effect. Here in America, Trader Joe's stores have led the way in introducing American wine drinkers to inexpensive own-brand wines. Because shopping at Trader Joe's is cool, trying Trader Joe's discount wines is cool, too (or at least not as uncool as buying Carlo Rossi at Kroger would be). You might ask "How good can a three-dollar wine be?" elsewhere, but at Trader Joe's it's "How *bad* can it be?"

TJ's lends its reputation to the wine, which is the key to all own brands. It is clear that Safeway, 7-Eleven, Target, Walmart, and many other chains that have introduced own-brand wines believe that they can do the same.

I call the second factor the Costco Effect. Costco, the big-box-store chain, is the largest retailer of wine in the United States. Although their selection of wines is surprisingly limited (generally fewer than 150 different wines in each store compared with one thousand to two thousand or more at a typical upscale supermarket), it draws people in with low prices, made possible in part by the fact that buyers pay annual membership fees for the right to shop. Costco has trained its upscale clientele to look for low prices, but that's not the Costco Effect I'm talking about here. Costco doesn't sell extreme-value wines—it leaves the bottom-feeding market to others.

The Costco Effect refers to the fact that shopping for wine at Costco is a lot like a treasure hunt. The wine selection changes all the time and so you need to come back often. Costco makes a point of stocking limited-production wines, which run out. So if you see something you like, you better buy it now. I have friends who have scored one or two spectacularly good buys on impossible-to-find iconic wines at Costco and who are now completely addicted—they stop by as often as they can just to see what might be in the bin today. Costco's success with its treasure-hunt strategy has generated a group of upscale customers who find the hunt almost as pleasant as the wine they buy. It's a big step but not an impossible one to go from Costco to Grocery Outlet, since both position themselves as happy hunting grounds.

The final piece of the demand puzzle is the recession, which made most of us stop and think about what we are paying and what we are getting. The data indicate that trading down (lower price), trading over (adopting a more casual and lower-cost wine lifestyle), and drinking up (drinking from the cellar rather than buying expensive wines) are significant effects. Paying less for wine doesn't carry the social stigma it might have in the boom-boom days, and it doesn't dent your personal wine identity as deeply, either.

When you combine these three effects, you get a market where extreme-value wines can enter the mainstream. The demand for these wines is increasing, with different wine buyers responding to different motivations. It will be interesting to see if the market shift is permanent or if wine buyers will go back to their old habits.

Extreme wine isn't solely an American phenomenon, of course. In fact you could argue that the US wine buyers are latecomers to the extreme wine party. Reports from Australia and New Zealand suggest that their version of this phenomenon is much better developed. Australian bargain hunters look for "cleanskin" wines, which are wines with all but the most basic wine-type information removed. Significantly, while the label might tell you that this is a Shiraz from Barossa, it won't say who made it, which makes buying cleanskins even more of a treasure hunt (or is it a scavenger hunt?) than a trip to Costco. The wine could be great, not so great, or really pretty bad. I wonder if the Aussies do what some Trader Joe's customers do in the US—buy one bottle and then step outside to take a sip. If it's good, run back in and buy the rest of the case.

Bargains are relative, and here in the US an entrepreneur named Cameron Hughes has become a wine world celebrity by taking the cleanskins model upmarket. Hughes buys up premium surplus bulk wines from California (and increasingly from other parts of the wine world) and labels them, like the cleanskins, with information that both informs (the type of wine, vintage year, alcohol content, etc.) and conceals (who made the wine). The conceal-ment is meant to protect the actual maker, who presumably wants to sell an identical or nearly identical product for much, much more. The wines are sold online and sometimes in stores, including both Costco and Grocery Out-let. As I was writing this, one of the online features was a typically mysterious 2009 Napa Valley Cabernet Sauvignon sold under the generic name Cameron Hughes Lot 247. Here's the website's description of the wine.[6]

> *Taste:* Lot 247 is an opulent wine with velvety, silken tannins. Concentrated blackberry and cherry intertwine with cherry infused fruit. Black licorice, espresso and integrated oak shimmer in the background of this elegant moun-tain fruit Cabernet. With fine-grained tannins and framing acidity, this wine shows old-world grace and plenty of fruit on the palate.
>
> *Cameron Confidential:* Lot 247 is quintessential Napa Cabernet from the ter-rific 2009 vintage. The wine comes to us from a relatively new winery with a lot of money behind it and plans to grow. The facilities are brand new in the last decade and the vineyards are all top notch, boasting properties in Rutherford, Calistoga, and St. Helena. They came to us last Fall and opened up their doors to their cellar as they simply had way more wine than they could sell—their

prices start at $60/bottle. Sam and Mike spent weeks feeling out the right blend and have really put together a great wine.

Can you guess who might have made the 9,800 cases of this wine that Cameron Hughes received? And can you guess what price it might have sold for? In their original labels, Napa wines like this can sell for sixty dollars or more (sometimes a lot more). But you can buy Lot 247 for eighteen dollars. Or you could have bought it. Lot 247 had already sold out by the time I finished writing about it. Now that's extreme!

What should we think about extreme-value wine? It is easy to conclude that the extreme-value trend is a bad thing for the wine industry. People are paying less for wine, buying more generic wine and less of the quality product. I don't see this as a completely negative trend, however. At least they are buying *wine* and not switching to other beverages. That would be ugly. This is part of the story of the collapse of wine demand in Europe. Wine became just another beverage and faded away as a quotidian pleasure. That hasn't happened here, at least not yet.

I am actually hopeful that the extreme-value trend will ultimately benefit the wine world, although I admit that my viewpoint is backed up by anecdotes more than hard data. I spoke with a young couple at the local Grocery Outlet who seem to me to be an optimistic view of the future of wine in America. They had parked their shopping cart (with two small kids) in the wine corner and were busy picking out three or four bottles of wine from the huge selection of inexpensive bottles. Do you buy wine here often? Yes, every week. We try different wines, which is fun. Some of them are disappointing, but it doesn't cost very much to try them, and we can always buy something different the next time. It's been a long time since we found something that made us want to come back and buy a case, but that's OK—it's still fun. What I like about this couple is that they use the extreme-value store as an opportunity to experiment, and they have the confidence to trust their own taste rather than some wine critic's ratings. If they keep this up I think they will work their way out of the bargain bin. But I hope they never lose their sense of fun and willingness to take a chance on something different.

Wine is a serious business, but it is a mistake to take it too seriously. Wine can be intimidating, that's for sure, especially the high-stakes wine game. It might be a healthier business in the long run if more people learn to love its treasure-hunt side. If mainstreaming extreme-value wine helps accomplish that, I think it is a positive development.

THE CHEAPEST WINE

A friend of mine (now sadly deceased) used to brag that he never paid for wine. Free wine is a pretty good deal, so I asked him how he managed to drink well for nothing. His secret, he said, was that he bought wines that he thought would be more valuable in the future, and for every case he drank he set one aside for the auction house. The profits from the sales on average covered the total bill. It is a great strategy, but not something that most of us are likely to try. The market for cellar-aged Yellow Tail Shiraz or Two Buck Chuck Chardonnay is pretty limited, so if wines like these are your regular tipple, I think you have to pay for them yourself. You're going to have to go big to make this strategy work, and most of us aren't prepared for that sort of investment.

The next best thing to free is cheap, and so I asked Michael and Nancy, my official senior cheap and good-value wine research assistants, to tell me where in the world the best wine bargains can be found. They should know. They spent twenty years aboard their forty-four-foot sailboat *Serenity* circumnavigating the globe. At each port of call they'd buy an inexpensive local wine and, if they liked it, try something just a bit cheaper. If they liked that, they'd try another bottle that was cheaper still. Down, down, down the price ladder they would go until they hit a wine that just didn't make the cut. Then they'd step back up, confident that they'd found the cheapest drinkable wine around. It was sort of like choosing a wine by Braille, but using their sense of taste, not touch, to guide their progress.

I asked Michael and Nancy to tell me their most memorable bargain wines. The wines of Israel, they said, because they were so surprised by the quality and variety. They settled on a $1.50 Riesling as the "house" wine on their boat and impressed fellow cruisers who imagined that it cost much more (and would never stoop themselves to buying such a cheap wine). Turkey was another port of call with surprising wines at excellent prices, they said. Their approach was always to purchase local products made for the local market and avoid paying the "Chardonnay tax" that is imposed on heavily promoted wines from multinational producers. And, like the nice couple I met at the Grocery Outlet, they were unafraid to experiment, learned to live with occasional disappointment, and trusted their own tastes rather than going with the crowd.

The advice I give when people ask me about finding bargain wines is to look at what everyone else is drinking and try something else. For me, as a Riesling lover, this has worked well in recent years because poor Riesling is misunderstood and underappreciated (people think that it's all sticky sweet, which it isn't, and that sweetness is always a bad thing, which it's not). You can often buy really excellent Rieslings for the price of an ordinary Chardonnay.

And I tell people to think global but drink local when they can. For example, some of my favorite bargain wines from Washington State are Lembergers. Lemberger? Isn't that a stinky cheese? No, it's a grape variety (also called Limberger or Blau Limberger) found chiefly in Austria (where it is Blaufränkisch) and Washington. People drink it up at winery tasting rooms, but it gets lost and ignored on store shelves. Although you'll never find it in the Two Buck Chuck price range, it's always a good value, and you'll never pay a popularity tax to drink it.

THE 1 PERCENT SOLUTION: EXTREME WINE VERSUS OPERA

Now it's time for me to reflect upon the extreme wine phenomenon. Or maybe this is just a rant. You be the judge. We've surveyed the extremes of wine prices from top to bottom, and what have we learned? Even if the rise in trophy wine prices has slowed down a bit, it sure looks like these wines have become the domain of the "1 percent." Which is fine, I guess, but it does change things. Is Bordeaux (and are the other trophy wine types) still relevant? Relevant to us 99 percenters, I mean. Bordeaux used to define fine wine, but now even 1 percenters in the US don't seem to buy much of it—the momentum's shifted to Asia. Export data suggest that interest in Bordeaux has dropped off sharply in the US, now the world's biggest overall wine market but no longer a powerful player in the Bordeaux game.[7] It's just another "brand" to many Americans, and one that is not as successful as it once was.

I was thinking about all the fuss that there is about Bordeaux, the annual en primeur circus, and the critics' ratings of these wines, and suddenly I found myself humming an opera tune. What can opera teach us about Bordeaux wine? Maybe nothing! But please read on anyway. Bordeaux's problem is that it is so expensive. Opera has that problem, too. Opera is arguably the most expensive form of art. Large capital expenditures are required (have you priced an opera house recently?). The sets and costumes used in high-end opera are so expensive that they are stored for future use and rented out to earn a few extra bucks. Opera is enormously labor intensive, too. You need soloist singers, a chorus, and an orchestra and conductor. Dancers are often also required. Most of these artists have trained for years and years, so we might add in human capital costs, too. There may be some type of regularly produced art that is more expensive to make, but I don't know what it is. It isn't a surprise, therefore, that opera evolved into an art for rich elites, and the opera houses became gilt palaces of conspicuous consumption. The tunes made it out onto the street, of course, and into the parlor, too, when sheet-music publishing caught on, but the focus was on grand opera, the elite patrons who watched it, and the elite artists who performed it.

Opera soon went global as the influence of European elites spread to the Americas and Asia. You can still see evidence of this cultural flow in the beautiful opera houses scattered across the world wherever colonial centers emerged and in faded news articles about the famous (if fading) touring opera stars who performed in them. Then technology in the form of broadcast radio and recordings (and then television, DVDs, etc.) brought opera to the masses. Opera on the radio here in the US began in 1931 with the first Metropolitan Opera broadcasts. The regular Saturday performances, sponsored for years by Texaco, became part of the shared experience of American life. Opera really meant something. But technology, which initially democratized opera, eventually became a corrosive force, too. Technology allowed opera to move from free broadcast media to pay-to-listen satellite radio and pay-to-view high-definition opera showings in movie theaters. More significantly, however, communications technology opened up an alternative universe of tunes to whistle and performances to enjoy.

Opera lost its privileged status and became just another artistic niche. Attention was paid, as it must be, because of the quality of the works and the sacrifices of those who organized and performed them, but opera's high cost became harder to justify. Attention became focused on the tried-and-true "warhorses" that would be certain to sell tickets. New operas were still written and sometimes performed, but not as often as one might hope. Opera still means something, but it is not the same.

It seems to me that the attention given to Bordeaux bears more than some superficial similarity to our attitude toward opera, although I naturally do

not want to push the analogy too far. Bordeaux, like opera, used to be a signi-
fier of taste among both elites who could afford it and the masses who could
not. (And it probably still is in Hong Kong and China.) Like opera, top-flight
Bordeaux is a victim of its successes and excesses—now so expensive that even
rich Americans balk at the prices. The focus is on those wines at the top of
the Classification of 1855 and a few others that have been identified by Parker
and other critics.

But Bordeaux is not the only game in town. The globalization that made
Bordeaux prices soar has also opened up a world of excellent alternatives.
There are a lot of great wines; maybe Château Lafite is as great as *La Traviata*,
but only a few will have the money, taste, and opportunity to sample either
one at its best. Is extremely expensive Bordeaux still relevant? I have decided
that it is, but in the particular way that great opera is still relevant. Opera no
longer informs us about music (or culture) generally as it once did. Opera is
about opera now, and that is good enough. And Bordeaux is (just?) Bordeaux.

SUPERMARKETS AND OPERA HOUSES

This chapter started in the supermarket and ended up at the opera house, all
in an attempt to understand the complicated relationship between money and
wine. What have we learned? Well, money is such a strong force in the world
today that it would be quite a surprise if wine somehow escaped its impact.
But it doesn't affect all parts of the wine world equally. It's not really about
wine at the top end: the most expensive bottles like those famous Bordeaux.
Or at least it's not *just* about wine, and maybe it never really was. Big money
changes things quite a bit and not always for the better.

It's not just about the wine at the other extreme down there on the bottom
shelf, either, but I actually see something hopeful in what you might call the
cheap wine movement. Yes, I know that wineries need to make a profit to stay
in business, so if everyone bought their wine at Grocery Outlet the world of
wine wouldn't be nearly as rich as it is today. But there's something to be said
for people who don't put wine on a pedestal just because it is so expensive.
And there's something to like about wines that people buy just because they
like them.

Wines cheap and dear: either of these extremes by itself would destroy the
world of wine as we know it, but taken together they strike a healthy balance
that promises to keep wine relevant for decades to come.

6

Extreme Wine
Booms and Busts

More than two thousand wine producers, grape growers, and industry executives gathered in a massive hotel ballroom in Sacramento, California, at the end of January 2012 to learn the "State of the Industry." This is always the most popular session of the annual Unified Wine and Grape Symposium, the Western Hemisphere's largest wine-industry meeting and trade show, because unlike some other sessions that focus on particular technical issues in wine, this one is about money, which is always on everyone's mind.

Not that it has always been an "upper" to sit through these presentations. In recent years the silver lining (the emergence of the United States as the world's largest wine market) came wrapped in dark clouds. The Great Recession hit the wine economy pretty hard, for example. Sales of high-end wines had fallen (the market for wines above about twenty-five dollars was often called a "dead zone"), and discounted prices were almost universally the norm. A decade of global oversupply had driven wine-grape prices into the basement, and many winegrowers were "grubbing up" their vines and planting more profitable alternative crops like almonds and pistachios.

WHEEL OF FORTUNE

I wasn't really sure what the audience was expecting when I stepped up to the podium to moderate the session, but I could sense a lot of tension in the room. And for good reason, because the facts and figures that the distinguished panelists revealed represented a dramatic sea change. The wine "wheel of fortune" had taken a new turn, and the American wine industry had entered a new phase that was as surprising as it was predictable.

For all its upscale pretensions, wine remains essentially a dirty-fingernail, bib-overall agricultural product. The wine you drink ultimately depends upon the grapes that some farmer somewhere in the world has managed to grow. Wine suffers all the natural and economic threats and uncertainties as other farmed goods, and one of the most interesting of these is a tendency toward cycles of boom and bust. The Turrentine Brokerage company, a California-based grape and wine brokerage company, calls it the Wine Business Wheel of Fortune, and like *Wheel of Fortune* hostess Vanna White's famous television wheel, it goes round and round, spinning off winners and losers.

The wine cycle is easy to understand but frustrating to deal with. It is based on the fact that, because wine is a farm good (or made from farmed grapes), the supply at any particular time is limited by past vineyard production decisions and cannot be easily expanded in the short run. This fact makes the market prone to exaggerated price cycles. Suppose, for example, that wine and wine-grape prices are relatively high, as they were in the United States in the late 1990s. High prices discourage demand growth, of course, but provide grape growers with a strong incentive to expand by planting new vineyards and renewing aging ones. New vines take root, but it takes several years before they can produce commercially acceptable wine grapes. The high prices of 1998–1999 therefore set the stage for huge increases in supply in 2002–2004, when the new vineyard production hit the market. Grape and wine prices fell as large surpluses appeared, and plans to further expand production came to a sudden halt.

Prices stayed low year after year as new vineyards, planted back in the good old days of higher prices, continued to mature. And then the Great Recession hit, depressing prices yet again. Wine consumption continued to grow, powered by discount prices and other factors, but vineyard expansion (with only a few exceptions) did not.

SPIN THE WHEEL

This set the stage for the 2012 wine symposium. The two massive screens behind the speakers showed that demand had finally overtaken supply. Bust (for many of the wine-grape growers in the room) had turned to boom. Looking down the road a year or two (or more), there just weren't going to be enough wine grapes to meet demand. Prices were already on the rise in 2012 and large-scale producers were scouring the globe for sources of market-quality bulk wine to put into bottles and bags and boxes to satisfy American wine consumers. The problem seemed unlikely to go away soon because the shortage of wine grapes even extended to nursery stocks necessary for new plantings, which also take time to produce. The boom for wine-grape growers, of course, represented a squeeze on producers, who now faced the problem of trying to sell more expensive wine to cost-sensitive consumers who had become accustomed to bargain prices.

The wine wheel was turning from surplus to shortage in 2012, but it was likely to turn again eventually. The lure of higher prices was certain to encourage new wine-grape plantings, which might all eventually come on the market at about the same time, overwhelming demand with greater supply and pushing price back down again. That's how markets have always worked in agriculture, and that's how the wine market works, too. The Turrentine Brokerage reckons that there have been three complete rotations of the Wine Business Wheel of Fortune in the last thirty years, of which the current boom and bust are perhaps the longest in duration and maybe even the broadest and deepest in terms of economic impact.

Every wine region in the world has ridden the wheel through its boom and bust cycles. Sometimes it's just like riding in an old pickup truck down a bumpy road, but sometimes the booms and busts get bigger and bigger until finally the whole vehicle collapses and the government has to come in to clean up the mess. What do these cycles tell us? Well, as I said a few paragraphs ago, they tell us that wine is still fundamentally a farm good despite evidence to the contrary and is subject to agricultural cycles. They might also tell us why so many wine businesses, even very large ones like Gallo, are still family-owned and not public corporations. You really need to think long term in wine, since the long wait from new vines to marketable wine is interrupted by the boom-bust cycles I've just described. Family firms that think in terms of generations are perhaps better suited to riding out the cycles of the wine business in some ways than public corporations that have to meet quarterly earnings estimates.

Yes, the wine wheel of fortune reveals quite a lot, but these cycles are the norm for wine, and this book isn't very interested in what's normal. It's the extremes that we are looking for. With that in mind, here are three nominees for the most extreme wine boom and bust!

AUSTRALIA: AN EXTREME HISTORY OF BOOMS AND BUSTS

While the winemakers and grape growers in Sacramento were listening to news about how their world was changing—for the better for some and for the worse for others—similar groups in Australia were considering their own circumstances. They were so "down under" (excuse the pun), the only way for Australian wine was up. Certainly Australia's cycle of boom and bust has been both extreme and especially interesting because in retrospect it seems so utterly predictable. But, as I'll explain in a moment, it is Australia's long history of wine booms and busts that qualifies the country for inclusion in this chapter.

The Australian boom went according to plan, at least at the start. The plan (an actual plan), which was released in 1996, was called *Strategy 2025*[1] and outlined a bold export strategy for "Brand Australia" wines aimed to achieve dramatic growth. "The vision is that by the Year 2025 the Australian wine industry will achieve $4.5 billion in annual sales by being the world's most influential and profitable supplier of branded wines, pioneering wine as a universal first choice lifestyle beverage."

Persuaded by the strategy, enticed by the seemingly endless export opportunities of an expanding global economy, and powered by the success of best-selling brands like Jacob's Creek in the UK market and Yellow Tail in the US, Australia achieved its 2025 goals twenty years sooner than projected. What was projected to be long-term growth became instead a short-term boom as vineyard and winery capacity exploded.

Sensing perhaps that expansion was out of control, the industry released a second report in 2007 titled *Directions to 2025*, which outlined a plan to guide and control growth and develop markets for Australia's regional wines and not just the big-vat bulk products that had proved so popular in the past. *Directions* had the right idea in wanting to steer Brand Australia away from its high-growth strategy, but its timing was off. The implicit warning came too late, and then a perfect storm of problems turned Australia's soaring boom earthward.

Changing tastes were the first troublesome factor. The market turned away from Brand Australia's signature Shiraz and Chardonnay wines. Wine critic

Oz Clarke blamed it in part on the main character in the film *Bridget Jones's Diary*, who drowns her sorrows in big glasses of Aussie Chardonnay. Bridget is a loser and so it became loser wine—who would want to drink that? Of course it wasn't as simple as that, but the one-note simplicity of the cheapest Brand Australia wines tainted the reputation of the better products as consumers turned toward new boom wines—New Zealand Sauvignon Blanc (especially in Australia itself, where it became the best-selling white wine) and Malbec and Pinot Noir in the United States.

The Great Recession that began in 2008 did nothing to help Australia's situation by reducing demand in some markets and growing demand in others. Exports fell by more than 20 percent or eight million cases in two years, with higher-quality wines especially hard hit as the twenty-five-dollar-plus "death zone" took its toll on sales. Pressure to reduce price intensified everywhere, and exports began to shift from higher-priced bottled branded wines to lower-cost bulk products shipped out in huge 24,000-liter Flexitank wine bladders stuffed inside ocean freight containers meant to be bottled, often with a private brand, in the US, UK, and even China.

The message was clear: Australia had too much wine, and it cost too much to produce. That message was delivered loud and clear in a report called *Wine Restructuring Action Agenda*.[2] "Comprehensive analysis and consultation suggests at least 20% of bearing vines in Australia are surplus to requirements, with few long-term prospects," the report stated. "On cost of production alone, at least 17% of vineyard capacity is uneconomic." The collapse of the Australian wine industry, both in the vineyards and in the production facilities, gained speed.

And then, incredibly, things got worse! Australian vineyards were hit by one natural plague after another. Drought increased the price of irrigation water, making wine grapes even more uneconomical to produce. Heat waves baked the vineyards and reduced grape quality. Brush fires gave the grapes and wines an unpleasant (and unmarketable) smoky taint. And then torrential rains and flooding left many vineyards with moldy, rotten grapes. What a mess. The silver lining to all these disasters was that, by reducing harvest yields, the drought, heat, smoke, and then rain allowed the huge surplus wine lake to slowly diminish, making an ultimate balance of demand and supply seem realistic.

DUTCH DISEASE?

And then came more bad news: Dutch disease and parallel imports. Dutch disease is the name economists give to the problem of too much good news in one industry and its negative impact on the rest of the economy. If one sector of the economy gets hot on the global markets (think oil exports, for example), one effect can be that export sales increase the demand for the country's currency, causing it to appreciate in real terms. The rising currency value makes all the nation's other products more expensive on foreign markets, sending them into a tailspin.

That's how good news in one part of the economy can backfire. The *Economist* magazine apparently invented the term to describe the dilemma of the Netherlands after a big gas field was found there in 1959. The good news/bad news in Australia was clearly the fact that China's economy is growing rapidly and sucking in the natural resources that Australia has in considerable abundance. But big purchases of the Australian dollar needed to pay for these products have pushed the currency up, making Australian wines more expensive here in the US and elsewhere.

That's just what the shell-shocked Australian wine industry needed—higher prices or slimmer margins in key export markets! But then the bad news got even worse—the strong Aussie dollar drove down wine prices in Australia's domestic market and slashed producer margins there, too. How? Through "parallel import" programs that crafty retailers put into effect. Some large retailers there discovered stocks of lower-priced Australian wines in other countries, including Brazil, Malaysia, and the US, and imported them back into Australia to sell for less.

Some Australian producers were thus getting a double squeeze in their home market. They were exporting wine at the slimmest of margins only to see the wine shipped right back and sold by local retailers, undercutting their plans for profitable home-market sales. Why do they call these "parallel imports"? I imagine it is because the imports and exports form two parallel lines, with cargo ships full of outbound and inbound wine containers crossing midocean.

And so you can see why I said that for Australia the only way is up. And up it will surely rise as adjustment progresses, but, I hope, not into another boom. Because it isn't the magnitude of Australia's boom and bust that make it noteworthy, it is the awful regularity. You see, nearly all of Australia's wine history has been boom and bust.

AUSTRALIA'S FIVE WINE BOOMS (AND BUSTS)

University of Adelaide wine economist Kym Anderson recounted Australia's serial wine-cycle story in his 2004 book *The World's Wine Markets*.[3] Each cycle is the same in its basic architecture—vineyard boom followed by a long plateau with persistently falling prices—but the details are so different that they are worth your attention.

The first boom lasted from 1854 to 1871 and was followed by a decade of decline. It was provoked by the Australian gold rush, which attracted thirsty riches-seeking immigrants who came for the gold and stayed for the wine. Interestingly, the California wine industry got a big boost at about the same time for similar reasons; the first California gold was found on the American River at Sutter's Mill in 1848. Supply gradually exceeded domestic demand, and the resulting surplus could not be profitably sold abroad because of the combination of high transportation costs and foreign-trade barriers. The growing wine lake spelled eventual bust for the burgeoning Australian industry.

The next cycle played out a bit differently, although the result was the same. Exports boomed this time, supplementing rising domestic demand in the second boom (1886–1896) and subsequent bust (1896–1915). Cheaper transport and a more open international marketplace were important factors in the industry's growth.

The third cycle (boom 1915–1925 and bust 1925–1945) was more complicated. Government policies played a significant role. Postwar soldier settlement policies and land development subsidies expanded the potential agricultural base for wine. The advent of irrigation further increased production. An export subsidy for fortified wine combined with a 50 percent British "Imperial Preference" on these wines increased supply and export demand simultaneously. It all unraveled in the Great Depression, however, as demand fell, subsidies fell, trade barriers rose, and the fundamental premises on which the boom was built slowly collapsed.

Domestic demand grew slowly for many years before the fourth cycle (1968–1975 boom and 1975–1987 bust), which was rooted in the Australian market itself. Retail sales reforms (much like those that erupted in Britain in about the same period) expanded the effective domestic market for wine. Per capita consumption of wine soared, fueled in part by the advent of "cask" or bag-in-box wine technology. Australian winemaker Thomas Angove invented the basic one-gallon box-wine container in 1965, and the Penfolds winery perfected the technology in 1967 by adding the now-standard plastic dispenser tap. The corrugated paper casks "democratized" wine to a certain extent, broadening and deepening the consumer base and even developing a previously undiscovered domestic market for white wines.

There are many interesting features of the four wine booms I've just described. First, each of them was set off by a disruptive development—gold, globalization, subsidies and irrigation, wine packaging technology. Half of the booms were domestic, and half were based on international demand. All of them, according to Anderson, ended with more of a whimper than a bang: production peaked, then plateaued, with a long period of falling returns. The most recent boom, the fifth, was different mainly in its extent, being driven by rising global demand, and I think in terms of the consequences. No plateau here. The collapse of wine is Australia has been surprisingly sudden and deep.

Given all this it will be interesting to see what the next boom looks like, because I am quite sure that another boom is on the horizon. Booms seem to be utterly irresistible. My evidence that hope will triumph over experience comes from a paper that Kym Anderson wrote with one of his students, Robert Osmond, back in 1998—just two years after the *Strategy 2025* plan was released.[4] The paper asked "How long will Australia's wine boom last?" and answered by saying that maybe it might last a little bit longer *this time*. Maybe domestic and international conditions were aligned to support rapid growth for a little longer than in the past. It put the most cautiously optimistic possible spin on things, that's for sure. But the implication of the analysis was clear. Booms end and this one will (and did) end, too. If the Australians can't escape the boom-bust cycle after their long history of rise and fall, what chance for the rest of us?

EXTREMELY FRENCH

No one will be surprised that France is number one in the world of wine. Although it has passed the torch as the largest consumer of wine to the United States (who will in turn eventually cede the honor to China, I am told), it remains at or near the top of the table in terms of area planted to grapevines

(817,000 hectares or nearly two million acres), volume of wine produced (over four billion liters), and value of wine produced (more than 22 billion in US dollars).[5] And of course France has the number-one reputation, based upon its many world-famous wines. Millions of people think wine when they think about France and France when they think about wine.[6]

So it should come as no surprise that France would appear in this chapter about booms and busts. But *which* French boom and bust is most extreme? It would be easy to tell the tale of France's postwar wine boom, which was encouraged in part by the huge payments given by the European Community's Common Agricultural Policy. Wine production was subsidized to provide jobs, incomes, and economic stability in heavily wine-dependent parts of France and Europe. The fact of a production boom (at the same time that domestic consumption was rapidly falling) was no surprise. Nor is the current "bust" restructuring, with thousands of acres of vines "grubbed up" to cut excess capacity and reduce budget outlays. The current crisis is pretty extreme, I admit, but it's not the most extreme.

An even bigger boom happened right at the start of wine in France when, following in the footsteps of the Greeks, Julius Caesar and the Romans brought vines to Gaul, or the Rhône region, as we call it today (Pliny the Elder is one source of information on Roman vineyards in France, including tasting notes). The original plan was that Rome would sell its wine to the French colonies and turn a tidy profit, but the Gallic vineyards expanded quickly. Too quickly, from the Romans' point of view. The direction of trade reversed, and Gallic wines threatened influential Roman wine producers. The boom turned to bust in 92 CE when Emperor Domitian ordered the Gallic vines (and in fact vines throughout the empire) ripped out, ostensibly to ensure more room to grow the grains necessary for Roman food security but probably mainly to protect Roman wine interests.[7] An obvious collapse followed, although evidence suggests that the order was only partially carried out and that those who managed to escape the edict benefited from the predictably higher prices that result from falling supply. Even wine busts have silver linings, I guess. The Gallic boom and bust were huge, but there was an even bigger one.

THE FRENCH CONNECTIONS

Transportation has been a limiting factor in the wine industry for most of its history. Ports, canals, railroads, highways—these are the infrastructure necessities for the development of a wine market and, until the middle of the nineteenth century, these were necessities that France distinctly lacked. As Graham Robb explains in his wonderful book *The Discovery of France*, what we think of today as France was for hundreds of years really a mosaic of towns and regions that were poorly connected and often spoke mutually unfamiliar languages and dialects.[8] The Languedoc region, for example, got its name because its inhabitants didn't speak French at all. They spoke Occitan, where the word "yes" was not the French *oui* but the local *oc*, hence Languedoc's *langue d'oc*.

In this highly localized world, wine production was distinctly small scale and local, too, constrained by the practical limitations of oxcart transport. Wine booms and busts were weather driven, not market based. Since wine was consumed just about everywhere in France, it was produced pretty much everywhere, too, in amounts scaled to the size of the local population. And then, suddenly, everything changed.

Economic historians compare the coming of the railroad in the nineteenth century with the advent of the Internet today: change that creates, destroys, disrupts. The railroad arrived in Languedoc in 1855. The first line went north through Lyon to Paris, and a second soon appeared, going to Bordeaux and its Atlantic port. Railcars dramatically expanded the market for strong, dark Languedoc wines. The big cities of the North, which had previously been supplied by vineyards in the surrounding area, were suddenly fair game for wine producers in the South. And new vineyards appeared to fill the big pipeline that the railroads made possible. Languedoc, which arcs across the South of France, became the world's largest vineyard area (a distinction it holds even today—the single French region of Languedoc has more area under vine than all of the regions of Australia combined!).

The railroad-driven wine boom created, destroyed, and disrupted. It created the vast vineyards of Languedoc; it destroyed many vineyards in the North, which were previously protected by transportation barriers and could not compete with the wines of the South; and it disrupted the way wine was sold. Middlemen called négociants appeared to buy up wine from thousands of small producers, blend and age it, and market it to big-city workers. As I explained in *Wine Wars*, this shifted the power away from producers, who found themselves in cutthroat competition selling a base commodity, and put it in the hands of the sellers.

Wine really boomed in the Languedoc. Wine production doubled and nearly doubled once again in the years between 1850 and 1869. And then came the bust, and it was even bigger than the boom. The bust, like the boom, was caused by a "French connection," but whereas the increased connectivity *within* France led to the big wine boom, it was increased connectivity with the New World that gave us the bust. The source of the bust can be stated in one word: phylloxera.

Phylloxera (*fil-ox-era*) is a tiny root-feeding aphid that arrived in France in 1863 on the roots of some American grapevines that were planted in an experimental vineyard. Ironically, it was transportation technology that created the problem. American grapevines had been shipped across the Atlantic to Europe for years, but the ships were so slow that the phylloxera dried up and died before making landfall. Faster ships meant that they were still alive when planted in French soil and the rest, sadly, is history. Native American vines were phylloxera resistant, but the European *vitis vinifera* vines were not and quickly lost vigor. The aphid spread slowly across Europe, destroying vineyards and wine industries in its path.

The Oxford Companion to Wine sums up phylloxera's impact by comparing it to the Irish potato blight. More than six million acres of vines were destroyed, throwing whole communities and regions into poverty. Total wine production dropped from more than 2,200 million gallons in 1875 to less than 24 million in 1889. That, my friends, is a bust![9]

Like the potato famine, the crisis forced many to migrate to phylloxera-free areas where wine making was still possible. Thus did some Bordeaux and Champagne winemakers set up shop in Spain, for example, and thousands of vignerons moved from Languedoc to Algeria, France's North African colony, where they established vineyards to supply thirsty French markets. (Ironically, many of these families migrated back years later, when Algerian independence made them and their wine unwanted.) All sorts of experimental remedies were attempted but the surest response turned out to be grafting of European vines onto American rootstocks. Many Europeans resisted this solution, despite its obvious effectiveness, because they feared that the wines would not taste the same. Indeed, some still believe that grapes grown on their own rootstocks produce different wines than grapes from grafted vines, and so this debate goes on. There are regions of the globe (Chile, for example, and parts of Australia, Argentina, China, and Washington State) that are so far phylloxera free and where, therefore, ungrafted vines exist in commercial quantities, but these are the exceptions, not the rule. Phylloxera is still a threat—even in America. Winegrowers in Napa Valley, California, have had to replant almost all of their vineyards over the past thirty years because of the unfortunate and widespread decision to use the (supposedly) phylloxera-resistant AxR1 rootstock in their vineyards.

I believe that the French boom and bust of the nineteenth century is the most extreme in terms of wine volumes and perhaps also in terms of economic, political, and social impact. The trains created the modern wine industry and phylloxera destroyed it, or at least knocked it for a loop. The effects were large and long lasting. Indeed, you can see one echo of the boom and bust on almost any label of commercially produced wine that you purchase anywhere in the world! If you look closely at the label, you will almost surely see some sort of narrow or broad geographic designation. These designations or appellations, as they are known, are regulated in different ways by each wine-producing country subject to international protocols and agreements. This "DaVino Code" is the direct result of the combination of railroads and vine aphids. As phylloxera sapped the vitality from French vineyards, increasingly desperate winemakers began surreptitiously to stretch their diminishing wine stocks with cheap and plentiful wines brought in from regions such as Spain and Algeria, as yet untouched or much less affected by the vine scourge. The resulting adulterated wines often bore little resemblance to the fine wines of previous years and threatened to undermine the regional reputations. French vignerons organized to stamp out these debased wines. The first *appellations contrôlée* were thus intended to stop production and sale of the fraudulent wines that phylloxera made necessary and that the efficient railroad transportation system made possible. Thus does the world wine system of today pay its respects to the nineteenth-century French boom and bust!

PROHIBITION: THE IRONY OF BOOM AND BUST

The Eighteenth Amendment to the US Constitution prohibited the manufacture, sale, or transportation of intoxicating beverages in the country. America was officially a dry country from January 17, 1920, until December 5, 1933. You might assume, given this chapter's focus, that I'm going to tell you about the way that Prohibition caused wine to boom and bust—and you'd be right. But the facts might still surprise you.

The Volstead Act, which set down the rules for enforcing Prohibition, specified that anything with more than 0.5 percent alcohol by volume was an intoxicating beverage, so it is obvious that wine was included in the ban (much to the annoyance of proponents of wine as a "temperance drink"). So it seems obvious that the bust would occur during the Prohibition years and the boom would follow repeal, when wine would once again be legal. Some of the facts support this version of the story. Commercial production of wine fell from twenty-five million gallons in 1919 to less than four million gallons in 1925. Most wineries went out of business, with those few that survived taking advantage of loopholes that permitted legal production and sale of wine for medical and sacramental purposes. The four million gallons reported for 1925 is a lot of wine given the limited legal use—I guess there must have been a lot of sick and religious people in America in those years!

Commercial production of wine recovered after 1933, and the number of wineries quickly expanded—boom! But this fact disguises the real story, the one that makes Prohibition a candidate for a chapter about extreme booms and busts. It is ironic that the real boom in wine occurred *during Prohibition* and the bust after its repeal.

Although commercial wine production nosedived during Prohibition, wine-grape production nearly doubled. How is this possible? There were actually three wine loopholes in the Volstead Act. Commercial production of medical and sacramental wine was allowed, as noted before, but so was limited home production of wine for "nonintoxicating" purposes. What this meant in theory is difficult to understand, since even homemade wine is obviously going to exceed the one-half percent of alcohol that defined an intoxicating product. Maybe it was the assumed purpose—homemade wine for temperate home consumption?—that made it "nonintoxicating." But what it meant in practice was clear: each "head of household" in America was legally entitled to produce up to two hundred gallons (or one thousand bottles) of wine each year for home consumption. Wow. Now that is a loophole big enough to drive a wine truck through. And that's just what happened.

Home production of wine soared; wine was far more popular during Prohibition than it was either before or after. California vineyard acreage expanded rapidly to provide grapes for home winemakers in the East, but the types of grapes planted and the way they were farmed changed dramatically. Whereas in other circumstances wine grapes are harvested and quickly transported to cellars, where the fermentation process begins under the watchful eye of trained enologists, during Prohibition the grapes were loaded onto trucks and railcars for a long journey before enthusiastic amateurs took them home and tried to make wine. Delicate grapes like Pinot Noir would never survive the long journey, so sturdy grape varieties and those that could produce strong, deeply colored wines were favored. And I imagine they were picked a bit early, too, since very ripe grapes would be less likely to arrive in good shape after the long, hot rail journey from vineyard to final destination hundreds or even thousands of miles away. Still, producing and selling the grapes sustained a lot of wine-industry families during the dozen-plus years of the Great Experiment, including such now-famous names as Gallo and Mondavi.

You can only imagine what the wines must have been like—tough, under-ripe grapes that had survived (or not) a long railway journey were crafted by untrained hands in improvised and possibly unsanitary conditions into homemade wine. I am sure some first-class wines were produced, but the general standard must have been quite low. And some of the wines were probably downright sickening due to bacterial contamination.

If the wine *boom* happened *during* Prohibition, the wine *bust* followed as soon as commercial wine was made legal again. Consumption of wine dropped, as you would guess, as consumers switched from mediocre home wine to now-legal beer and spirits that quickly came to the market. Commercial wine production resumed, of course, but wine production cannot be ramped up as quickly as beer and spirits.

The real wine bust was not so much about quantity as quality. Many California wineries had reserve stocks of wine made before Prohibition, according to James Lapsley's wonderful book *Bottled Poetry*, but they were by this time well on the road to vinegarville.[10] Even so, some winemakers tried to blend in these old wines with the new to stretch the stocks. The resulting wines could not have been much of an improvement over home production.

Not that the new wines were that much better. The raw materials—the grapes—did not lend themselves to high quality. A 1934 survey of Napa Valley vineyards found that 40 percent of acreage was planted to sturdy Petite Sirah (a.k.a. Durif), 25 percent to Alicante, 15 percent to Zinfandel, and 11 percent to Carignane—all deeply colored shipping grapes.[11] You *can* make quality wines from these grapes, but that's not why they had been planted.

And in any case, quality wine just wasn't in the cards. It was a matter of supply and demand.

Much of the technological skill in making quality wine disappeared during Prohibition. Apart from the few professionals who hung on making medical and sacramental wine, wine making faded away as an occupation in the United States, and it would take a few years for cellar arts and crafts to renew themselves. But it's not clear that there would have been much demand for quality wine in the 1930s even if such products were available. It was the Great Depression, remember, and discretionary incomes were sorely stretched. The American wine palate, if I can even speak of such a thing, was in any case badly corrupted by Prohibition. Wine had become an insipid (and sometimes sickening) drink valued by many more for its alcoholic content than for its artistic concept. There is no quality wine without a demand for quality wine. And the demand just wasn't there, and it took years for it eventually to develop. Hence the post-Prohibition quality bust.

But wait, it gets even worse. The end of Prohibition did not mean the emergence of a free national market in wine as you might expect. Instead many aspects of alcohol regulation were turned over to the states, and each one implemented its own system, effectively fragmenting the market and stifling its growth. Wine in America then (in a way like wine in Australia today) had nowhere to go but up. The vibrant American wine culture of today is even more impressive when viewed from the depths of the post-Prohibition bust.

BOOM VARIETAL

The boom-bust cycle is so much a part of the world of wine that it is almost impossible to escape. I was reminded of this when a film crew showed up at my office door. I didn't really know what to expect when Sky Pinnick contacted me about being interviewed for the documentary he was making. He wanted to talk about Argentina and its hot Malbec wines, and I guess it was logical to talk with me since I write about the Argentinean wine industry frequently on *The Wine Economist* blog. Certainly Argentina and Malbec are two of the great wine success stories of the last twenty years, so I guessed Sky would be interested in that perspective, especially since the film was being backed by Kirk Ermisch, an Oregon-based wine importer who owns a winery in Argentina.

We talked about all sorts of things, and Sky even asked me to give a video tasting note, which thankfully didn't make it into the film. But the main topic of conversation was right down my alley—boom and bust. Because, you see, Argentina has a history of wine booms and busts to match any of the examples I've provided in this chapter.

Argentina is really an Old World country, at least in terms of wine, mistakenly located in the New World. It has long been one of the world's largest wine-producing nations, boasting at one point the largest winery in the world! But you never saw its wines here in the US until just a few years ago. You didn't see them in part because the Argentines drank them all (their per capita wine consumption rivals Italy and Spain, whence many of their families emigrated), and the quality wasn't up to international standards. A combination of falling domestic wine consumption (mirroring the European trend), economic reforms that encouraged foreign investment, and an economic crisis that transformed the industry together helped create the vibrant Argentinean world of wine you see today.

And so the recent boom, which has spread the fine wines of Argentina to the US, Britain, and even China, has changed Argentina's reputation in the world of wine, even if the mediocre old wines of years past still hold a tight grip on the domestic mass market. Good wines and a great story of rebirth (some of those Malbec vines are nearly one hundred years old) and discovery.

And yet, because this is wine and this is Argentina, a long shadow dampens the celebration. How long will the good times last? Even the film's title, *Boom Varietal: The Rise of Malbec*, raises doubts—intentionally, I think, and not just for dramatic purpose.[12] As a winemaker says in one scene, where there's boom, there's bust.

EXTREME BOOM AND BUST?

And so I guess it is time to confess that there is nothing very extreme about booms and busts in the wine world. As we have seen in this chapter, cyclical booms and busts of the type that the Wine Business Wheel of Fortune describes are unexceptional. Because wine is an agricultural product, it is almost necessarily prone to agricultural cycles. In fact, wine may be more prone to these ups and downs than most farm goods because the time lag between when decisions are made and when the results hit the marketplace is much longer—three years or more for wine, but just a year or so for corn, wheat, or soybeans, for example. That makes the cycle longer and more complex and probably makes the peaks and valleys more extreme, too. And of course wine is now a global industry, and while this might in theory reduce fluctuations if cycles in one part of the world balance out opposite phases in the other, I don't see much recent evidence that this has happened. In addition to these cycles, we have seen that bigger booms and busts can be set off by all sorts of events—gold rushes, railroads, vineyard pests, and government policy.

Taking all this into account, it is clear that booms and busts are part of business as usual in the wine industry. What is extreme and therefore unexpected is stability! This realization gives me new respect for family-owned wine producers who have managed to ride out the booms and busts successfully. The Antinori and Frescobaldi families of Italy (which date wine production back to 1385 and 1303 respectively), for example, or here in the New World the much younger Catena family of Argentina and Gallo family of California. The persistence of family businesses like these in a turbulent world is more noteworthy than most of us realize.

7

Extreme Wine People

The International Pinot Noir Celebration (IPNC) has been held on the campus of Linfield College in McMinnville, Oregon, every summer since 1987. It is a short (three days) but very intense gathering of the inhabitants of Planet Pinot. Sue and I were pleased to participate in the 2012 event, where I gave a class as part of that year's University of Pinot program.

Pinot Noir is a sensuous wine. Bordeaux is famously an intellectual wine that is appreciated above the neck, while sensuous Burgundy—made from Pinot grapes—is felt down below, so this event is perhaps better understood through literature than statistics, but "IPNC by the numbers" nonetheless gives you a good sense of what went on.

Each year's celebration mixes together about eight hundred registered participants with about 140 representatives of the seventy featured wineries. An additional five hundred Pinot lovers attend an open-air tasting on the final day. Wines from Oregon, France, Canada, California, Chile, New Zealand, and Argentina were represented on the 2012 list. Chefs from more than four dozen restaurants worked with a team of more than three dozen professional sommeliers and an almost uncountable number of volunteers to produce and serve thousands of plates and portions of delicious food showcasing the region's summer bounty. More than nine hundred diners enjoyed the three-course Grand Dinner on Friday night and about one thousand feasted on

Neah Bay salmon roasted over an open fire in the traditional Northwest Native American way at the Saturday-night barbecue.

IPNC reckons that guests have the opportunity to taste over 250 wines. In addition to the seventy wines that the featured wineries provide, there are more wines to taste in the seminars and at meals where each table features a winemaker host pouring his or her most interesting wines. Indeed, IPNC seems to be an excuse for winemakers to bring out their favorite bottles to share with guests and each other. It is impossible to drink this much wine (impossible for me, at least), so spitting and dumping onto the lush lawns is encouraged and vigorously embraced. I think the grounds of Linfield College must be the most lavishly (and expensively) irrigated fields in the world during the International Pinot Noir Celebration.

People come to the Pinot celebration for all sorts of reasons. Most come for the wine and the chance to meet wine producers from around the world. We met one woman who has come twenty-five years in a row with no plan to terminate the string, and I don't think she was alone. This devotion is tribute to both the wine and the event organizers, who manage somehow to make each year's program both fresh and familiar. Some come, I'm sure, for the food, which was fabulous. No shame in that. How many people say they visit Italy for the art and culture but really go for the food? If you are honest, you might admit to this motive yourself, and IPNC's attendees are probably no different.

Many people come to do business, of course. The list of "wine trade" people I found in my registration packet had about 350 names, including all of the winery participants, of course, distributors, retailers, and representatives of various hotels, restaurants, and trade associations, plus all the main wine media, including blogs, newspapers, wine magazines, and even television (the food editor of *Every Day with Rachael Ray*) and cinema (a documentary about *A Year in Burgundy* was previewed at the event). I counted more than a dozen US states plus six foreign countries (France, Canada, New Zealand, England, Japan, and Switzerland).

My motive? I came for the people. Wine is a relationship business, and meeting new people and renewing old friendships is one of the most important reasons that all these people travel to Oregon. The wine and food are great, but they are to a certain extent simply a delicious excuse for all these assorted groups to come together. But I was after more. I came to IPNC in search of extreme wine people to populate this chapter's pages, and I found them. Here is my report, presented in the sort of rapid-fire style that characterized that weekend, as I wandered from event to event, table to table, chatting with old friends and making new acquaintances before circling back and starting again. If this chapter seems a little disorganized, it's only because I'm trying to capture that real-time extreme wine people experience. Grab a glass and come along!

EXTREME WINE GEEK

The keynote speaker and leader of the Grand Seminar wasn't a famous winemaker (although some winemakers have played that role at IPNC in the past, including Lalou Bize-Leroy, the "Queen of Burgundy"), or even a famous wine critic (Jancis Robinson did the honors a few years ago). No, he was what I would term—with great respect—an extreme wine geek: Allen Meadows.

The old joke (which was told on this occasion) is that the way to make a small fortune in the wine business is to start with a large one, and Allen Meadows is a good example. His career in finance spanned twenty-one years and included senior executive positions at Great Western Bank. Then, in 1999, he decided to turn his big fortune into a small one by giving up money and embracing his true passion, wine. Not just any wine, however. The wines of Burgundy, often considered the wine lover's equivalent of crack cocaine for their ability to cloud the mind and empty the bank account.

Meadows's plan was simple. He'd move to Burgundy and write a book about the people, places, and wines. This plan has evolved only slightly. He now lives in Burgundy for four or five months a year and writes a quarterly journal for a subscription-only website called Burghound.com that covers Burgundy, of course, as well as developments in Pinot Noir in Oregon and California, with annual reports on Champagne. Four quarterly electronic issues plus access to the online database runs $145 per year—more than most online publications but, to put it in perspective, much less than you might pay for a single bottle of a great Burgundy. He finally published his book in 2010, *The Pearl of the Cote: the Great Wines of Vosne-Romaneé*. It includes beautiful maps and photographs (how could a book about Burgundy not be sensuous?) as well as extremely detailed (did I say geeky?) information about the vineyards, the winemakers, and the wines themselves. Appropriately for an extreme wine book, Meadows reports on what might have been the greatest single wine tasting of all time—seventy-four vintages of Domaine Romaneé-Conti from 1870 to the present.

After thirty years of collecting and studying Burgundy and more than a dozen years of full-time work on the book and journal, you would think that Allen Meadows knows all that there is to know about his favorite wine. And hearing him talk, you begin to think this might really be true, but obviously he doesn't believe it because he's still pushing ahead to learn and do more.

Meadows' Grand Seminar was billed as a walk through the vineyards of Chambolle-Musigny, Echézeaux, Gevrey-Chambertin, Nuits-Saint-Georges, and Vougeot. Meadows set the stage and served as translator for the guest winemakers Bertrand Ambroise of Maison Ambroise, Grégory Gouges of Domaine Henri Gouges, Jacques Lardière of Maison Louis Jadot, and Philippe and Vincent Lécheneaut of Domaine Lécheneaut.

The particular wines (I hope you are ready for the geeky details) we tasted were these:

- Domaine Lècheneaut: 2008 Chambolle-Musigny 1er Cru and 2008 Chambolle-Musigny
- Domaine Henri Gouges: 2007 Nuits St-Georges 1er Cru Clos des Porrets Saint-Georges and 2006 Nuits-Saint-Georges 1er Cru Les Pruliers
- Maison Ambroise: 2010 Echézeaux Gran Cru and 2008 Echézeaux Gran Cru
- Maison Louis Jadot: 2006 Gevrey-Chambertin 1er Cru Clos Saint-Jacques and 2001 Chambertin Grand Cru Clos de Bèze

If you know Burgundy, this is clearly an interesting exploration of Burgundian terroir, probing differences in time, place, and maker style. It is impossible to say everything there is to is to say about Burgundy in eight glasses (or eighteen or eighty), but this is a start. If you do not know your Burgundy, then just staring at the names of the wines listed above is enough to give you a sense of how complicated Burgundy is—vintages, villages, vineyards, and vineyard classification—and how much time and effort it must take to understand the wine to the depth and extent that a wine geek like Allen Meadows does. Allen is extreme in this sense, but not unique. There are other Burgundy geeks, and there are geeks who take delight in Bordeaux, Rhône, and Champagne wines, to name just a few French regions, and wines all around the world. They are one type of extreme wine person that you will meet.

EXTREME WINE IMPORTER

All of us who attended the Burgundy seminar had good seats, but the best seat of all, right at the head of a long table in front of the speakers, was reserved for another extreme wine person, Robert Kacher (or Bobby, as everyone seems to call him). Kacher is a wine importer, and two of the featured wineries that day were in his stable.

Kacher is a "roads scholar." Instead of going to college he grabbed a backpack and traveled French roads, learning about that country's wines and wine culture at the grassroots. His intense study launched him on a career in wine, working at Continental Liquors in Washington, D.C., and then at World Shippers and Importers. Finally, he broke away and formed his own company, Robert Kacher Selections, which focuses on "quality and authenticity" through a portfolio of small producers from all the main wine-making regions of France. Kacher's website suggests that his style is very hands-on. He doesn't simply import and sell the wine, but rather he works closely with the winemakers to improve their wine and develop their businesses. He was certainly treated with great respect at the Pinot conference due to his detailed knowledge of French wine, his contributions to the industry, and of course his commercial clout. In the complicated world of imported wine, a label that says Robert Kacher Selection has a market advantage—a sort of *Good Housekeeping* seal—that differentiates it from the hundreds or even thousands of wines that, whatever their real merit may be, lack such an outward indicator of quality. Kacher was awarded the title Chevalier de l'Ordre du Mérite Agricole in 2004 in recognition of his contribution to French wine as mentor, cheerleader, gatekeeper, and importer.

Bobby Kacher is a prime example of a particular kind of extreme wine person who combines knowledge, passion, business sense, and an ability to communicate to create a personal brand that allows minnow-sized boutique wineries to swim among the global wine whales. Leonardo LoCascio, the founder and CEO of Winebow, is another member of this group. He left a successful career at Citibank to found Leonardo LoCascio Selections, an importer specializing in Italian wines, especially from Tuscany, Piedmont, and the Veneto.

Any list of extreme wine importers must also include Terry Theise, Neal Rosenthal, and Kermit Lynch. Theise swims against the tide. His wine portfolio (part of the Michael Skurnik Wines list) focuses on terroir wines like Riesling from Austria and Germany and small-production grower Champagnes (sparkling wines made by the Champagne grape growers themselves, not produced by the huge luxury conglomerate Champagne houses). I have tasted many of Theise's wines, and they are a paradox. They speak for themselves in the glass, so clear and distinctive are their expressions, but they must be devilishly difficult to sell. Few consumers know about grower Champagne, which lacks the marketing muscle of the big name brands, and even fewer appreciate the Austrian and German white wines—until they taste them. So Theise has necessarily become advocate and educator as well as importer, helping these surprising wines find an otherwise quite improbable market.[1]

Neal Rosenthal has the distinction of being the only extreme wine importer to appear in the documentary *Mondovino*, where he illustrated clearly the paradox of this extreme genre. When we think about fine wine, we imagine sunny vineyards and dank, atmospheric cellars where you can almost smell and taste the romance of wine. But extreme wine importers inhabit a gritty parallel universe of delivery vans, loading docks, hand trucks, and industrial warehouses, where romance is a scarce commodity and the sun is supplied mainly by fluorescent tubes. The industrial serves the natural in this case, not the other way around, as in so many other cases, and Rosenthal personifies the process.[2]

Kermit Lynch is perhaps the best-known extreme wine importer in the United States. His shop in Berkeley, California, and the many fine French and Italian wines that carry the Kermit Lynch Selection label have made his trademark famous. His newsletter is so informative and the tasting notes so lyrical that some people actually collect them to read and read again. Like the others I have put in this category, his extreme devotion to a particular idea of wine has transformed in some ways both the production of wine in Europe and its image and status in the United States. (And like Robert Kacher, Lynch has also received the Chevalier de l'Ordre du Mérite Agricole.)[3] Apparently unable to resist the temptation, he now owns vineyard property in France.

Some people say that wine is made in the vineyard and others that wine comes from the cellar. This group of extreme wine people shows that it is also made far away by those who import, distribute, promote, and sell the wines, since without them (and their sometimes extreme vision of the wines and devotion to them) the vineyards and cellars might not still exist.

NOT QUITE OPPOSITE EXTREMES

One of the pleasures of the International Pinot Noir Celebration is the opportunity to dine with winemakers in small groups and to talk with them about their craft. Two not quite opposite extremes were revealed at lunch and dinner on the Friday of the event.

We lunched with Scott Paul Wright, the owner of Scott Paul Wines in Carlton, Oregon, and his winemaker Kelley Fox. Wright is a self-confessed Burgundy geek who makes Pinot Noir in Oregon and also imports small-producer wines from France. Although he started out in radio, at one time playing a notorious "pirate radio" character named Shadow Steele, wine and some sort of French connection were apparently in his blood. He was managing director of Domaine Drouhin Oregon, the Burgundian Drouhin family's Willamette Valley outpost, before starting his own winery in 1999.

As the first course was cleared away, Wright pulled out two bottles of Pinot Noir, and while they were both delicious, one especially caught my eye. It was the 2008 Scott Paul Dom Denise, and it showed Wright to be a winemaker willing to go to a historical extreme. Pinot makers seem to worship Burgundy, as I have said before, with its finely delineated terroir and long history of wine making. Clos Vougeot is one of the most famous and historic sites in Burgundy, and apparently the Cistercian monk Dom Alexandre Denise, who was responsible for wine making there in the eighteenth century, kept detailed notes on his practices and techniques. Wright got the extreme notion to try to make Oregon Pinot using the Dom Denise recipe.

Four tons of Pinot from the Momtazi Vineyard's D block were accordingly loaded into a fermenter (with 25 percent whole clusters, as per historical practice) and . . . left alone for nine days. None of the usual punching down or pumping over that is so typical of modern Pinot, although eventually a worker climbed in and mixed skins and juice with his feet as specified by Dom Denise's instructions. The wine was drained into barrels when the fermentation was almost but not quite done, and it sat in the oak untouched for the next ten months.

Was the wine different? Yes, said Wright, different in a subtle way. Earthier with more spice and complexity. We thought so, too. We liked the wine, the idea of the wine, and the kind of crazy extreme that drove this winemaker to produce it.

The grapes for Dom Denise came from Moe Momtazi's vineyard, and by happy coincidence we sat with Moe and Flora at dinner that night. Moe's story is extreme in a completely different way. Moe and Flora are elegant and refined, so it is not very easy to imagine them screaming through the night on motorcycles, their arms wrapped around the waists of the drug smugglers who were smuggling them out of Iran. Flora was eight months pregnant at the time. It is a story that Katherine Cole tells in *Voodoo Vintners*, her book about Oregon's biodynamic winemakers.[4]

Moe and Flora made their way to the United States, where Moe had studied civil engineering at the University of Texas, and eventually they found themselves in Oregon, where Cole says they fell in love with Pinot Noir. They have a five-hundred-acre vineyard outside McMinnville and a winery called Maysara (Farsi for "hour of wine") where their Davis-trained daughter Tahmiene (who survived that wild motorcycle ride in her mother's womb) now makes the wine. The Momtazi story is certainly extreme, as is their devotion to the vines and wine making. But it is their firm embrace of biodynamics that makes them seem extreme to outsiders (and it is the reason they feature so prominently in Cole's book).

Biodynamic viticulture is controversial—do a simple Google search for the phrase "biodynamic viticulture debate" and you'll see what I mean. There is even a blog with the unambiguous title *Biodynamics Is a Hoax*. I once wrote a column about the debate on *The Wine Economist* that used the term "DooDoo VooDoo" to characterize some of the controversy. Organic viticulture sort of adopts Google's motto: "Don't Be Evil." Eliminate chemical fertilizers, sprays, and so forth. Biodynamics takes a different and more proactive approach that considers vineyards the way the Gaia hypothesis thinks of the earth, as a living organism. Just avoiding harm is not enough! If you want healthy grapes, you need the entire environment to be healthy and growing, from the dirt and its microorganisms on up.

This sounds good enough, but then there are the cow horns and other unexpected elements of the system. Rudolf Steiner, biodynamic agriculture's Austrian founder, prescribed certain treatments, sprays, and practices that strike many as more black magic than agricultural science. Any recipe that begins with burying a cow horn filled with manure (that's DooDoo) in the vineyard and involves special stirring instructions for the resulting organic tea to harness cosmic energy before it is sprayed on the vines (VooDoo?) is bound to have skeptics.

Some wine people declare that biodynamics is bogus. Others approach the concept with almost religious reverence. I spent an hour walking the Alto Adige vineyard rows with Italian biodynamic guru Alois Lageder in 2011, and the depth of his faith was hard to miss . . . or to resist. He's a true evangelical biodynamic fundamentalist, and there are many who share his faith.

Moe Momtazi seems cast from a different (but still quite extreme) mold. All 540 acres of his current vineyard have been certified biodynamic by Demeter, the agency that regulates the biodynamic designation. This must make Momtazi vineyards one of the largest single biodynamic vineyards in the country, if not the world. But Moe Momtazi's commitment to DooDoo VooDoo wine growing is probably based on more than faith (or principle, if you prefer)—after all, he is a civil engineer, and I'm pretty sure that he didn't rely entirely upon faith or mysticism to support the many structures he designed over the years. Either way the wines are delicious, and I suppose that's the real test.

MAD SCIENTIST

Jason Lett's business card reads "President, Winemaker & Curator," and it is true that he performs all three tasks at The Eyrie Vineyards. The first two jobs are easy to understand, but curator? Yes, of course, since Eyrie is an important part of Oregon's wine history, and Lett's challenge is to preserve the heritage without choking off the innovative spirit that defines the place.

Three jobs are a lot, but maybe Jason Lett should add a fourth to his business card: mad wine scientist. The scientist part is uncontroversial—Lett has scientific training, and he seems to approach wine and life with a scientist's combination of curiosity and discipline. The "mad" aspect . . . well, I'll leave that up to you to decide. Maybe it's not madness so much as innovation and experimentation taken to the extreme. Either way he seems to belong in the extreme wine file.

Sue and I ran into Jason as we circled around talking to old friends at the salmon barbecue at IPNC. We had previously visited Jason at Eyrie in 2011 when I was giving lectures at Linfield College. Jason invited us to visit the winery (housed in a converted turkey-processing plant), and when we arrived he asked if we wanted to taste through the current releases or check out some of his experiments: No question, we said. Take us to your laboratory. And so we learned about and sampled three different extreme wines.

Oregon is Pinot country—everyone knows that! But let me tell you a secret. It's Pinot Gris, not just Pinot Noir. Pinot Gris is Oregon's number-two wine-grape variety, and it's a darn useful one, too. Pinot Gris is what I call a Château Cash Flow variety, since the time from harvest to market is shorter than that for Pinot Noir, and the production expense (think expensive oak barrels) is lower, too. But there's that respect thing. White wines seem to get less respect than reds in most parts of the wine world, and probably nothing can match the status of Pinot Noir, so Oregon Pinot Gris is the "second wine" in more respects than vineyard acreage. No wonder a group of winemakers has come together to create OregonPinotGris.org in an attempt to get their grape the recognition it deserves.

Eyrie was the Pinot Gris pioneer in Oregon, but these wines (which account for 60 percent of Eyrie's production) suffer from the recognition problem, too. ("Oh, it's *just* Pinot Gris?") So Jason Lett decided to try to do something to change the perception of Pinot Gris—by tweaking it in a modestly extreme way. The result is the 2008 Pinot Gris Original Vine Rosé, which has three unusual qualities according to Lett: (1) all "original vine" (first planting in the US, circa 1965), (2) 100 percent skin-contact fermentation, like Pinot Noir, and (3) three years age sur lies. It was Pinot Gris all right, but a very different take on it. More serious? Maybe. It certainly made me think about Pinot Gris differently, which is what extreme wines are supposed to do.

The second extreme wine was actually more interesting than delicious . . . but that's not a criticism, because it was *very* interesting. It was the history of Oregon wine in a glass, and it came about through Lett's curatorial duties. Eyrie's wine library contains Chardonnay vintages going back to the very first year, when Jason's legendary father David Lett made his first wines. Jason Lett went through these wines sorting out the good wines, the ones that had gone bad, and some interesting wines in the middle—oxidized ("sherried" I guess you'd say) but still drinkable, with a certain distinct character. Lett mixed these middle wines from all forty vintages along with some fresh 2009 Chardonnay and a little eau de vie made from estate grapes. The wine *tasted* old because of the oxidization, but made me think about how *young* the Oregon wine industry really is—so young that you can drink a slice of its history this way. An extreme nonvintage blend. Very memorable.

The final extreme wine was the result of a mad experiment. Lett knew about Clark Smith's theories of wine and music. Wine's taste can change depending on the music you are listening to, according to Smith. Although this sounds a bit wacky, some of my students have experimented, and they say that there is some effect. There's a potential scientific basis, too, since music stimulates some parts of the brain that are also active in the sensory perception of wine. So far, so good.

But Jason Lett decided to take the next step. If music makes a difference when you *taste* wine, then how about when you *make* wine? You know, the way that they say it is good for pregnant women (or, to be more precise, for their unborn babies) to listen to Mozart—it is supposed to help the baby's brain develop. (Alois Lageder has his "pregnant" wine barrels listen to Mozart played at a very low speed.) There has even been some scientific research on the effect of music during fermentation (in Austria, Rudolf Steiner's home, I believe).

So Lett set up an experiment. Identical grape juice and yeast, but with different music. One fermentation listened to music (what I would describe as chants, although there is probably a better musical term) by Hildegard of Bingen while the twin tank grooved to the jazz of John Coltrane. Incredibly, the two fermentations developed differently (the Hildegard started first), and the wines taste different, too. Or at least that's what Sue and I thought as we tasted back and forth. Hmm. Maybe there's something to this music thing! Sue challenged Lett to take the next step. Does the Hildegard *taste* different listening to Hildegard than to Coltrane? Does the affinity for the music extend all the way down the line?

GRAPE TRANSFORMATIONS

Jason's father, David Lett, is one of my heroes. I met him early in my teaching (and his wine-making) career when he was still working his day job as a college textbook salesman to finance his winery dreams. He was part of the group they call the Pioneers, who transformed Oregon from a place known for fruit and nuts rather than grapes to a region frequently mentioned in the same breath with Burgundy.

Lett's story is remarkable. Trained at the University of California–Davis, he came north looking for terroir where he could make Pinot in the Burgundian style. His first Pinot vines were planted in 1965; 1970 was the first Eyrie Pinot vintage. After one or two false starts he hit pay dirt. Great wine. But from Oregon? Rainy old Oregon probably seemed like the last place on earth to make world-class wine in the 1970s. Then came the Wine Olympics of 1979. This was a competition, sponsored by the French food and wine magazine *Gault Millau*, that featured 330 wines from thirty-three countries tasted blind by sixty-two judges. The 1975 Eyrie Pinot Noir Reserve attracted attention by placing tenth among Pinots. A stunning achievement for a wine from a previously unknown wine region.

Robert Drouhin of Maison Joseph Drouhin, a Burgundy négociant and producer, was fascinated and sponsored a further competition where the Eyrie wine came close second behind Drouhin's own 1959 Chambolle-Musigny. Thus was Eyrie's reputation set (and Oregon's, too). It wasn't long before Domaine Drouhin Oregon (DDO) was built in the same Dundee Hills as Eyrie's vineyards—a strong endorsement of the terroir and recognition of the achievement.

Writing about David Lett got me thinking about a particular kind of extreme wine person that I associate with "Grape Transformation" (pardon the pun)—individuals who have transformed the way that people think about wine or a particular wine region. Jesus is at the top of my list, of course, since he changed water into wine, the ultimate grape transformation. And there is a reason that we think of this as a miracle. As the always insightful Ken Bernsohn reminds me, inertia is a very strong force in the world of wine (and elsewhere). This is obviously true in the vineyard itself, where years are required to "turn the supertanker" from one grape variety to another. It is also true in the marketplace, where a visible iceberg of wine drinkers interested in trying new things sits atop an invisible bulk of consumers with preferences and habits that are frozen in place (most of them drink no wine at all). So it really is a miracle (although not in the "fishes and loaves" class) when wine makes a big turn. Who are some important examples for my Grape Transformations file? Please pardon a brief digression while I examine this type of extreme wine people.

Let me begin with Robert Mondavi, if only because I discussed his case at some length in my 2011 book *Wine Wars*. Here's how the section on Mondavi begins:

I like to say that Robert Mondavi tried to do for American wine what Julia Child (public television's "French Chef") tried to do for American cuisine: revolutionize it by convincing Americans that they could not just imitate the French but maybe better them at their own game. Julia Child succeeded, although not by herself of course. American cuisine was transformed by her books and *The French Chef*, which aired from 1963 to 1973. She changed the idea of food in America. American ingredients, French techniques. Bring them together and cooks could be chefs.

Robert Mondavi did the same thing for wine. He was convinced that American grapes and Old World techniques could produce world-class wines. And he was right. When the Robert Mondavi Winery opened in Oakville in 1966, it was the first major new investment in Napa Valley in decades, and it changed everything (not by itself, of course) and paved the way for a distinctly American vision of fine wine that coexists today along with a Gallo-tinted image of mass-market wines. Mondavi wasn't alone, and he didn't do it by himself, but I think it is fair to associate Robert Mondavi with the Grape Transformation of American wine. Quite an accomplishment.

I think of Nicolas Catena as the Robert Mondavi of Mendoza, although I admit that the similarities only go so far. Catena's transformation of Argentina's wine industry is perhaps even more significant because the previous wine-making baseline was so low. Laura Catena tells the story in a very personal way in her excellent book *Vino Argentino*.[5] She explains how and why Argentinean wine changed in terms of her family history. A broader and more detailed account, Ian Mount's illuminating *The Vineyard at the End of the World*, places Nicolas Catena's accomplishments in a bigger context, changes the Catena story a bit, and raises new questions, but does not alter our view of the transformative force he helped launch.[6]

I admit to prejudice in this matter because of the courtesy we were shown when we visited Mendoza and met with Catena and Luca (Laura Catena's project) winemakers. Nicolas Catena has a PhD in economics and was a visiting professor at the University of California–Berkeley when trips to Napa winemakers (and a meeting with Mondavi) transformed his idea of what New World wine could be. It was a special treat when, during our winery visit, I was given the opportunity to browse for just a moment through Catena's personal collection of economics texts.

Accept for the sake of argument that Mondavi and Catena belong on the Grape Transformations list. What can we learn generally from their two specific cases? Something, I think, but n = 2 is a small sample size, so we shouldn't press too hard. Robert Mondavi and Nicolas Catena have little in common in terms of personality from what I have read. Catena seems be as pensive as Mondavi was outgoing. Both were driven, I suppose, and perhaps that's the critical factor. Both took big risks, and that seems like an important characteristic. And I think that they both felt that they had little choice but to take risks, although for different reasons and from different perspectives. Mondavi left the family business and forged out on his own relatively late in life. He didn't have a plan B—his new winery had to succeed. And it did.

Nicolas Catena, on the other hand, unexpectedly ended up with the family business (ruining his plans for an academic career). But Argentina's wine markets were in a funk—export was the only route open, and he (and those who worked for and with him) had no choice but to remake the wine and the business if they were to avoid collapse. No plan B here, either. Finally, it is interesting that family is such a powerful theme in both stories. In both cases the transformations that they led began as internal revolutions, dramatic changes within the family way of doing business, and rapidly spread outward.

The family theme continues today. Laura Catena is now the face of the family business, even though she still maintains her "day job" as an emergency-room doctor in the San Francisco area where she and her family live. The Mondavi sons carry on the family business tradition, but not of course the actual family business—Constellation Brands purchased the Robert Mondavi brand back in 2005.

ITALIAN EXTREMES

A visit to Italy's Piemonte region prompted me to add two more names to the list of extreme transformative winemakers. You have probably already guessed the first name: Angelo Gaja, who is associated with the transformation of Barbaresco. The second name? I'll leave you in suspense for a few paragraphs. See if you can figure it out.

Angelo Gaja changed the way the world thinks about Piemonte wine (and to some extent Italian wine in general). Joe Bastianich (writing in his book *Grandi Vini*) says that Gaja is "the most famous Italian wine producer in the world" (this may come as news to the Antinori and Frescobaldi families, but I'm sure Joe knows what he is talking about).[7] Barbaresco was seen as the plain little sister of sexy Barolo until Gaja changed everything.

Exactly what Gaja changed and how is a matter of opinion, although the achievement is clear. Bastianich looks to the vineyard, the development of particular vineyard sites, and the production of "cru" single-vineyard "terroir" wines. He also praises Gaja's efforts to travel the world promoting his wines and the other wines of the region. The power of Gaja's personality is clearly part of the story here. Matt Kramer, writing in his book *Making Sense of Italian Wine*, tells a different story.[8] For him Gaja's contribution was in the cellar even more than the vineyard, where he introduced an international style to the wine by using small French oak barrels (Gaja also controversially introduced international grape varieties to the family's vineyards).

Gaja's second and perhaps even greater achievement, Kramer suggests, was to charge outrageous prices for his wines. "While few people know about wine, *everybody's* an expert on money: Could this Gaja . . . really be worth *that* much money? The sheer chutzpah was captivating and so, too, it turned out, were the wines." Gaja became a role model for Piemonte and perhaps for aspiring winemakers throughout Italy.

As much as I admire Angelo Gaja, enjoy his wines, and respect his innovations, he is not alone on the Piemonte Grape Transformations podium. The second "tornado" is someone who did for democratic Barbera what Gaja did for aristocratic Nebbiolo. The achievement may be even greater. Nebbiolo, the noble grape that is responsible for the great Barolo, Barbaresco, and Langhe Rosso wines, is far from the most planted Piemonte grape. It has the best reputation, but perhaps because it ripens so late and requires specific site characteristics to excel, it is not as widely planted as you might imagine. There is fifteen times more Barbera than Nebbiolo in Piemonte.

Barbera! Making this humble everyday wine respected and even fashionable today is a signal achievement. This is the claim to fame of the late Giacomo Bologna of "Braida" winery in Rocchetta Tanaro, just a few miles from Asti. Barbera is not finicky like Nebbiolo—it will grow pretty much wherever you plant it in Piemonte, both where it produces outstanding grapes and where quality is not so high. There was not much of a premium for quality grapes in the early postwar era, when wholesalers would buy indiscriminately and lump them all together. Giacomo Bologna thought he could do better and set out to achieve excellence beginning in the 1960s, when Gaja was also picking up steam.

The old Barbera was nothing special, but by focusing on specific sites with old vines and low productivity, engaging in aggressive cap management, and aging the wines in small French oak barrels, Bologna was able to create both a new Barbera wine and a new image of Barbera wine. The top wines, including the famous Bricco dell'Uccellone, redefined the region and jump-started the quality wine movement.

We visited Braida in June 2011 when were in Italy for the wine economics conference in Bolzano. Nadine Weihgold led us on a tour of the winery, pointing out the many ways that Giacomo Bologna's vision and plans have been fulfilled by his wife Anna and his two children Raffaella and Giuseppe (both of whom are enologists) since his untimely death. We tasted the single-vineyard wines and then Ai Suma, an extreme version of Bologna's idea of Barbera that is only produced in special years. These are wines of distinction and reputation and so popular in Italy that a surprisingly small amount leaks out to the rest of the world.

Giuseppe Bologna happened to pass through on his way to the barrel room and, hearing the wine economics conversation, sat down to join us. "Is there anything else you'd like to taste?" Nadine asked. Embarrassed and apologetic, I confessed I wanted to follow these great wines with their vivacious but less prestigious little sister—La Monella, the frizzante Barbera that was the company's first success. A simple wine, but with style and quality. Were they offended? No, just the opposite. Grinning with obvious pleasure, Giuseppe went to work, corks started to fly, and soon were we chatting away in mixed Italian and English.

Ai Suma might be literally the summit of Giacomo Bologna's mountain, but his son Giuseppe has his own dreams and plans—and they include Pinot Noir. Pinot is a blending grape in this part of Italy, but Giuseppe has hopes that it might someday learn to stand on its own as Barbera has. He called for a barrel sample, and the wine was very interesting—not an imitation of Burgundy, Oregon, or New Zealand, but something different, still developing, full of potential. Pinot Noir in Baroloville? Giuseppe Bologna must be nuts. But then they probably said that about Giacomo Bologna and Angelo Gaja back in the day.

GROWERS: THE INVISIBLE EXTREME

Giuseppe Bologna's Pinot dream brings me back to the Pinot Celebration in Oregon and all the types of extreme wine people I met there. Pinot Noir brings out the extreme in the wine community, which is why it is a good springboard for this chapter, but one extreme remained invisible until brunch on the very last day of the event: the winegrowers.

When I started working on this chapter I asked my *Wine Economist* readers for ideas. Who are the most extreme wine people? I received many nominations, but one particularly caught my attention. It came from a Californian who asked that winegrowers be included on the list. Everyone says that wine is made in the vineyard—and some growers go to real extremes to make that happen—but it is the winemakers who get all the attention. The Pisoni family was cited as an example. Fruit from Pisoni Vineyards goes into some of the best wine in California, although only a little of it is bottled under the Pisoni name.

Good point. A quick search on Robert Parker's website turned up a long list of Pinot Noir and Syrah with the Pisoni Vineyards designation (Parker calls it a grand cru vineyard in one review). The 2008 Pisoni Estate Pinot earned the highest score (ninety-eight!), but all the reviews were strong. Clearly there's something special about this vineyard and the people who farm it.

And the Pisoni family is not alone. The wines we tasted at IPNC were top drawer, and I think that almost half of them were vineyard designated—all the grapes came from one particular vineyard (in a couple of cases, from a specific block within a particular vineyard). The best of them reflected a unique terroir, but all of them were the products of farmers with a rather single-minded devotion to growing outstanding grapes.

The growers. Their work is always there in your glass, although it is only sometimes recognized on the label. They are the real extreme wine people, and I didn't meet anyone who was a pure grower (and not also a winemaker) until Sunday brunch, when a quiet young couple joined us at our table, happy to enjoy the great food, sparkling wine, and general conversation, but in a shy way that suggested to me that all the fancy trimmings felt a bit foreign to them. They were all about growing the grapes and took satisfaction in that. They reminded me that, while I have a lot of great memories of our trip to the IPNC, perhaps the most important one was of a small block of struggling vines and the extreme winegrowers who planted and nurtured them.

We visited Anne Amie Vineyards twice during our Willamette Valley weekend, first to attend a casual food and wine reception and then again for a "magical mystery tour" seminar and luncheon. We've been to this place on many occasions, starting about thirty years ago when it was called Château Benoit after Fred and Mary Benoit, the Oregon wine-growing pioneers who planted the first vines on this spot. We liked the wines then, especially the sparkling wines as I recall, and it has been interesting to watch the place evolve as the region's wine industry developed. Much has changed. We called it Château Benoit (pronounced Ben-OYT) when we first visited because that's how the founders said it, but I understand it morphed into a French-inflected Château Ben-WAH later on. And it 1999 it became Anne Amie when Portland businessman Robert Pamplin bought the operation and named it after his two daughters.

More than the name has changed—Pamplin has invested much energy into developing Anne Amie's Pinot Noir program, as you might expect in Oregon—but much has remained the same, including some of the original vineyards. As we drove up the long road to the hilltop winery, we passed the original (1979) block of Müller-Thurgau vines that produced the grapes that went into the wines we tasted on our very first visit. It has taken a good deal of persistence to maintain these vines, because they have faced a lot of challenges. The first is economic—there's not much of a market for Müller-Thurgau here in the United States. It might make economic sense to pull them out and put in a more marketable variety.

And then there's nature. The bottom of the hill gets pretty cold in the winter, and these old vines sometimes suffer and struggle. And I think I remember that they've been hit with phylloxera, too, but were nursed along rather than grubbed up as you might expect. This particular Müller-Thurgau vineyard is singled out for special mention in *Wine Grapes* by Jancis Robinson, Julia Harding, and Jose Vouillamoz, and it is easy to see why—only extreme winegrowers would have planted and nurtured it. I like the wine that is produced from these grapes—crisp and clean—but more than that I appreciate the perseverance that is behind it. It is a tribute to extreme wine growing even if wine making gets most of the attention.

EXTREME THINKING (INSIDE THE BOX)

It is commonplace to say that a creative person "thinks outside the box," and I am sure that this happens in the wine business, too. But it seems to me that all of the extreme wine people we have met are actually noteworthy in a different way. Wine is a natural product, a sensory experience, and a business, too. It defines itself by its constraints: natural limits in the vineyard, technical limits in the cellar, and the market's stern discipline. You can push those limits, but you can't ignore them. If you truly think outside the box these lines form, you will make bad wine or no wine at all.

So extreme wine people necessarily turn their passion and creativity inward. They find the box that suits them best (Pinot Noir, for example) and then follow their passion to the ultimate extreme. Wine has so many boxes that it seems to be able to accommodate all sorts of extremes. Or at least that's how it seemed on that sunny summer weekend at the IPNC.

8

Celebrity Wine

The Chinese are known for their passion for French wines, especially Bordeaux and especially the famous châteaux of the Classification of 1855. Lafite. Latour. Margaux. Haut-Brion. Mouton-Rothschild. Wines of substance and reputation that have garnered international recognition and stood the test of time. Great wine in China is red, not white, and French. Anything else is just an imitation. This might be a bit of a caricature of China's image of fine wine, I admit, and attitudes toward wine in China are changing quickly, but the cartoon bears more than a resemblance to the real thing.[1]

So it comes as something of a surprise to learn that what might be the most celebrated wine in China today doesn't come from France and doesn't have a reputation that spans centuries. It comes, in fact, from Napa, California, and is made by a start-up winery headed by a first-timer in his early thirties. It's red, I'll give you that, and made using the same grape varieties as the famously French Bordeaux, but otherwise it's very much a thing apart.

BIG IN CHINA

The head of the winery has one unquestioned distinction. He is the tallest winemaker in the world. He stands seven feet six inches (2.29 meters) tall. The winery website describes him as a "global humanitarian and recently retired NBA star," and in November 2009 his company released Yao Ming® 2009 Napa Valley Cabernet Sauvignon. Most of the five thousand cases of the first vintage went directly to China, where they sold for the equivalent of $289.[2] There's also a smaller-production (and even more expensive) reserve bottling. Pernod Ricard, the French wine and spirits multinational that has a big presence in China, is the exclusive distributor.

Yao Ming (I don't think I need the ® sign when I talk about the person, only the product) is already a Chinese sports legend. He has played basketball for the Shanghai Sharks (a Chinese professional team that he now owns), the Houston Rockets (he was named to the all-NBA team five times), and of course the Chinese national basketball team. How did he get interested in wine? He learned from his fellow National Basketball Association team members, he says. He'd pay attention when they ordered wine at dinner and ask lots of questions. His unlikely mentor in this seems to have been a Congolese player named Dikembe Mutombo, who stands a mere seven foot two.

When Yao retired from the Rockets, he asked his business agent, BDA Sports International, for help starting a winery in Napa Valley. Yao, like most sports stars today, has many business and charitable interests (he's Apple's face in China, for example) and is therefore the central figure in a complex management structure. I don't think that they had much trouble finding people to help out. Tom Hinde, a well-connected winemaker, joined the team. Classic Bordeaux-variety grapes were purchased from various sources (no estate vineyard or winery yet), new French oak barrels were filled, and an attractive label was designed that "features a hand-drawn illustration of Napa Valley with the ancient Chinese character for 'Yao,' elegantly representing both cultures Yao Ming has made his home," according to the winery website.[3] The very first bottle of Yao's wine was revealed at a 2011 charity auction in Shanghai, where it raised more than thirty-one thousand dollars for the Special Olympics.

The wines are apparently very good. The 2009 Cabernet received a silver medal in the *Decanter* world wine competition and *Wine Enthusiast*'s California editor Steve Heimoff gave the Cab a score of ninety-five and the reserve a ninety-seven. I'm not surprised that the wines score so well—celebrity wine projects, when they are well designed, can bring out the best. I'll bet everyone was happy to join Yao's team—it's just good business, as well as good wine. Good for Yao, good for Pernod Ricard, good for his vineyard and winemaking partners. It's even been good for the Special Olympics, which got money and helpful publicity, too. It's also been good for Napa Valley and the California wine industry. In fact, I suspect that the biggest beneficiaries of Yao's new wine venture are the dozens of top-drawer producers of Napa Valley Cabernet. Yao's new wine will do wonders to publicize the region's brand and to validate the quality and importance of their wines. They already have a foot in the door of the Chinese market, but Yao's big size-eighteen sneakers will open it so much wider than they ever could by themselves. Yao is big in China, and I think everyone hopes to ride on his coattails into this growing market.

THE AGE OF CELEBRITY
We live in the age of Celebrity with a capital "C." People are celebrated for their achievements in sports, politics, and the arts. Celebrities are everywhere—in the news, on TV, and all around us through ads and product endorsements. So we shouldn't be surprised that there are celebrity wines, too. Some wines simply use a celebrity name as a marketing tool, but other celebrity wines are more than just marketing projects (although having a famous name doesn't hurt). There are so many celebrity wines available that there's a Wikipedia page devoted to them.[4] More than seventy wine-making celebs make the list, but I know there are more, since both Martha Stewart and Paul Newman wines were somehow missed, and new ones seem to show up almost daily. (How long have the Rolling Stones had a wine? It was hard to miss their Forty Licks brand at the wine shop, with its colorful tongue and lips logo.)

Sports stars like Yao Ming figure prominently on the Wikipedia list, of course. American football legends like Mike Ditka (a winery in Mendocino Country), Dick Vermeil (Napa Valley), Dan Marino (California), Joe Montana (Napa), and Charles Woodson (Napa again) are on the list, along with Tom Seaver (baseball, Napa), and Wayne Gretsky (hockey—his winery is on the Niagara Peninsula in Canada). Golf stars like Nick Faldo (Coonawarra, Australia), Arnold Palmer (California), Ernie Els (Stellenbosch, South Africa), and Greg Norman (South Australia and California) and auto racers such as Mario Andretti (Napa Valley), Jean Alesi (Côtes du Rhône, France), Jeff Gordon (Napa Valley), Richard Childress (North Carolina), and Jarno Trulli (Abruzzo, Italy) seem particularly attracted to the celebrity wine game.

The music industry supplies its share of wine celebs, such as Cliff Richards (his winery is in Algarve, Portugal), Boz Scaggs (California), Dave Matthews

(Charlottesville, Virginia), Mick Fleetwood (Lake County, California), Olivia Newton-John (South Australia), and of course Madonna (the Ciccone Vineyard and Winery on the Leelanau Peninsula, Michigan). Then there are the actors and actresses, including Dan Aykroyd (both Ontario, Canada, and Sonoma, California), Drew Barrymore (Italy), Antonio Banderas (Ribera del Duero, Spain), and Sam Neill (Central Otago, New Zealand), and a few politicians, like Nancy Pelosi (a vineyard in Saint Helena, California) and Jacques Parizeau (a winery in Languedoc, France). There's even one Nobel Prize–winning economist who owns a vineyard—Daniel McFadden, who famously theorized about asymmetric information and the "market for lemons." You've heard of him, haven't you? McFadden is a big celebrity among wine economists, although admittedly that's a pretty small group of people.

Sprinkled among the famous names are a few celebrities from the food and wine industry, including cookbook author and chef Lidia Bastianich (she owns a winery in Friuli in partnership with her restaurateur son, Joseph), Iron Chef Mario Batali (La Mozza Winery in Tuscany, which he owns in partnership with Joe Bastianich), and the wine critic Robert Parker. Parker owns Beaux Frères Winery on Ribbon Ridge in the Chehalem Valley, Oregon, in partnership with his brother-in-law.

Celebrity wines are hot, or at least that's what the indicators say. A couple of years ago *People* magazine asked Gary Vaynerchuk, a celebrity wine critic, to rate the wines of four celebrity winemakers.[5] Hip-hop artist Lil Jon's Little Jonathan Winery Chardonnay ($15.99) scored a solid eighty-nine points. *Sopranos* star Lorraine Bracco's Italian-made Pinot Grigio ($11.99) earned an eighty-six-plus rating. Mötley Crüe rocker Vince Neil's nine-dollar Petite Sirah was an eighty-eight-point good buy, Gary said. And the twenty-dollar Victory Rosé from Olympic figure-skater Peggy Fleming's winery, Fleming-Jenkins, received eighty-seven points. (Fleming donates two dollars to breast-cancer research for each bottle of this pink wine she sells—a use of celebrity clout that is difficult to criticize.)

Maybe you aren't entirely comfortable taking wine recommendations (or wine market analysis) from the pages of *People* magazine. If so, then a study released by the Nielsen Company (market-research experts) a few years ago might interest you.[6] The Nielsen data indicated that grocery-store sales of celebrity wine grew by nearly 19 percent in 2007, albeit from a low base (the celebrity wine category is still a small market segment—less than 1 percent).

The average price of the celebrity wines, $8.50, was higher than the super-market average of $5.75, according to Nielsen. Unsurprisingly, the Nielsen report focuses on marketing and distribution (not the quality of the wines themselves) as the key factors driving sales growth. Several factors fueled the growth of celebrity wines, according to the report. "First, existing brands are expanding and gaining new distribution through new line extensions. Second, more celebrities have launched their own brands in the past year or have had suppliers launch products under their names. As these brands have proven themselves, they've gained distribution in other retail outlets, which has fur-ther stimulated growth. And third, savvy marketers leverage the 'celebrity' benefit into expanded marketing programs via in-store vehicles, outdoor events and traditional and online media."[7]

CELEBRITY WINE MYTHS

Like the "critter wines" that they superficially resemble, celebrity wines are associated with a number of myths that should be briefly considered.

Myth 1: Celebrity wines are an American phenomenon. Alas, no. As the list above indicates, the celebrities come from pretty much everywhere, and their wineries are everywhere, too. America has no monopoly on celebrity wines or any other celebrity product.

Myth 2: Celebrity wines are bad wines. No again, although I admit I haven't tried very many of them. The studies I have found suggest that celebrity wines are just like wines generally: you can find examples that are good or bad, and maybe even a few that are ugly (hey—good, bad, ugly—that would make a great name for a line of Clint Eastwood wines!). Because celebrities have an incentive to protect their personal "brands," I suspect they try to avoid as-sociating their names with really foul products. At least some of the celebrity winemakers take a real personal interest in their products, which is likely to make a difference in quality.

Some celebrity wines are excellent, which is easy to understand. Celebrity is a powerful force in today's world and celebrity winemakers can often lever-age their fame through connections and associations that contribute to wine quality. You know what I mean—privileged access to quality grapes, personal advice from talented professionals, and so forth.

Myth 3: Celebrity wines are bad for the wine business. Celebrity brands draw attention away from "real wine," this argument goes, and only cheapen and commodify the idea of wine. There is obviously some truth to this, especially if we consider multiproduct lifestyle brands that have expanded to include a wine component in their portfolios—Martha Stewart, for example, and Sir Richard Branson's Virgin empire. It seems to me that these associations diminish wine as a distinct product by reducing it to "just another" Martha S. or Virgin lifestyle label. No offense—that's just how it seems to me. You might disagree. (I acknowledge that there might be little difference between these celebrity brand portfolios and store "house brands" that also span many product categories. Costco's Kirkland Signature brand includes both wine and toilet paper, for example.)

But most celebrity wines that I've seen don't fit this mold and create a different kind of celebrity association. These products may benefit the wine market by attracting new customers and encouraging wine drinkers to try new types of wine. They also probably distort the market a bit, making it marginally more difficult for noncelebrity wines to get distribution in some market segments. On balance, the influence of celebrities is probably positive, since they draw public attention to wine. Even the readers of *People* now know a little more about wine thanks to a profile of Lil Jon's wine.

Celebrity wine represents an extreme edge of the wine world, but one that is as diverse as wine itself. I think the best way to study it is through brief profiles of different types of celebrity wine experiences. Our first stop is California, home to so many celebrities and to some pretty good wine, too.

KING OF THE WINE FRONTIER

Coonskin caps—hats made from raccoon skins (or made to look like it) with the tail hanging down the back. If you were around in the 1950s, 1960s, or 1970s and I say this celebrity winemaker's name, a number of vivid images will flash before your eyes, but the much-prized coonskin cap will be the strongest of them. I'm talking of course about Fess Parker, the film and television star who portrayed many characters in his long career, but none more famous than Davy Crockett (on TV and in movies in the 1950s) and Daniel Boone (a 1964–1970 TV series).

Fess Parker (1924–2010—incredibly, it was his real name) studied drama for a year on the GI Bill and got his first speaking part in film providing the voice of Leslie the chauffeur in *Harvey* (1950), which starred Jimmy Stewart and a six foot three-and-a-half-inch tall invisible rabbit. He seems to have found steady work on stage and in films, but his big break came when Disney hired him to play Davy Crockett, King of the Wild Frontier.[8] Crockett, in the Disney version, was the classic American frontiersman and patriot, and Fess Parker's Texan take on the character was immensely popular. The later Daniel Boone series changed the name, but not the person behind it.

Fess Parker was good enough at acting, but he was even better at business. He became famous for plowing his acting fees into landholdings in the Santa Barbara area north of Hollywood. One of his investments is familiar to anyone who has visited that seaside town—the Fess Parker Doubletree Resort and Conference Center. In 1987 he bought a big ranch in the Santa Ynez Valley near Los Olivos. The *Sideways*-driven Santa Barbara Pinot Noir boom was still years away, but Parker and company decided to plant some grapes (White Riesling) on the land, which was originally intended to be a cattle ranch and residence. One thing led to another, and pretty soon a vineyard named Ashley for Fess's daughter was in place, and his son Eli was making wine. It would be wrong to say that the Fess Parker Winery put Santa Barbara on the map (there are several noteworthy wineries that can claim part of that fame), but certainly the celebrity connection did not hurt the cause. A Fess Parker Pinot even had a nonspeaking part in *Sideways*! The Parkers bought the Grand Hotel in Los Olivos in 1998 and rechristened it Fess Parker's Wine Country Inn and Spa.

Wine was serious business for Fess Parker and still is to his family. The wines have seen a few peaks and valleys over the years according to critics, but they are seriously good today, with several receiving scores in the ninety to ninety-three range from *Wine Advocate*. The business side is serious, too, and it seems to me that the whole enterprise has made the key celebrity transition. Once famous mainly for the coonskin cap association, the winery, vineyard, and hospitality facilities are now famous on their own, well known among younger folks who never saw the classic video scenes. Fess Parker's celebrity built a business and helped build several industries in the Santa Barbara area.

THE GODFATHER OF CALIFORNIA WINE

It's a bit of a stretch, but I'm going to name Gustave Niebaum the godfather of California wine, or maybe Napa Valley wine. I'm not sure I can make the designation stick, but I have my reasons, so work with me on this. It's an unlikely title to give to a Finnish sea captain who made his fortune in the

Alaskan fur trade and then settled down in Napa Valley. He purchased a vineyard there in 1879 and built a beautiful house and then eventually a winery, too. He called the place Inglenook and set about making the finest wines in California. He may have achieved this goal before his death in 1910, but that's not why I call him the godfather. Rather, it is because of his most important innovation: estate bottling. Before Niebaum, most Napa wineries were really in the bulk business. They'd ship their wines to négociants in San Francisco and elsewhere who would age, blend, and bottle them under their own labels, thus effectively capturing the economic rents that established brands accrue. Niebaum rebelled against this system (much as French growers were doing at about the same time) and against the market power of the négociants, too. And so he bottled his own wines and put the Inglenook label on them. The Napa Valley that we know today, with its focus on quality and individuality, is at least in part "Godfather" Niebaum's legacy.

It's just as well that the captain didn't live to see what Prohibition did to his winery and vineyards, and it fell to John Daniels Jr., Niebaum's wife's grand-nephew, to pull things back together once again starting in 1939. The Inglenook team produced some stunning Cabernets during this time and raised the winery's reputation to the heights. The story took a bad turn in the 1960s, however, when Inglenook was acquired by Allied Grape Growers, who were in turn swallowed up by Heublein and on and on through various mergers and acquisitions. Somewhere along the line the corporate wise men latched on to Inglenook as a good name for a brand of inexpensive jug wines they were rolling out. And thus did Inglenook fall from the top shelf of California wine to the bottom tier in one marketing-driven tumble. After a while no one—or almost no one—remembered the high quality that Inglenook once stood for. Then fate stepped in.

Francis Ford Coppola was flush with cash when he first spied the old Niebaum estate in 1975. A screenwriter and director, his *Godfather* films had made him both rich and a celebrity, too, and he was looking for the perfect summer house in which to relax, enjoy family and friends, and, in the Italian style, make a little wine for home consumption. I'll bet the sea captain's house was a real fixer-upper, but Coppola took on the challenge. There, surrounded by the vineyards in the heart of a Napa Valley that was exploding with new people, new ideas, and new wineries, Coppola got the wine bug. Stomping grapes for homemade wine soon made way for more serious projects funded by his income from the film industry. In 1994 he was able to purchase the old winery on the site and he began to produce Niebaum-Coppola wines, linking the historic name with his own famous moniker. The top wine was called Rubicon, and eventually he renamed the winery Rubicon Estate. He couldn't call the wines or the winery Inglenook, which would have made sense, because the trademark belonged to the corporation that was cranking out the jug wines of that brand.

Finally in 2011 Francis Coppola pulled it all together: the vineyards, the winery, and the brand name—Inglenook. The director of *The Godfather* restored the godfather's vision, a signal achievement and an unlikely outcome for what we must admit is a celebrity winemaker. You don't think of celebrities as having a sense of history, but I guess Coppola is the exception to the rule.

Coppola has built a substantial wine empire, with Inglenook at its peak. For example, there is a Francis Ford Coppola Winery north of Santa Rosa that features a bit of Hollywood (or is it Disneyland?) flair in addition to the classic Niebaum estate. The Diamond label and Director's Cut wines sell at popular prices. There is a sparkling pink wine called Sofia after Coppola's daughter that you can buy in bottles or little "mini" cans. Coppola has clearly used his fame to make money as well as wine, but I will always remember him for restoring a piece of California wine history.

ART IMITATES LIFE 1: GÉRARD DEPARDIEU

"Grenouille d'hiver" means "winter frog" and it is the title of a short film by the director Slony Sow that was first broadcast on French television in 2011. It's not in commercial release as this is written, but is making the rounds of film festivals, including Cannes, so I haven't seen it yet, except for the short trailer on YouTube. It stars the venerable Gérard Depardieu in an emotional role. "Benjamin, grower, sees his wife die in his arms following a long illness. Only one way out for him: death. But a young Japanese girl, came especially for its wine tasting, will bring it gently to mourn a series of symbols and exchange between two cultures," according to the film's official synopsis as translated by Google.[9]

Gérard Depardieu has played many roles in his long career—over 170 of them since he began in the 1960s, according to his French Wikipedia page. He's played everything from Cyrano the big-nosed patriot of the classical play to Obelix the big-nosed patriot of French cartoon fame. He's worked with the iconic directors like Francois Truffaut, has won most of the top awards, including the César and the Legion of Honor, and his acting career shows no signs of slowing down now that he is in his sixties, with more than a dozen roles (including the wine-growing Benjamin) since 2010. He is scheduled to portray libertine French socialist politician Dominique Strauss-Kahn in an upcoming film.

Depardieu has played so many roles that there seems to be nothing exceptional in his role as Benjamin. Except that the vines he stands among as he contemplates harsh fate and his own mortality are actually his own on his vineyard estate in Anjou. And I'm pretty sure the wine he sips with the young Japanese visitor, which opens the door to grief, is his, too. Depardieu has owned Château de Tigné in the Coteaux du Layon appellation since 1989. He owns the facilities, which include the fourteenth-century castle, and oversees things in the way that a busy global superstar can, leaving the actual day-to-day wine making to an old friend.

The wines, with names such as Cuvée Cyrano and Confiance, as well as more conventional titles, are made with the traditional Loire Valley Chenin Blanc, Grolleau, and Cabernet Franc grape varieties along with Chardonnay and Cabernet Sauvignon. An attractive line drawing of Depardieu's familiar face adorns each bottle, along with "Vins Gérard Depardieu." The estate is big by local standards—one hundred hectares—and produces about four hundred thousand bottles of wine each year.

Although it is tempting to jump to the conclusion that Château de Tigné is just another celebrity winery conceived in a marketing meeting and executed to cash in on a famous name and face, I get the impression from all that I've seen that this Depardieu winery—the first one—was not an act but rather a quite sincere project driven by an authentic interest in wine, food, and everything that goes with them taken on by someone who could afford to make such an extravagant action.

First winery? Yes, there are more, although I'm not really sure how many because they seem to get bought and sold a bit. In 2001, twelve years after his relatively modest Anjou purchase, Depardieu teamed up with the high-powered Bordeaux producer Bernard Magrez to develop new wineries in France and around the world. The wines are united under the brand Le Clé du Terroir (the key to terroir).

Going through the tasting notes on the *Wine Advocate*'s website I found evidence of projects in Argentina (a dry Malbec called Gérard Depardieu Mi Diferencia), a Bordeaux blend from Haut-Médoc called Gérard Depardieu Ma Vérité Cuvée d'Exception, a Tempranillo from Castilla y Leon, Spain, called Gérard Depardieu Toro, and Gérard Depardieu Priorato from Priorat, Spain. Gérard Depardieu Passion d'Une Vie is a powerful red blend with an Amarone-like nose from Roussillon in the South of France. Gérard Depardieu Ma Preference comes from the Pays d'Oc. Gérard Depardieu Lumiere De l'Atlas is from Morocco, and Gérard Depardieu Domaine de Ste. Augustin Cuvée is from Algeria. The wines have only a few things in common besides Depardieu's involvement. First, they are apparently very good—the *Wine Advocate* reviewers give them high marks. Here's a tasting note from a 2004 review of an Algerian wine.

> The rich, full-bodied 2002 Cuvée Monica is a revelation for its place of origin. An old vine blend of Syrah, Carignan, and Grenache, boasts an inky/purple color along with a spectacular nose of blackberries, crème de cassis, melted asphalt, a hint of bacon fat, and voluptuous flavors. It is a tour de force in wine-making as well as a tribute to Depardieu's vision of quality from this backwater area of North Africa.

The most recent review of a Gérard Depardieu wine continues with the same gushing enthusiasm. "Another brilliant effort, the 2011 Confiance is composed of 97% Merlot and 3% Malbec. It possesses lots of black raspberry and black currant fruit intermixed with hints of charcoal and damp earth. Dense, rich, full-bodied and textured with abundant glycerin, it is atypically rich and fleshy for a 2011." Depardieu's wines share a reputation for quality (and, if these reviews are accurate, a certain sensuality), which is not a bad thing, given that the wines come from three continents and five countries! The other thing that they have in common, according to critics, is that they are not the wines Gérard Depardieu says he likes. They do tend to be the sort of wines associated with the flying winemaker Michel Rolland, who is known to consult on at least some of Depardieu's projects (although not the original Anjou winery, according to the actor—not enough money to be made there). It weakens Depardieu's case a bit if the wines he endorses aren't necessarily the wines he says he loves (and perhaps makes at his home winery), but if this is true it must be said that he would not be the first winemaker to pay attention to the market (and to critics) in making a wine.

While Fess Parker's celebrity helped shape a region's development and Francis Ford Coppola's celebrity has ultimately set history right, Depardieu's celebrity is perhaps a bigger thing, casting a shadow across a wide swath of the wine-making world. Some of what he has done in wine reminds me of an actor playing a part—like the character Benjamin that he plays in "Grenouille d'hiver." But I can't help feeling this is art imitating life, because it seems to me that there is something of that vigneron in Depardieu's true character—a romantic notion for an economist, don't you think?

ART IMITATES LIFE 2: ANDY WARHOL AND DOM PÉRIGNON

In the future, everyone will be famous for fifteen minutes—Andy Warhol is the author of this famous statement, which I used to open chapter 4, but he wasn't a very good example of his own theory. The future is now, and Warhol's fame has hardly diminished. Of course he's not "everyone" or "anyone," but he is better evidence for fame's ability to persist than its short half-life.

Interestingly, much of Warhol's fame came from his calculated use of fame and celebrity. I'm talking about his serigraphs of famous people and products done up in unusual colors. They are some of the most familiar images of our time. If you do a Google images search for "Warhol serigraphs," you will see what I mean. The many Marilyn Monroe images flood the screen, along with Chairman Mao and Elizabeth Taylor. I like the John Wayne and gunfighter Elvis works a lot and nothing can really compete with the Campbell's Soup cans. Warhol's durable celebrity is based on the lasting (more than fifteen minutes) fame of his subjects.

I'm not sure if Andy Warhol ever made a Dom Pérignon image, but we know that he drank a lot of it at Studio 54 and his other haunts. There's even an entry in his notebook about a plan his friends hatched to wall up two thousand bottles of Dom to be unsealed at the turn of the millennium. What a party that would have been.

If you do a Google images search for Warhol + Dom Pérignon, you'll turn up an array of images of the familiar fat bottles decorated with red, yellow, and blue Warhol-inspired labels. They are life imitating art—Dom Pérignon's tribute to Warhol, produced in cooperation with the Andy Warhol Foundation. The Design Laboratory at Central Saint Martin's School of Art and Design was commissioned to come up with the colorful images that adorn a special 2002 cuvée that sells for between $150 and $200 here in the United States. You'll need to buy all three label colors to get the full Warhol effect, of course, and the bottles and their bright boxes are works of art that will persist (like Warhol's fame) long after you've drained the sparkling wine itself.

It is appropriate that Andy Warhol should give us a different twist on celebrity wine. Who is the celebrity—Warhol or his subjects? Both, I suppose, each gaining notoriety from the other. It's hard to know who made whom in the sense of fame. And it's hard to know who really made the Warhol Dom Pérignon edition. Certainly Dom Pérignon made the wine itself, and the design team produced the colorful labels, but isn't it actually Warhol's posthumous work? Certainly it could not have been produced without him. Without Warhol's touch, it would be just ordinary Dom Pérignon (if there is such a thing) dressed up for Halloween. It kind of confuses the whole celebrity (and celebrity wine) business, don't you think?

CELEBRITY WINE, HIP-HOP EDITION

I guess the Warhol case shows that celebrities can "make" a wine in several different senses of the word. This explain why I'm including Moscato wine in this chapter. The hottest segment of the US wine market in 2011–2012 was the previously unexceptional Moscato. Not Moscato D'Asti, the famous white wine from the Italian Piedmont. Oh, the Italian Moscato was doing fine, but the US demand was booming so strong that available supplies from Italy and California combined could not satisfy the American demand, so resourceful wine companies began to search for Moscato supplies from around the world. There are many different "Moscatos" made from Moscato plus its close grape-variety relations Moscadello, Moscatel, Muscat, and Muscatel. They come from many different countries and are made in many different ways, including white and pink; dry, sweet, and very sweet. All of them were "hot" when this chapter was being written. Barefoot, a Gallo brand, was the market leader with four different Moscato entries, and the bottle I found at the local supermarket said the wine came from Argentina. The wine inside was probably diverted to fill American glasses from its more typical path over the Andes to Chile, where it would otherwise be distilled into a spirit called pisco, key ingredient in the pisco sour.

The Moscato boom is a real puzzle for people like me who look to rational explanations for market changes. Why the sudden interest in wines that are usually sweet rather than dry, with relatively low alcohol? Most of the wines are not expensive, but they aren't Two Buck Chuck cheap, either (except, of course, for the Two Buck Chuck Moscato, if there is such a thing). Why Moscato? Why now?

The answer, my students suggest, lies not with the usual facts and figures but rather with a group of hip-hop artists by the names of Drake, Ab-Soul, Kanye West, and Lil' Kim.[10] They have served Moscato wines at their parties and have used the word (which has a nice rapping beat—say "Mo-sca-to") in their songs. Moscato is suddenly hip because of its personal association with these hip-hop celebrity artists, and that has brought a whole new group of consumers to wine. Compared with the mainstream wine market, Moscato drinkers are disproportionately urban, young, female, and online, with a somewhat lower average income. Young and urban are the key descriptors here, since women are more likely to drink wine than men in any case, and once you put young and urban together the remaining factors quickly fall into line.

The Moscato boom is exceptional because it is so broad: it's not just a single brand of wine, but a whole category, and the boom isn't just among the young and hip (although there is growing agreement that they got it started), but now older and more digitally challenged consumers are taking it up, too. It has even stimulated a parallel demand for sweet red wines and "chillable reds" that was not previously significant. "Moscato is a pop wine in the truest sense; its popularity is fueled by its simple, welcome taste," according to analyst Robert Haynes-Peterson. "The aromatics and flavors present a cornucopia of easy-to-love elements, from flowers and honey to tropical, citrus, lychee, melon, apple and stone fruits (especially peach), with upfront sweetness providing an overall family resemblance . . . Moscato is refreshingly easy to say, sip and buy. It's a happy wine." And who wouldn't want to be happy! Maybe this trend will have "legs" and be the start of a durable new wine trend. Or maybe it will be a flash in the pan like Jay-Z and Cristal.[11]

As I mentioned briefly in an earlier chapter, the artist Jay-Z stirred up interest in Cristal Champagne a few years ago through a combination of conspicuous consumption at parties and concerts, product placement in music videos, and pointed references in his lyrics. Cristal, a prestige cuvée from Louis Roederer, doesn't have very much in common with Moscato. Its production was first commissioned in 1876 by Tsar Alexander II, and the clear crystal bottles are both a luxury and serve the practical purpose of making it easier to inspect the bottle for adulteration (a plot against the tsar!). It is expensive where Moscato is relatively cheap, dry instead of sweet, and elite instead of mass-market. But it was hip and very appealing to members of the hip-hop community with money and a desire for status.

Jay-Z wasn't the only rapper who embraced Cristal as a symbol of wealth and power. Puff Daddy paid eighty thousand dollars for four six-liter Methuselah bottles of Cristal during a vacation in Saint Tropez and set up six Cristal fountains for his birthday party at Cipriani in New York at a cost of five hundred thousand dollars. The makers of Moscato are presumably happy with their sudden celebrity-driven popularity, but I guess the people at Louis Roederer had mixed emotions about being associated with these celebrities, and a spokesman apparently suggested at one point that the company wouldn't mind if hip-hoppers switched to some other brand of bubbles. Jay-Z declared the comment racist and publicly switched his loyalty to a previously obscure brand called Ace of Spades made by Armand de Brignac. I looked for it online—$250 and "out of stock" at one major seller's website, so I guess it must be selling pretty well.

CELEBRITY WINE: THE MORE THINGS CHANGE . . .

Among the many vintage wine advertisements you can find on YouTube is a thirty-second promotion that the famous British actor James Mason filmed for Gallo's Thunderbird wine back in the 1950s or 1960s. Dressed for a country weekend in ascot, shirt, and blazer, Mason pours himself a glass of Thunderbird on the rocks and pronounces it a very good drink—not like anything he's ever tasted before. And it probably was a completely different experience for him, given Thunderbird's citrus-flavored white Port nature. James Mason and Thunderbird, what an odd couple!

And that's how I thought the whole celebrity wine business would turn out when I started working on this chapter. But I'm sure that you can tell that I've changed my mind a bit. Yes, celebrity wines can be and perhaps often are examples of rather ruthless or sometimes desperate exploitation of a famous name. Just what you'd expect! But on further review, I am both surprised and delighted to say, celebrity can at least sometimes mean more when it comes to wine. Not what I expected at all. I guess that's what makes it extreme.

9

Extreme Wine at the Movies

If there is one thing I have learned from studying wine's extremes it is that the media is frequently part of the equation. No surprise there. We live in a media-driven age. The X Games, which are in a sense the inspiration for this book, are of, by, and for media use and attract extreme attention (and probably extreme profits, too) on that account. So a chapter on extreme wine media—this chapter—was always in the cards.

But "media" is a very broad category. In my original outline, this chapter was going to focus on print media, especially wine magazines and newspaper wine columns, since these are the wine media sources that I grew up with. But as I started to line up the periodicals (*Decanter, Wine Spectator, Wine Enthusiast, Gambero Rosso*, and so forth) it dawned on me that there is nothing particularly extreme about them anymore (except for the extremely large physical format of some of them). No offense, but as much as I love to hold them in my hands and leaf through the pages, the world is slowly passing them by. To find the cutting edge, I decided, I would need to move off the page and onto the screen. Since screens take many forms in today's world, we have a lot of territory to cover. Let's start by going to the movies.

WHAT WE TALK ABOUT WHEN WE TALK ABOUT WINE

You might think that wine's sensuous nature would make it a very popular film subject. But you would be wrong. The most surprising thing about wine in the cinema is not how few extremely good wine films have been made, but how few wine films have been made, period. So a film about wine or where wine plays a really central role is almost by definition extreme.[1]

The best known and probably the most popular wine film of recent years is *Sideways*, a 2004 film by Alexander Payne starring Paul Giamatti, Thomas Haden Church, Virginia Madsen, and Sandra Oh. The film, based on a novel by the same name written by Rex Pickett, follows two men on a wine-tasting tour of the Santa Barbara area. I think it is the only film that has ever been credited with creating a wine boom (Pinot Noir) or blamed for a wine bust (Merlot). That's good enough for admission to the extreme wine film club.

Sideways is a visually beautiful film, but the most memorable moments are not all very pretty. There's the famous "dump bucket" scene where Miles, Giamatti's character in the film, almost literally drown his sorrows by swilling down a tasting-room bucket full of discarded drinks. A high "yuck" factor, indeed. And then there's the burger-joint scene, which is yucky in a different way, when Miles once again drowns his sorrows, but this time by drinking his prize possession—a bottle of 1961 Cheval Blanc—from a Styrofoam cup while wolfing down a cheeseburger at a fast-food restaurant. What a horrible way for a great wine to die. It is also an ironic death, since Miles famously prefers Pinot Noir to all other wines and will not allow mere Merlot to wet his lips. This is ironic because the Cheval Blanc he treasures is mainly Merlot (and Cabernet Franc). Ouch!

Wine certainly brings people together in this film, sometimes in the "sideways" way that happens when boys and girls act like boys and girls. But in spite of the couple of dozen bottles that are opened in this film (the labels lovingly captured by the camera in pure product-placement mode), this is not really a wine story at all. Wine is just the language that is used to express hopes, fears, and emotions. When the characters in *Sideways* talk about wine, they are really talking about themselves. What could be more interesting? Let me show you what I mean.

The key scene in the film from my perspective takes place on the back porch of Stephanie's (Sandra Oh's) house. She and Jack (Thomas Haden Church) are in the bedroom, noisily getting "sideways," leaving Miles and Maya to sit and talk. Why are you so crazy about Pinot Noir, Maya asks?

Miles: I don't know. It's a hard grape to grow. As you know. It's thin-skinned, temperamental, ripens early. It's not a survivor like Cabernet that can grow anywhere and thrive even when neglected. Pinot needs constant care and attention and in fact can only grow in specific little tucked-away corners of the world. And only the most patient and nurturing growers can do it really, can tap into Pinot's most fragile, delicate qualities. Only when someone has taken the time to truly understand its potential can Pinot be coaxed into its fullest expression. And when that happens, its flavors are the most haunting and brilliant and subtle and thrilling and ancient on the planet.[2]

Of course this is a pretty good description of Miles, or Miles as seen and felt by Miles himself. Fragile, delicate, but capable of blooming with a little TLC. Who hasn't thought of themselves in this way, I wonder? Who couldn't relate to a wine with those same qualities? No wonder filmgoers embraced fragile Pinot Noir and turned away, at least for a while, from promiscuous, unsubtle (like Jack, I suppose) Merlot.

Maya has her moment, too. Maya uses wine to tell a powerful "circle of life" story and to express her own fragile mortality.

Maya: . . . I do like to think about the life of wine, how it's a living thing. I like to think about what was going on the year the grapes were growing, how the sun was shining that summer or if it rained . . . what the weather was like. I think about all those people who tended and picked the grapes, and if it's an old wine, how many of them must be dead by now. I love how wine continues to evolve, how every time I open a bottle it's going to taste different than if I had opened it on any other day. Because a bottle of wine is actually alive—it's constantly evolving and gaining complexity. That is, until it peaks—like your '61—and begins its steady, inevitable decline. And it tastes so fucking good.

The way they use wine to talk about themselves makes the characters of Maya and Miles more human. Wine is a powerful part of this story, but it's not really about the wine, it's all about the characters.

Most people don't know about the Japanese remake of *Sideways*, which was released in 2009. It is set in Napa Valley, not Santa Barbara, and the characters lust after sturdy Cabernet Sauvignon (and each other), not delicate Pinot Noir. The dump bucket scene is replayed with the same yucky hilarious effect, and some of the same beautiful imagery is employed. But somehow it's not the same. Maybe it's one of those "lost in translation" situations and the English subtitles simply let me down. But I think it is because the language of wine isn't as effectively deployed. When people talk about wine in this film they simply talk about wine, not themselves. What could be less interesting?

BOTTLE SHOCKED

The meaning of wine was explored in a different way in Randall Miller's 2008 film *Bottle Shock.* Bottle shock is a technical wine term—it refers to the way wine is disturbed by the violent process of filling the bottle. It just isn't itself for a while after bottling—it needs a little time to pull itself together. The term is used differently here, however: the shock isn't so much about the wine as about how we think about the wine and the people who make it.

Bottle Shock is loosely based on Steven Spurrier's famous 1976 Paris tasting of French and California wines, which George M. Taber wrote about so well in his book *The Judgment of Paris.* Napa Valley wines (Château Montelena Chardonnay and Stag's Leap Wine Cellars Cabernet Sauvignon) were top rated at the tasting, and this surprising result is said to have put California wine on the map. This event shook up the French and forced Americans to reconsider their opinions of California wine. Come to think of it, bottle shock isn't a bad way to describe what happened.

Sideways was actually a pretty good movie (not that I am qualified to judge), whereas *Bottle Shock* strikes me as a less serious effort. A fruit bomb of a movie, if you know what I mean, but not a lot of depth or complexity. It is Merlot to *Sideways*'s Pinot Noir. Alan Rickman is funny in a sort of Terry-Thomas way as Spurrier, but the two main male characters seem to be slightly modified younger versions of the *Sideways* cast—one is an oversexed surfer dude with a good heart (think Jack), while the other is, well, fragile and thoughtful (like Miles?). Do you see the resemblance? The female love interest is obviously a younger version of the *Sideways* charter Maya. Not much character development here, and many of the plot elements are predictable and cartoonish. This is not necessarily a barrier to commercial success, however.

The movie says that it is based upon a real story (the one that Taber covered for *Time* magazine), but it takes incredible liberties with the facts. Most of the nouns (people, places, things) are wrong in some way, although some of the numbers are correct (1976—check—got the right year). Château Montelena's winemaker, Mike Grgich, is left out entirely, even though he is a central figure in the true story. Warren Winiarski, the winemaker at Stag's Leap, is nearly as invisible. I feel sorry for others, like George Taber and Paul Draper (who made the Ridge Monte Bello), who appear only as crude caricatures. Artistic license, I suppose.

Perhaps the biggest error is the most basic: who won? Although California wines came out on top in both red and white competitions, they also came dead last. In fact the bottom two Chardonnays were from California (Veedercrest and David Bruce), as were the four (out of ten) bottom Cabs (Heitz, Clos du Val, Mayacamas, and Freemark Abbey).

If the Paris tasting was judged as a team competition, France versus California, rather than as a rating of individual wines, I think you might reasonably conclude that the whites were a dead heat, while the French won the battle for the reds, depending upon how you calculated the team scores. The variations among the judges were almost as great as among the wines, so clear winners and losers are difficult to determine. Toss out a couple of judges or bring in some new ones and the rankings could change quite a bit. The movie didn't do anything to correct the record in this regard, but that would be asking too much of a simple film. Instead it concludes with the Spurrier character's prediction (with 20/20 foresight) that soon we'd be drinking wines from all over the world: Australia, New Zealand, South America, South Africa, and so on. So globalization was the real winner of the competition.

I don't think there was a widespread *Bottle Shock* effect that can be compared with the *Sideways* effect in the wine market, although the specific wines featured in the film experienced a boom. This means Château Montelena more than any other wine, because it is the focus of the film. For a while at least Château Montelena offered its visitors a *Bottle Shock* tour of the place that echoed the *Sideways* tours that still operate farther down the coast. Why was *Bottle Shock*'s impact so modest? At the end of the day it may be because while the actual event—the Judgment of Paris—was extreme (and extremely important), the film is just a film, after all. The fictionalization of the circumstances diminishes somewhat the reality.

ALTERED REALITIES

If *Sideways* and *Bottle Shock* are the mass-market wine films that (almost) everyone has seen, what are the cult wine films—the *Rocky Horror Picture Shows*—that are viewed again and again by a small number of insanely devoted fans?

Well, I'm not really sure there are cult wine films, but if there are, then the list of them is short and almost certainly includes *Mondovino* and *Corked! Mondovino* is Jonathan Nossiter's 2004 documentary on how globalization is undermining wine's integrity and authenticity. (I wrote about the film at some length in my 2011 book *Wine Wars*, so I'll be brief here.)

Mondovino is extreme in several respects. It is a fairly long film, running 135 minutes in the English version and 159 minutes in French. Both versions are short, however, compared to the "director's cut" version released to Australian television and DVD: 576 minutes (more than nine and a half hours). No wonder it took Nossiter months in his Paris studio to edit his raw footage down to a length suitable for commercial release.

Mondovino reveals to us many of the wine world's greatest human extremes—the wealth of French and American wine moguls is contrasted, for example, against the abject poverty of small winegrowers in remote Brazil and Argentina. The influence of American wine critic Robert Parker is set alongside the force of fascists Hitler and Mussolini, which certainly invites an extreme response. The noble dogs of Old World terroirists are contrasted with vulgar New World canines.

Some people get vertigo watching *Mondovino*—a side effect of the jittery handheld camera documentary technique employed, apparently, before the days of affordable image-stabilization systems. Others find their heads spinning for other reasons. Whatever it is, people seem to love *Mondovino* or hate it—I haven't met many who stake out a middle ground. If you haven't seen *Mondovino*, it is time you did.

Although Nossiter has written that he did not go into the film with a clear idea of its message, it is very clear (to me, at least) that by the end, as he edited long hours into shorter hours, he knew exactly the points he wanted to make, and the many interview subjects (and the boisterous soundtrack) are deftly deployed to this end. Some of the characters are transformed into (or perhaps revealed to be) caricatures of themselves. But what ultimately makes *Mondovino* an extreme wine film is the serious way that the characters and the audience approach wine. It isn't just a mildly intoxicating delicious beverage, it is a civilization itself, under assault from the unstoppable forces of capitalism, globalization, and Americanization. All of the characters in the film take wine *very* seriously, nearly all of them see it as something much more than a simple consumer product, and most of them are angry when they consider how much they and we have to lose as the soul of wine drowns in a money-green sea.

Such earnestness calls out for a response, and the call was answered in 2009 in the form of a farce by Ross Clenenden and Paul Hawley called *Corked! Corked!* is what they call a mockumentary—a fake documentary designed to make fun of the real thing. *This Is Spinal Tap* and *Best in Show* are mockumentaries, and when I first read about *Corked!* I thought it might directly take an *Mondovino*, but it didn't. Instead it tells the story of a documentary crew that shows up in Sonoma, California, to cover a wine awards ceremony (featuring a famous wine critic with the initials RP, only this time it is Richard Parsons, not Robert Parker). It satirizes the New World wine figures they encounter rather than poking fun at the documentary makers themselves, as I had hoped.

The film pretends to take viewers behind the scenes to see how wine is really made, and I don't have to tell you that what they find isn't pretty, starting with the dead body in the fermentation tank and ending with one of those awful dump bucket scenes. While most of the characters are difficult to like, I admit a certain fondness for the middle-aged wine tourist couple who dream of working the harvest, casually picking delicious grapes in the warm autumn sun. Their romantic notions quickly meet harsh reality.

Incredibly for two films so different in every way, *Mondovino* and *Corked!* end up making very similar points: Wine may be noble, but some of the people who are attracted to it as a business are ridiculous. Their motives are base, their tastes even baser, and their market-driven methods are beneath contempt. *Corked!* takes the extreme *Mondovino* to the next level as a commentary on the cynical business of wine.

WINE? WHAT WINE?

Watching an extreme wine film, an earnest one like *Mondovino* or even a satiric one like *Corked!*, can be disheartening. If the romance of wine is a sham (*Corked!*) or simply doomed (*Mondovino*), then what's the point of living? Might as well give up any attempt at serious thoughts and simply try to be entertained. That's what I did as I worked my way through a list of famous wine films that I found on the Internet. And what could be less serious than this: a 1969 film by Stanley Kramer called *The Secret of Santa Vittoria* starring Anthony Quinn, Anna Magnani, and Virna Lisi?

Based on a best-selling novel by Robert Crichton, *Secret* is a comedy in the spirit of *It's a Mad Mad Mad Mad World* (also by Stanley Kramer) about a little Italian village in the closing months of World War II. Town drunkard Quinn is unexpectedly anointed mayor just as word arrives that German troops (real Nazis this time, not metaphorical ones as in *Mondovino*) are about to occupy the town and seize its only significant asset: a million bottles of wine produced by the town cooperative and stored deep in the city hall cellar. Losing the wine would mean losing everything, and so the townspeople unite behind their heroic buffoon of a mayor and his cockamamie plan to hide the wine in ancient Roman caves beneath the village. In what is one of the film's most memorable images, the million bottles are transferred from hilltop village to deep Roman cavern one bottle at a time via a vast human chain. Hand to hand to hand for a thousand hands, a million bottles snake up from the cellar, out across the square, down the steep mountainside, and deep into the caves. Truly an image of how wine can bring people together!

Incredibly the ruse works, although not without some sex and violence of the modest kind that reminds us how much things have changed since 1969. Despite its mainly madcap tone, what comes through in the film is how really important wine is to these people who depend upon it (and upon each other through it). *The Secret of Santa Vittoria* isn't its hidden wine, when all is said and done, but rather its hidden ability to bring people together, if only when the chips are down. The perfect antidote to *Mondovino* and *Corked!* and their cynical attitudes, and not just an entertaining diversion after all.

NOT NECESSARILY REALITY TV

Television is the logical next stop on the extreme-wine media tour and, as with film, the biggest surprise is wine's tiny impact compared to fashion, food, and home decor. I keep waiting for a wave of wine television to wash over me, but it hasn't really happened yet. A couple of years ago I read an article about a reality television project called *The Winemakers* that filmed one or perhaps two seasons of shows.[3] Like *Top Chef* or *Master Chef*, the idea was for a dozen aspiring winemakers to compete in a series of wine-making challenges that would both educate the audience about how wine is made and also entertain them. As the series's publicity blurb says:

Set in California's wine country, *The Winemakers* takes viewers inside the making of one of the world's most storied beverages. The contestants plunge headfirst into one of the most challenging yet rewarding (and often romanticized) professions to experience every aspect of wine making—from viticulture and enology to sales and marketing. A seasoned panel of top winemakers, educators, columnists and culinary celebrities oversee the true-to-life challenges the prospective winemakers would face in the real world.

Can the aspiring vintners learn new skills quickly? Do they have enough drive and dedication? In the end, the judges decide who advances to the next set of challenges and who goes home.

At the end of the series, one contestant gets to become a real winemaker and make his or her own wine. A dream come true. It's a reality-television format that seems to work in every country, but it took several years before I finally found a few episodes hidden in one of my cable TV provider's back alleys. The show lacked the quick pace and high tension that I associate with reality shows. Maybe wine just doesn't lend itself to elimination competitions, I speculated. Or maybe it's just that the first episodes were filmed back in 2008 and 2009 and the art (if you can call it that) of reality television has come a long way in the meantime. In any case, I wish the producers luck—better luck than Texan Ross Outon, who won the competition but lost everything except his determination to make wine along the way. According to one report, "his rocky path included start and stop filming for two years, divorce, loss of his house to the bank, loss of his job, the unexpected passing of his beloved dog, threats of legal actions to obtain his prize money, other prizes never honored and post harvest unemployment."[4]

Most of the other TV wine programs I have seen are fairly conventional in approach—like the History Channel's 2008 *A Brief History of Wine*, which covers wine's origins and development in an informative but not exactly heartstopping one hundred minutes.[5] John Cleese's *Wine for the Confused* miniseries (2004) leveraged the Monty Python comedian's talent and fame to demystify wine for its American audience.[6] *Uncorked: Wine Made Simple* did the same thing a few years later with Food Network celebrity Ted Allen as host.

I am a big fan of a miniseries that Jancis Robinson made for the BBC back in the 1990s called *Jancis Robinson's Wine Course*.[7] In fact, I still show it to my classes because, despite the passage of years, most of the timeless material is still relevant, and the opportunity to travel the globe with Jancis in search of wine is hard to resist. Robinson tries to demystify wine, too, but she goes well beyond that as she takes us to vineyards and cellars Old and New, North and South, meeting famous people and offering her own quite pointed opinions.

Completely different is *Oz and James's Big Wine Adventure*, the most ambitious English-language wine television series to date.[8] *Big Wine Adventure* aired on BBC in the 2006 and 2007 seasons and was later shown in the US on the BBC America cable channel. It is widely available on DVD and on YouTube as streaming video. The idea behind *Big Wine Adventure* is extreme. Take one world-famous wine expert, Oz Clarke, and send him off to tour the wine regions of France (2006) and then California (2007) in the company of a television celebrity who finds the rituals and romance of wine totally annoying: James May, best known as cohost of the long-running BBC auto series *Top Gear*. Clarke and May hit the road in a Jaguar convertible (France) and a motor-home caravan (California) in search of wine, "wine facts," and general wine enlightenment. The result is wacky fun that appeals to people who don't care a fig about wine, just as the *Top Gear* series finds an audience among folks with no particular passion for cars.

As wine entertainment this series is hard to beat, even if it doesn't have quite the depth of Jancis Robinson's videos in terms of wine education. Incredibly, however, I think the end effect of the project is exactly the opposite of the stated goals of some of the other television projects. Where they try to demystify wine, Clarke ends up convincing May that wine's mysteries are real and worth mastering for the most part. Wine's not like Coca-Cola, where all is revealed in the first sip. You've got to work a bit to get its magic to reveal itself and, if you are successful, the rewards can be profound. And that, as James might say, is an extreme wine fact.

AN ASIAN TWIST

Oz and James's Big Adventure is about as popular as wine television gets in Britain and the United States, but it only earns a bronze medal in my Extreme Wine TV competition. The top two finishers take a completely different approach to wine. Instead of being lectures or travelogues, they propose wine as soap opera, full of mystery, romance, and intrigue. Interestingly, they come from two countries not necessarily known for their wine: Japan and South Korea.

My silver medal goes to *Kami No Shizuku*, a nine-episode series shown on Japanese television in 2009.[9] It is based on the manga graphic novel series of the same name that swept Japan, then France, and then finally the United States. The television series has everything—sex, drama, mystery, intrigue, and romance. The plot is driven by an unlikely competition between two young men who must identify a series of wines in a blind tasting. For one, the prize is wealth and fame: the keys to the greatest wine cellar in Japan and the prestige that comes with its ownership. For the other, the real prize is enlightenment and understanding as successive glasses of wine unlock memories and conjure forth emotions. Wine isn't mysterious, the lesson seems to be. *Life* is! And wine, with its rituals and traditions, is part of that life and embodies liquid memories through its taste, smell, and texture. It's the same realization that James May has in the BBC series, but taken to an Asian extreme. Backed by the popularity of the graphic novel on which it was based, the *Kami No Shizuku* series took Japan by storm in 2009, although my informants there tell me that the effect was broader than it was deep. A booming interest in wine (especially the particular wines of the television series) faded when the series reached its end, much as our fascination with a particular bottle of wine fades a bit when the last glass is drained.

The prize for the most extreme wine television program goes to South Korea for a twenty-part drama that aired in 2008–2009 called *Terroir*.[10] When I first read about *Terroir* I dreamed of viewing it, but how was that ever going to happen, apart from a few YouTube scenes? Where was I going to find Korean television drama here in the United States? Much to my surprise, I did find it, just a few miles away at the local public library. They had seven copies in their DVD catalog (we have a large Korean American population!), and although most of them were checked out, I finally managed to view one.

The television series's story is complicated (how else can you justify twenty episodes?) and the title comes from the French name of a Korean restaurant that is central to the plot, which at its heart is a clash between globalization and terroir. Two precious wines feature in the story. The first is the most valuable wine in the world—Château Mouton Mayer 1945. It represents wealth, power, status, and taste. Most important (to my mind anyway), it is an iconic product that is essentially foreign to traditional Korean culture but that Koreans find themselves tempted by and fascinated with now that they are an integral part of the global economy and are even (see chapter 11) a rising force in the world of wine. To crave the fictional Mouton Mayer is to seek a position atop a global pyramid.

The other wine is not French and is not even made out of grapes. It is Bokbunjajoo, a traditional Korean fruit wine made from rare wild mountain blackberries or black raspberries.[11] It also "represents" by symbolizing Korea's deep roots, which are challenged now by the glittering stars of globalization. The problem of the protagonists, which is also the problem of modern-day Koreans and of the rest of us, too, is how to live with our feet in two different and sometimes contradictory worlds—the local and the global—and how to reconcile the resulting tensions.

The problem begins (and a romance is kindled) in *Terroir* in the most commonplace of ways when two similar suitcases are mixed up on a Paris-to-Seoul flight, one containing that impossibly precious Mouton Mayer 1945 and the other a bottle of grandfather's black raspberry wine that is precious in a different way. Getting those wines back to their rightful owners and making sense of it all isn't easy, but it all works out in the end.

Why do I find this television series so interesting? The fact that it is so unexpected is certainly part of it. Wine in Korea? Really? But the global-local tensions are completely universal, so why not Korea? And the fact that wine is a plausible container for these quite different values and aspirations is also quite profound. Oceans separate the (eventual) lovers, but wine brings them (and us) together. Irresistible!

WORLD WINE WEB

Globalization and the World Wide Web aren't the same, but they are related. The web expands our ability to communicate and exchange information, intensifies the connections, and speeds everything up. I'd use the same words to define globalization, but globalization goes beyond information to include production, consumption, and so on. One of the things that I have learned about globalization in the many years I have studied it in my other life as a university professor is that it has two types of effects: it transforms and it magnifies. Globalization can alter human relations, but more often it simply magnifies what's already there. I think the same may be true of the web and maybe especially of wine on the web.

The magnification effect means that, whereas the choices were pretty limited when I went looking for wine in cinema and on television, wine is virtually everywhere on the web. You can buy, sell, and rate wine as well as tweet, like, post, and link about it. There are millions of wine stories on the World Wide Web—more than 164 million this morning, if the numbers supplied by the Google search engine mean anything—and they come from all over the world and from every imaginable source. Just for fun, for example, I decided to search for "prison wine"—the most unlikely combination of terms I could think of—and Google yielded up thirteen thousand references, mainly about a cell-made (homemade seems like the wrong term) alcoholic drink called pruno or prison wine that is apparently surreptitiously produced in some penitentiaries from sugar, fruit, and ketchup (with moldy bread added to supply the yeast). Who knew?

It has become conventional wisdom that wineries, wine merchants, wine writers, and others must have a presence on the web. It is easy to understand why: the numbers are impressive. Gary Vaynerchuk developed a fanatical following for his *Wine Library TV* daily video blog, attracting an average of more than ninety thousand viewers to his one thousand posts between 2006 and 2011.[12] CellarTracker.com, an online wine-cellar-management website, boasts more than 240,000 users.[13] Eric LeVine, the guy who created the site and keeps it going, was named Wine Person of the Decade by DrVino.com in 2010. I'm pretty familiar with the power of the wine web, both as a consumer of information and as an active contributor. I first started *The Wine Economist* blog because I wanted to work out ideas in public, where I could meet people and hear their ideas.

Much has been written about how the web has "democratized" communications, and I think this is true for wine, too. Although the big players in wine media all have websites (Decanter.com, WineSpectator.com, and so on), little guys have access, too, both through blogs and websites and through the simple "comment" function you'll find on many web pages. This broader access is great, and the proliferation of voices is positive, too, but the world is not (yet) flat. As with other media forms, the top 1 percent of websites attract enormously more readers than most of the 99 percent that remain. The web has both transformed wine media by giving more people access and also magnified the system's inherent inequalities. Is this a problem . . . or a solution? Well, it depends. Predictably the question came up in an exchange on the web, and while the answer takes us a little bit off track, I think it's worth a brief detour.

OCCUPY WINE: A DIGRESSION

One of my loyal *Wine Economist* readers wrote to suggest that I take advantage of my place in the wine media spectrum to organize an Occupy the Vineyards movement. The purpose? To protest that part of the wine world that focuses on iconic wines for elites. What about the rest of us? he says. What about the other 99 percent of wine drinkers who are looking for good, affordable quotidian wines and don't really care about impossibly expensive one-hundred-point wines?

It is a very Wagnerian idea (the reference here is to Philip Wagner, who promoted a democratic notion of wine here in the US, not the more famous aristocratic composer), and I am very sympathetic toward it. Wagnerian wines don't have to be cheap cheap cheap, they just need to be good, drinkable, affordable wines. Wine food, not wine porn, if you know what I mean. A sensible idea. So I started fooling around on the Internet, searching for titles like "Occupy Napa" and "Occupy Bordeaux." I figured that a catchy name would help make the point. But they were already taken—by groups affiliated with the Occupy Wall Street movement. Occupy Napa held weekend protests at a Napa, California, town square. Occupy Bordeaux seems to be part of the broader Occupy France movement. (Wait. I thought France was already occupied by the antiglobalization movement . . .) A CafePress web page sold Occupy Bordeaux souvenirs, including T-shirts and water bottles, but I don't think it was directly affiliated with the group in France.

I like the idea of promoting a more casual idea of wine, but I guess I won't be using the "occupy" trademark, since it would be too easy to confuse the wine group with the larger transnational advocacy movement. But I think that what I am calling the "occupy principle" probably applies to both. Usually we think that movements need to stand for something quite specific—to have a clear agreed-upon agenda—and in the long run I think this is very important. But in the short run sometimes it helps if a movement is a little ambiguous, with a flexible identity that can lend itself to several different purposes and attract a good many followers, which generates media coverage. I think this ambiguity helped the Occupy Wall Street movement to gain initial attention and to spread as it did. The Occupiers I have read about resent and oppose unequal wealth and power (the gap between the 1 percent and the rest) but differ in many other respects. It will be interesting to see if a clearly focused agenda ever emerges and, if it does, what specific goals are adopted. Perhaps, of course, the protest itself and the consciousness-raising it provokes are sufficient as a first step. Maybe it's just a media thing in the end.

A wine movement for the 99 percent would surely bring together the wine-world equivalent of "strange bedfellows," too. Some supporters are just cheap (or thrifty, if you will) and want a little respect for their self-restraint. Others may be against an elitist idea of wine or oppose conspicuous consumption. So if there were to be an Occupy Wine protest, where would we gather, and what would we do? That's a bit of a problem, since the places that sell the most wine (including supermarkets and wine shops) often have a lot of choices for the 99 percent—not much to oppose there. Costco is the largest wine retailer in the US, and although it does sell some icon wines, most of the products are more affordable. Most 99 percenters probably view Costco as friendly territory because of its policy of marking up wine only 15 percent for most bottles and 17 percent for house-brand Kirkland Signature wines. I suppose that we could protest in front of high-end restaurants that sell superstar wines at supernova prices. But I think restaurant wine markups are an issue of their own. And besides, the smell coming out of the kitchen would probably make me crazy. We could meet at Trader Joe's to acknowledge the Two Buck Chuck phenomenon, but it wouldn't be the same.

No, we would need to occupy the "commanding heights"—which in the case of wine means the wine media, where the 1 percent wines are praised and raised to an often unreachable altar. But there are flaws in the plan to occupy *Wine Spectator*, too. First, all the popular wine magazines are making efforts to reach price-sensitive "99 percent" buyers in the post–Great Recession world, even if they also run stories about 1 percent wines. Even Robert Parker's *Wine Advocate* identifies good values, and I have seen box wines and house brands included in some wine-magazine reviews.

The other problem is that I am not sure that there is a market for an alternative *Occupy Wine* magazine that would focus on everyday wine values and ordinary wine lifestyles. The target audience probably wouldn't buy it—they'd rather spend their money on wine than wine literature. And in any case

there are several wine blogs that cater to the good-value audience. Maybe . . .
and this is only speculation . . . maybe we have *already* occupied wine and we
just don't realize it? The wines are there and so are we, the 99 percent.

Occupy Wine is a *fait accompli?* Who knew! Spread the word.

A FINAL UNEXPECTED EXTREME

This chapter is almost complete, but I can't stop until I tell you about one
more type of wine media extreme. As I was working my way through wine
in the cinema I came across a 1959 film by Henry King called *This Earth Is
Mine.*[14] It stars Rock Hudson, Jean Simmons, Dorothy McGuire, and Claude
Rains, and if you are interested, you can watch all 124 minutes on your smartphone or tablet courtesy of YouTube. The film is set in Napa Valley during
Prohibition, and I was initially attracted by the vineyard and winery footage,
which gave me a very dramatic sense of how much the area has changed in
the last fifty years (and how little it had likely changed in the previous fifty).
Apparently all the famous wineries of the day, including Beringer, Beaulieu,
Inglenook, Christian Brothers, Louis M. Martini, and Sebastiani (which is
actually in Sonoma, not Napa), were used as settings for various scenes. Shot
in glorious Technicolor, *This Earth Is Mine* is a visual treat.

The story is pretty interesting, too. It's about the Rambeaus and Fairons,
two fictional wine-growing families, and the intergenerational conflicts as
Prohibition squeezed the fine-wine business (leaving only sacramental wine
to be made) and distorted the grape business (as I discussed back in chapter
6). It was interesting to watch the film, but puzzling, too. It just didn't make
much sense, like a jigsaw puzzle with a few pieces missing. I guess that's why
I was still looking for a sense of closure even after the happy ending (yes, boy
does get girl) and the screen credits rolled. What was I missing?

So I reversed course and went to the opposite extreme—the dusty old
shelves of the library stacks. There I discovered the well-used remains of the
first edition of a 1942 novel by Alice Tisdale Hobart titled *The Cup and the
Sword*, the source of the film's story. All my questions were answered as I
worked my way through the book's four hundred pages. The names of the
characters were the same and the Prohibition time frame, too, but just about
everything else was altered.

The main action of the book isn't set in photogenic Napa Valley, where
California's fine-wine industry is centered today. The action takes place in-

stead in the hard-working unglamorous San Joaquin Valley, where most of California's wine grapes are still grown, destined for the bulk wines that fill everyday boxes, jugs, and blends. And the purpose of the book is clear: like one of those James Michener novels that it pre-dates, *The Cup and the Sword* is meant to capture the broad sweep of California wine-industry history from about 1900 through the Second World War. The focus is on the crisis years, of course, which would be Prohibition and the years that immediately followed it. And, since this is an American story, it is about the immigrant melting pot—French (the central Rambeau family), Spanish, German, Italian, and Chinese families.

The story told here made sense—more sense than the film—because of course all the pieces are there. The screenplay was obviously an attempt to sew together all the choice bits (along with a few additions) to make a two-hour film. But what was more important to me was how well the real economic history of the industry came through. I've read a lot about the development of wine in America, but hardly anyone does as good a job as this novelist in capturing the forces that shaped and reshaped American wine during these critical years.[15]

Really, *The Cup and the Sword* took my breath away as an extreme wine chronicle. I don't think this is great literature, but the true story behind the fiction is extremely interesting (exactly as the author intended). Which leaves me in an awkward position. Having examined quite a lot of evidence, the most extreme wine story I found isn't available to view on any sort of electronic device. Google Books tells you to forget about loading *The Cup and the Sword* on your iPad. You've got to go find a print copy like I did.

I guess it's not the medium that makes wine extreme, it's the message in the bottle that matters most.

10

Extreme Wine Tourism

My colleague Pierre returned from visiting his parents in Toulouse, and he brought with him the May 2012 special wine tourism issue of *La Revue du Vin de France*, which features "Les 35 meilleurs circuits du vin." Since I was drafting the outline of this chapter at the time, I couldn't wait to dig in.

So what are the thirty-five best wine tourism destinations? Well, given the French readership of *La Revue*, it should be no surprise that twenty-nine of them are in France itself. I'm sure that if *Wine Spectator* were to pick out the best wine-touring routes, there would be an American bias (out of practical concern if nothing else), although it might not be so extreme as this French case. But I can't really criticize the editors' choices, since France is so central to the world of wine.

I sensed a diplomatic hand at work in making the selection, however, as virtually every important wine region in France is singled out (so to speak) in one way or another for inclusion. I think you could organize a Tour de France–style bicycle race from these wine tourism suggestions. If you did, I suppose you'd want to stock up on Boisset's Yellow Jersey brand wine, made in tribute to the great race—the plastic bottle fits neatly in your bicycle's water-bottle cage.

Even Paris makes the wine tour list. You might wonder at this because vineyards are not frequently seen on Parisian hillsides, but that's not why wine tourists go to Paris. It's the shops and wine bars that are the attraction here. So

La Revue directs you to visit Galeries Lafayette in the ninth arrondissement to see the magnificent collection ("12000 bouteilles en cave") of Bordeaux wines there. Other shops are recommended for unrivaled access to wines from Burgundy, Champagne, and Languedoc and imported wines, too, from Germany, Hungary, and Spain. Although the idea that Paris is a wine tourist destination felt wrong at first, I can see the attraction. Follow the money, Deep Throat said. Follow the wine is good advice, too, and sometimes the best collections of wine are far from the sunny vineyard slopes (but close to where the money resides).

I am particularly interested in *La Revue*'s selection of wine tourism destinations outside France. I expected to see Napa Valley on the list; Napa is the second-largest tourist destination of any kind in California (after Disneyland) and so certainly the largest *wine* tourism center in the United States. But it didn't make the *La Revue* cut. Easy to understand, I suppose. When the French visit the United States, they may not be thinking of wine. New York, Miami, Los Angeles, and maybe Las Vegas—these are the most common European tourist targets I have heard. American wine country is a bit off that map. Or at least it is off *La Revue*'s map for 2012.

Porto in Portugal did make the list, however, along with Tuscany, Vienna, Geneva, the Rhine Valley, and Cape Town, South Africa. Cape Town is a spectacularly good choice for wine tourism, of course, and any list of the top global wine destinations would have to include Tuscany and Germany. But the competition for the final spots must have been pretty fierce, and it would be interesting to know how Vienna and Geneva beat out New Zealand, Australia, Chile, and Argentina (not to mention Napa and Sonoma). There are many amazing wine tourist destinations, and choosing just six outside France (or choosing just twenty-nine inside France) is necessarily difficult and controversial.

Wine tourism is a big industry here in the US. The Wine Institute estimates that 20.7 million tourists visited California wine regions in 2010 and spent 2.1 billion dollars. An economic impact statement prepared in 2012 by Stonebridge Research for the Napa Valley Vintners Association estimated that wine tourism accounted for more than eight thousand jobs in Napa Valley alone in 2011 (about as many workers as in all the 789 wineries combined) with total payroll of more than 200 million dollars.[1] Total wine-related tourism expenditures in Napa County were estimated to be more than one billion dollars. The economic impact is spread over hundreds of small businesses—wineries, of course; wine tour companies; hotels; restaurants; wine and food shops; and so forth.

Although it doesn't make the French magazine's list, Napa Valley is the industry leader in many ways. Surely many wine tourism programs around the world have been inspired by Robert Mondavi's example, which from the start aimed to create an experience, not just a wine tasting or buying opportunity. It's all about storytelling. Wineries use tourism as an opportunity to tell their stories, which visitors weave into their own lifestyle narratives.

The Oxford Companion to Wine's "wine tourism" entry suggests that Old World wine tourism development has been quite uneven. Wine tourists were long welcomed and accommodated in Germany's Rhine and Mosel River Valleys, for example. But in France . . .

> In France, wine tourism was often accidental. Northern Europeans heading for the sun for decades travelled straight through Burgundy and the northern Rhône and could hardly fail to notice vineyards and the odd invitation "Dégustation–Vente" (tasting-sale). (And it is true that a tasting almost invariably leads to a sale.) . . . Bordeaux was one of the last important French wine regions to realize its potential for wine tourism. . . . Alexis Lichine was mocked for being virtually the only classed growth proprietor openly to welcome visitors.[2]

Now, as this issue of *La Revue* indicates, the French are catching up!

OLD BOTTLES, NEW WINE (TOURISM)

The wine tourism industry, with its promotions, brochures, associations, and economic impact studies, is relatively new. But I think wine tourism itself has been around for a long time. It wouldn't surprise me to learn that the Roman naturalist Pliny the Elder (23–79 CE) did some wine touring in his day. He wrote of wine's medicinal value, but he couldn't resist giving his own sensory evaluation. Falernian wines from Campania are the very best, he wrote, particularly the ones from the Faustian Clos on the southern slopes of Monte Massico (Pliny was an early proponent of terroir).[3] I can imagine him making the trip to Monte Massico to see the vineyards and meet the winemakers and enjoy the old wines of their cellars. In fact, I cannot imagine that he did not go if he could. He was a man of such insatiable curiosity that he died in the eruption of Vesuvius, drawn to the area by his need to see for himself what was going on.

George Taber cites three famous early wine tourists in his wine tourism book *In Search of Bacchus* (which was the initial inspiration for this chapter).[4] The British political philosopher John Locke moved to the South of France in the 1670s—he hoped the warmer, drier climate would improve his health. Like so many after him, Locke became fascinated by the food and especially the wine and visited the vineyards and cellars, putting detailed questions to the vignerons, the answers to which he duly recorded in detailed notebooks. Thus among the nine volumes of John Locke's collected works you will find *Leviathan* (of course) and also *Observations upon the Growth and Culture of Vines and Olives* (written at the request, it says, of the Earl of Shaftsbury).[5] Locke lists the local names of a total of forty-one different wine-grape varieties that he uncovered in the Languedoc in the area around Montpellier. A few, such as Clarette (Clairette) and Piquepoul (Picpoul), are familiar in the Languedoc today, as is Unio Blanquo if it is really Ugni Blanc, a.k.a. Trebbiano, the world's third-most widely planted white wine grape, and the various Musquats (Muscat). Most of the rest are lost in history or perhaps just lost in translation.[6]

Thomas Jefferson replaced Benjamin Franklin as US ambassador to France in 1785 and served in that capacity until 1789. He was already a wine lover when he arrived on French soil and also a frustrated winegrower—his attempts to grow *vitis vinifera* at his Monticello home were depressingly unsuccessful (I wonder if it was phylloxera?), although visitors there today can see a modern re-creation of the vineyard Jefferson had in mind. They can also taste Virginia wines, as this is now a thriving wine and wine-touring region.

Jefferson set out to visit the French wine regions in 1787, and he seems to have made all the important stops. Like Locke before him, Jefferson marveled at Haut-Brion while in Bordeaux and took detailed notes on vineyard and cellar practices. And, of course, he made or did not make the notorious purchase at Château Lafite—the "billionaire's vinegar"—that featured in the earlier discussion of the "most infamous" wine.

Taber doesn't include him in the list of famous early wine tourists, but Adam Smith made the rounds of French wine regions a few years before Jefferson and even wrote about what he learned in *The Wealth of Nations*. Smith was taking Lord Townshend's son (yes, Townshend of the infamous Townshend Acts that provoked revolution in Jefferson's America) on the Grand

Tour that was part of every gentleman's education. Wine was part of the civilizing process, and Smith seems to have embraced it warmly.

A Scot like Smith, Robert Louis Stevenson (*Kidnapped* and *Dr. Jekyll and Mr. Hyde*) is the third early wine tourist in Taber's troika, and he is noteworthy for his visit to Napa Valley, which inspired an 1883 travel memoir called *The Silverado Squatters* and coined the term "bottled poetry" to describe the wines. Having lived in France through the worst years of the phylloxera scourge, Taber says, Stevenson thought that fine wine was dead in Europe and the future could be found in California. He was wrong about the wines, but not far from the mark if we are talking wine tourism: Highway 29, where Robert Mondavi built his destination winery, is just across the valley from Stevenson's Silverado Trail.

GOING TO EXTREMES

Taber's book makes a good starting point for any exploration of extreme wine tourism. His global tour stops in twelve countries—South Africa, Argentina, Chile, Australia, New Zealand, Spain, Portugal, Italy, France, Germany, Georgia, and the United States. Each chapter tells the story of wine and wine tourism ("Diary of a Wine Tourist") in a particular region and then recounts a particular day Taber spent performing some pleasant wine-touring task. In South Africa, for example, he enjoys the wines while going on a wildlife photography safari. He takes cooking classes in a thousand-year-old monastery in Tuscany.

One of the peculiarities of Taber's book is that he limits himself to a single wine region in each country in order to avoid, I suppose, *La Revue*'s problem with French wine regions. I guess wine regions are like potato chips—once you get started, it's hard to stop. So he goes to Tuscany in Italy, for example, but not Piemonte, Umbria, or Alto Adige. Rioja in Spain, but not Priorat. The Margaret River in Australia, not the Barossa Valley. The only exception to this rule is France, where he writes about Bordeaux but then walks in the Burgundy vineyards. I can see where it would be difficult (from a political angle if nothing else) to choose one of these iconic regions over the other, although even so he leaves out the twenty-seven other top French wine tourist destinations on *La Revue*'s long list.

Taber's global wine tour route intersects with my own personal map in several places, although we don't seem to do quite the same the same things in the same places, which I guess shows the great diversity of wine-touring options that are available. While in New Zealand, for example, Taber tackles the beautiful Central Otago wine region, and his "day out" diary has him bungee jumping off a bridge (there's even a photo showing him dropping headfirst into the abyss). That's a good choice, since bungee jumping was invented in Queenstown, New Zealand, in 1979 by A. J. Hackett (one possibly unreliable Internet source suggests that there was alcohol involved . . .). We spent more time in Marlborough and Hawke's Bay during our Kiwi wine trip. Our bit of adventure was accidental, when the combination of heavy rain, gusty wind, and an unexpected herd of deer put us and our rental car in a ditch while we were driving on the wild west side of the South Island. No one was hurt, and a friendly big-rig trucker pulled us out with a long, long rope—sort of bungee jumping in reverse.

While it may be thrilling to throw yourself off a bridge or drive into a ditch, it must be said that these are not exclusively wine tourist activities. Ordinary (if somewhat extreme) tourists also do these things. What is it that makes wine tourism special (and defines extreme wine tourism for the purpose of this book)? To try to find out, I searched through the "extreme wine tourism" entries on *The Wine Economist* blog. One entry took me north and another one south.

O CANADA: ICEWINE AND BEYOND

You are probably not surprised to find that Canada is missing from both *La Revue's* wine tourism list and George Taber's. Many wine drinkers find the very idea of Canadian wine a bit of a surprise, which is understandable, since only a handful of wineries have successfully navigated the process to get distribution outside the country. The wines themselves hold many surprises, if you can find them, and I'm not just talking about the famous Icewines. And then there are the wine tourism opportunities. Wow! For a lot of people, this will be the biggest surprise of all.

Wine tourism is naturally appealing—even if you omit the wine!—because vineyards and wineries are often located in areas of great natural beauty. But wine tourism in many regions has been slow to develop because vineyards are agricultural zones often lacking in the expected tourist infrastructure and amenities. And at some point, as more people arrive, there is tension between farming and tourism. The Okanagan wine region in British Columbia has a decided advantage over most winegrowing regions. Usually the wine comes first, and then the tourist infrastructure slowly develops. It's the other way 'round here. The Okanagan region has spectacular scenery with four-season sports and recreation opportunities that have long attracted visitors. At the center of it all is beautiful Lake Okanagan, a long narrow north-south body of water that feels like a fjord and has just about everything a tourist might desire, including a resident lake monster (a relative of the Loch Ness monster?) named Ogopogo.

Wine grapes are known to love to look down on lakes and rivers. People do too, of course, so the Okanagan developed its tourist infrastructure long before the current wine boom. We benefited from this timely development on our trip, staying right on the lake at the Summerland Waterfront Resort in Summerland, BC, and enjoying meals made from regional ingredients at Local, a restaurant just next door. Sipping wine in the evening with the fireplace roaring, looking out across the lake to the vineyards on the Naramata Bench—well, wine tourism does not get much better than this.

As this region's wine industry developed from the 1990s on, many wineries made very significant investments in wine tourist facilities, which elevated the standards of tourism generally in the region. Direct sales of the kind that wine tourists provide have historically been extremely important to wineries in this region. Every winemaker I talked with noted the cost and difficulty of getting distribution in other Canadian provinces, to say nothing of entering export markets. Direct sales are therefore key, and tourists from Vancouver in the west, Calgary in the east, and the US down south are a big part of that business.

Burrowing Owl Estate Winery in Oliver is a good example of a BC destination winery. Perched on a hillside, it is a beautiful facility in a great location that includes the winery, a tasting room, a restaurant, and an inn with a swimming pool. As a must-stop on the wine tourist trail, they count on cellar-door sales to move most of their substantial annual production. Tasting room fees are still very low in this region—amazingly low for anyone who has visited Napa Valley lately. Most of the wineries I visited offered free tastings for a limited number of wines. At Burrowing Owl, a two-dollar donation was encouraged—the money goes to a nature conservancy group.

The ultimate wine tourist destination in the Okanagan Valley must be Mission Hill Winery. Inspired by Robert Mondavi's iconic winery in Napa Valley,

Mission Hill sits high atop a peak and looks out over the lake. The winery is stunning, with an entry arch that immediately made me think of the Mondavi winery and a soaring bell tower. Everything inside is strictly first class, too, including comprehensive tours that end with sommelier-led tastings from your souvenir Riedel glass. Mission Hill is the cherry on the Okanagan wine tourism cake. Altogether, this wine region is quite a treat and is sure to grow in popularity as the word gets out.

As extreme as the Okanagan Valley is, with its unexpected combination of wine, recreation, and hospitality facilities, it is not the most extreme wine tourism opportunity in Canada. On the recommendation of a *Wine Economist* reader, I am adding the Niagara Icewine Festival to my wine tourist bucket list. Unlike every other wine festival I know, this one is held in the dead of winter. The deader (or colder) the better, because by law the grapes need to be frozen to at least minus 8 degrees Celsius or 17 degrees Fahrenheit to produce a natural Icewine of the kind that is celebrated here. Sounds like cold fun, but fun nonetheless.

THE ART OF WINE TOURISM IN ARGENTINA

Mendoza, Argentina, lies on a high plain at the foot of the Andes Mountains. Flying in over the drab desert landscape, you almost wonder if you've come to the right place. Where are the lush green vineyards? Well, they are there, but they are the product of irrigation canals that were first built by the Incas, which bring cold, clear water down from the mountains. Lots of green vineyards where the water is found, but mainly brown desert everywhere else. No wonder Taber's break from visiting the wineries was a desert asado—a meal featuring Argentina's great grilled meats (and wines, of course!). I can't criticize Taber's choice, but we took a different route.

We came to Bodegas Salentein because I wanted to see the state of the art in wine tourism in Argentina. Bodegas Salentein is a world-class operation and a tribute to the "if you build it, they will come" school of thought. What a miracle it is that thousands of wine tourists now flock to this remote area each year to visit Salentein and the other spectacular wineries that followed in its wake.

You approach Salentein, located in the Valle de Uco about ninety minutes by car south of Mendoza city, by driving up the long entry road. You arrive at the main hospitality center, which contains a reception center, gift shop, restaurant, and Killka, a spectacular modern-art museum built to display part of the owner's collection. Another beautiful building, the Chapel of Gratitude, is just down the road. Incredibly, you have not yet arrived at the winery. To get there you pass through the reception center and walk down *another* dramatic lane (this time through a vineyard) to arrive at one of two wine-production facilities on the property.

The winery's architecture is even more impressive than the museum's, especially inside, where wine making is organized around the "cathedral of wine" barrel room, laid out like a cross around a mosaic compass rose. Entering the vast space, you really do feel like you are in a cathedral. I could hear the click, click, click of our friend Scott's camera as he tried to capture every line and curve of the stunning building's architecture. Posada Salentein completes the package with a sixteen-room inn and gourmet restaurant that serves creative cuisine paired with estate wines. It is hard to imagine a better way to visit the Valle de Uco than to stay here among the vines and to exploit the restaurant menu to answer burning questions such as "How does Malbec go with fresh local trout?" (Perfectly, as it happens, based on our experience.)

Bodegas Salentein hosts twenty-five thousand to thirty thousand visitors per year according to Lorena Cepparo, who guided us through the facility. Salentein is a destination winery that is high on the hit list for every Valle de Uco wine tourist (O. Fournier is another must-see in the area.) The typical "day tripper" experience, according to Lorena, involves a tour, tasting of three wines, and lunch at the restaurant—an appealing combination. But the basic package is just a start and can be customized in many ways depending upon the particular interests of visitors. International visitors come from the winery's main export markets: the US, Brazil, Canada, and the Netherlands. The Netherlands? Well, yes. Lorena explained. The winery's owner is Dutch (Salentein is the name of a Dutch estate). And Holland's Princess Máxima is from Argentina, Lorena said, so the Dutch are understandably crazy about all things Argentine. Who can blame them?

It seems to me that Bodegas Salentein sets a high standard for wine tourism here in Mendoza and, as the first destination winery built in the Uco Valley, it has inspired others to try to match or exceed their facilities and services. Bórmida and Yanzó, the local architect firm that designed Salentein, has gone on to create an incredible collection of facilities here. The contrast between their cutting-edge architecture and the starkness of the high desert vineyards makes wine tourism here a unique experience.

WHAT MAKES WINE TOURISM EXTREME?

Wine tourism is obviously important both for wine enthusiasts and for the wine industry, too. But what produces an extreme experience? So far this chapter has followed the conventional wisdom that the three most important things (in real estate, business, life?) are location, location, and location, and certainly wine tourists can and do go to geographical extremes in search of Bacchus (to draw from the title of Taber's book), in search of the spirit.

But, having led you down this road, I think I must admit that, though location certainly matters, it's probably not the most important thing. I've followed the wine trails to some of the most beautiful and most unexpected places on the planet and, while a striking physical setting certainly makes a difference, it's not the whole story. What makes a tourist experience memorable or extreme is its ability to leave a lasting impression—to create an indelible memory. Any of the senses can be the critical gateway—sound, touch, smell, taste, feel, or sight—and when they all come up together at once, the impact can be devastating. Unlocking the senses like this is neither necessary nor sufficient for a moving experience, but it certainly opens the door, and that is the key.

If this is true, then I think that the way to think about wine tourism is not just in terms of the wine or just in terms of the place (or even the people), but rather in terms of the total impact of the experience. Inspired by Mondavi's early efforts to make his eponymous Napa Valley facility a destination, many wineries are giving very serious thought to designing an experience that will make a deeper impact on visitors. I visited one such experiment in extreme wine tourism on a sunny January day in 2012 when I stopped by to do a book signing at Raymond Vineyards.

Located in the famous Rutherford corner of Napa Valley, Raymond was founded by Roy Raymond and his family in 1971 using money from the sale of historic Beringer Vineyards to Nestlé. (Roy Raymond worked at Beringer starting as a cellar rat in the 1930s and worked his way up in the company, where he met and married his wife, Martha Jane Beringer.)[7]

The Raymond enterprise expanded over the years to over three hundred acres. They sold the place to Kirin, the Japanese brewing company, in 1988—

right at the peak of the Japanese economy's bubble, when foreign investment was rampant. The Raymonds stayed on to operate their facility until Kirin finally sold out in 2009 to Jean-Charles Boisset of the Boisset family of winemakers from Burgundy. Under Boisset's guidance, Raymond reclaimed its stature and received the American Winery of the Year award for 2012 from *Wine Enthusiast* magazine. Jean-Charles Boisset lives together with his wife Gina Gallo and their twin daughters in the old Robert Mondavi residence, one of the symbolic centers of Napa's wine world. It was his eccentric, flamboyant vision of wine tourism as expressed through Raymond that drew my attention there.

The Raymond Vineyards experience is unconventional. And I'm not just talking about the fact that a visit to Raymond includes the opportunity to take your pet to Frenchie Winery, Napa Valley's first *dog* winery, which seems to be run by or perhaps for Gina Gallo's dog Frenchie. Frenchie Winery features small French-themed suites with wine-barrel beds for dogs, whose owners can watch their pets via the Frenchie Cam while visiting Raymond. Frenchie features two wines, both red, from the 2009 vintage. Frenchie Winery is certainly out of the ordinary (more so than you might think—visit Frenchie's website to view the videos of Frenchie and Jean-Charles Boisset and you'll see what I mean), but it is only the beginning.

You actually begin the Raymond Vineyards experience by walking through a curtain into a garden, which is called the Theatre of Nature. A trail takes you through two acres of plants and exhibits that explain the principles of organic and biodynamic viticulture that guide wine growing at Raymond (and also up in the Russian River area at DeLoach, another Boisset property). Wine is made in the vineyard, and so the experience starts here, and if you think that biodynamics is a bit eccentric in a voodoo viticulture sort of way, then you should be ready for the next phase of the visit.

They say that wine is appealing because it stimulates all of our physical senses, and I think the Raymond experience mirrors this quality. The attractive tasting room allows visitors to stimulate their senses in the usual way, sampling the range of Raymond's wines, but that is only the beginning. The Corridor of the Senses, located just inside the winery's entrance, highlights wine's texture (how it feels on the palate) and aromas, including especially a sort of "blind" sniffing of scents, such as cherry and dark chocolate, associated with the wines. The darkened Corridor of the Senses leads to the Red Room, a private tasting facility for wine club members that assaults the senses, especially the visual sense. Red velvet covers the furniture, red flocked fabric covers the wall, red light seeps through red banners that drape from the ceiling around the crystal chandelier at the center of the room. A special wine (red, of course) that is only served here fills the glasses. The experience is unexpectedly intense and, walking out of the Red Room back into normal light, my vision seemed to be affected for a few minutes; anything red "popped" to my color-hungry eyes.

The Crystal Cellar is as bright and cold as the Red Room was warm and dark, its shining steel surfaces and dark oak barrels lit by seemingly dozens of Baccarat crystal fixtures. Visitors taste and feel how Raymond wines change when served from Baccarat crystal decanters. I signed books in the warm, woody, candlelit Barrel Room.

The craziest place in the winery is probably the Blending Room, where visitors don shiny silver lab coats and blend a personal cuvée with its own custom-designed label in an atmosphere that reminded me of a mad scientist laboratory. Like all the other elements of a visit to Raymond, the Blending Room is a bit over the top, pushing the limit of sensory overload. But it has a real educational purpose, too, and I'm sure that the visitors who take advantage of this opportunity share what they've learned with friends and family as they serve their personal blend of wine. The ultimate personal expression was not on the official tour—Jean-Charles Boisset's radical remodel of Roy Raymond's old pool house. We sampled some of Boisset's signature JCB Cremant de Bourgogne sparkling wine from Baccarat flutes as we surveyed a room filled with metal, glass, crystal, and leather. A huge flat screen blasted out a Lady Gaga music video (the only artist permitted on the pool house playlist, we were told, apart from Michael Jackson).

Jean-Charles Boisset seems driven to create a personal statement about wine, to give visitors an experience that threatens to overwhelm their senses. Raymond is a very popular stop for Napa Valley wine tourists, especially those who take the daily Napa Wine Train up from San Francisco. For about $150 each, wine train riders get a three-course lunch, an antique railroad experience rolling through the scenic vineyards, and a ninety-minute tour and tasting at Raymond (or Grgich Hills or ZD).[8]

IT'S ALL EXTREME

If a Raymond Vineyards visit seems a bit over the top to you, with its voodoo vineyard, doggy cellars, crystal chandeliers, and so on, well, I think you might be right. It is quite an experience. And that's what it is and is meant to be—an experience that perhaps intentionally overstimulates the senses in a world where our senses are constantly bombarded and leaves an impact for that reason. If it seems a bit gaudy, I would say that this is a question of taste. It is one expression of Jean-Charles Boisset's notion of a wine tourism experience, but not the only one.

If you head west from Raymond and take the Oakville Grade Road over the Mayacamas Mountains to the Sonoma Valley, then bear south on Highway 12, you'll come to another Boisset operation with a completely different wine experience. Founded in 1857, Buena Vista Winery was California's first fine winemaker, and its historic cellars defined California wine for many visitors, including Jean-Charles Boisset, who visited with his parents at age eleven. Its founder, Count Agoston Haraszthy, is credited with bringing the first *vitis vinifera* vines to California. Buena Vista could not be more different from Raymond in terms of atmosphere and environment, but the sensual impact is equally intense and profound.

The Buena Vista experience is all about the history of the place. The opportunity to walk in the footsteps of the California wine pioneers and especially to visit the famous old cellars, off-limits for decades because of structural concerns, is possible once more because of Boisset's ambitious restoration since he bought it in 2011. It is, along with Francis Ford Coppola's successful effort to reunite all the pieces of Napa Valley's Inglenook winery, quite the most extravagant tribute from one generation of winemakers to another. And it is quite a moving wine tourism experience.

What makes wine tourism so important is that it opens for the door for millions of people to find what they are looking for . . . in what? I was about to say "in wine," but as I hope I have convinced you, wine may be the reason that people travel to these beautiful or interesting places, but it may also be the excuse. Maybe we are all a bit like Miles and Jack, traveling down the wine tourist road but looking for destinations that aren't on any map. Looking for clues about who we are and what we think and believe. Talking about wine, as I noted earlier, as a way of talking about ourselves.

The fact that we seek very different things does not seem to matter. Different than we tell people, different than we tell ourselves. Wine simply opens the door. That's why wine tourism works in the vineyards or the aisles of Galleries Lafayette. That's why we go north to Canadian hilltops and south to

Argentinean deserts. You can jump off a bridge like George Taber, skid off the road with me, or follow in the footsteps of famous political thinkers. So long as we can justify it by the wine, we are free to do crazy things like Jean-Charles Boisset! I guess wine tourism brings out the wild Bacchus in all of us.

And for those of us for whom a deeper understanding of or appreciation for wine is the Bacchus we are seeking, wine tourism brings us together and gives us stories to share. The stories and memories, of the people, places, wines, foods, sights, sounds, aromas, and more—this is what wine tourism is all about.

Extreme wine tourism? Yes, of course—by definition. It's all extreme (or has that potential) once the door to your senses is opened wide.

11

Extreme Wine

The Next Generation

Extreme Wine is built on the idea that what's going on at the edge of the wine world can tell you a lot about what's happening all the way through to the center of the glass. I doubt that I'm the first person to think about extremes this way, although I believe that I'm the first person to write a book about how the concept applies to wine.

Jim O'Neill had a similar extreme idea back in 2001 when he was chief economist at Goldman Sachs. He wanted to understand globalization back then and to be able to advise Goldman's clients about how best to leverage global growth. The United States and the European Union were at the center of globalization, of course, since they were the biggest economic systems in the world. But were they really the key to the future? No, O'Neill concluded, the real action was out at the edge, in the "next-generation" nations of Brazil, Russia, India, and China. The BRICs, as he called them, were stirring the pot from the outside in, changing everything in the process. BRICs—that's where the action is, O'Neill said.[1]

Initially many people suspected that BRIC was just a gimmick—a way to package four very dissimilar countries into an appealing acronym that would draw investor interest. If it was a strategic maneuver, it was a brilliant one because of the way it captured the business world's imagination. "BRICs" is an attractive name for many reasons, perhaps especially because it sounds like "bricks"—solid building blocks—and because it looks like NICs—the newly industrialized countries of Hong Kong, Singapore, Taiwan, and South Korea that have been so successful in the global economy. There was some question initially about why these four particular countries were chosen and what, if anything, they had in common. Why Brazil and not Mexico? What about Turkey? Some Brazilians joked that they only made the list because O'Neill needed a "B" country and Bulgaria and Botswana really didn't work. But despite the controversy, the idea quickly caught on.

In this chapter I'm going to try to twist O'Neill's clever theory to serve my own purposes. The BRICs are certainly an unlikely group of countries to include in a book about wine . . . unless it's a book about *extreme* wine. Although none of these countries is included in the typical definition of Old World or New World winemakers, the idea that they are an active edge of the world of wine—part of the wine industry's "next generation"—is far from ridiculous. All four countries make wine and all four, because of their large populations and rapid growth, are seen as key potential wine markets. So, although this seems like an unlikely thing to do, humor me for a few pages while I try to deconstruct the future of wine BRIC by BRIC.

MISUNDERSTANDING BRAZILIAN WINE

Intuition isn't a very good guide to understanding the wine market in Brazil, so it is easy to misunderstand what's going on there. Nearly everything you might think you know about wine in Brazil is probably wrong. For example, a lot of people probably imagine that

- Brazil doesn't produce wine, or not much of it anyway. How could they? The country is covered with Amazonian rain forests (except for the beaches in Rio, of course).
- Brazil probably doesn't consume much wine, either. Everyone drinks those caipirinha things, don't they?
- If they do make wine, it is probably very bad. But I wouldn't know—I've never had any.

What's wrong with these statements? Where should I begin? Brazil produces a lot of wine—it is the fifth-largest Southern Hemisphere producer (after Argentina, Australia, Chile, and South Africa). Brazil's 340-million-liter production (2009) is more than half again as much as the corresponding figure for New World wine power New Zealand (204 megaliters).[2] While you might think of Brazil as a land of beaches and jungles, it is a very geographically diverse country with several major vineyard areas. The principal wine-growing region is the state of Rio Grande do Sul on the warm edge of the world wine-growing zone (roughly 30 to 50 degrees of latitude north and south). Serra Gaúcha has more than ninety thousand acres planted to vine. Wine is also grown in the São Francisco Valley, a hot desert area in the northeast just nine degrees south of the equator. Winegrowers there use plentiful irrigation and specialized viticultural techniques to more or less program grapevines to produce crops twice a year on a rolling schedule that keeps winery equipment in nearly constant use.

Wine in Brazil goes way back. Honest! The Portuguese planted grapes around São Paulo in 1532, and Jesuit priests established vineyards in Rio Grande do Sul in 1626. But it took a wave of immigrants from Italy in the late nineteenth century to firmly plant the vine in Brazil. The migrants came from Italy's northeast—Trentino and the Veneto—and were drawn to the climate and hilly terrain of the Rio Grande do Sul. They brought wine-growing knowledge and a taste for the wines of their homeland, especially sparkling wines (think Spumante and Prosecco). Their influence persists today. Although average wine consumption for Brazil is low—less than two liters per capita—Brazil's middle class is on the rise, and the wine market is growing beyond its traditional immigrant community base. Many people are betting on Brazil and hoping that it will become a more prominent player in the world of wine.

It is an old joke that "Brazil is the country of the future . . . and always will be." Champagne maker Möet & Chandon saw Brazil's potential, especially for sparklers, as far back as 1973, when it was making its big globalization push into the US, Australia, and Argentina. They invested in sparkling-wine production in Brazil, figuring that if anyone was going to sell domestic "Champagne" to fizz-happy Brazilians, it should be the Champenoise themselves. Möet & Chandon were soon joined by other wine/drinks multinationals, including Seagram, Bacardi, Heublein, Domecq, and Martini and Rossi, so the international presence in Brazil is quite strong.

Wine production one hundred years ago was focused on quantity instead of quality, as it was in most of the world, and that meant American hybrid grapes rather than European-style *vitis vinifera* varieties because of climate concerns. Economic problems led to the establishment of large cooperatives in the 1920s and 1930s as growers, many with tiny vineyards, struggled for market power. As in northern Italy, these cooperatives are still important today as the wine industry moves up the quality ladder. One of them grew so large that it became more or less the Riunite of Brazil. Cooperative Vinícola Aurora was receiving grapes from more than fifteen hundred family growers at its peak in the mid-1990s and producing (and exporting) very large quantities of wine. Even though you think you have never tasted a Brazilian wine, you may well have sampled the Aurora co-op's products. The name on the label wasn't Aurora—it was Marcus James!

Here in the US, Marcus James is now a multinational label in the Constellation Brands portfolio, but it began life in the 1980s as the Aurora co-op's brand. The very un-Brazilian name was derived from the first names of an Aurora executive and the son of his American business partner. The wines were simple and affordable (the Yellow Tail of their day?) and captured a substantial market. You probably tasted Marcus James if you were drinking wine in the 1990s, perhaps at a party or reception, even if you didn't actually buy any of it yourself. By 1996 Marcus James was selling more than half a million cases in the United States—more than the entire Argentinean wine sector at the time—and exporting to thirty other countries as well. The Aurora production facility was the largest winery in the Southern Hemisphere and one of the largest in the world. The brand was so successful that Constellation Brands apparently had concerns about the ability to meet growing demand, and when the contract came up in 1998 they switched wine sources to Argentina and eventually elsewhere, too. Marcus James continues to be a successful brand here in the US, selling Argentinean Riesling and Malbec as well as Merlot and Cabernet Sauvignon sourced from Spain and Chardonnay from southeastern Australia. I understand that Aurora still sells Brazilian-made Marcus James wine at home.

The Brazilian market is in transition today. *Vitis vinifera* grape varieties have replaced the hybrids in most places. As Brazil's wine market has opened up to imports, quality standards have risen, and although the bulk wine market is still large, the quality sector is expanding fast. In fact, Brazil is on every wine exporting country's short list of target markets as this is being written, due in part to the Brazilian economy's strong growth during the global economic crisis. Brazil's middle class is growing in size and perhaps also in its openness to wine and other upscale products. The fact that Brazil will host the soccer World Cup in 2014 and the Summer Olympic Games in 2016 adds to the growing optimism.

So the wine market is improving in Brazil and so are the Brazilian wines. Richard Hemming published reviews of Brazilian wines on the subscriber-only part of the Jancis Robinson website in 2009. He rated four Brazilian wines in the four-star seventeen-plus out of twenty category, with a 1998 Cave Geisse Brut sparkler topping the list. The tasting note for a Lidio Carraro Nebbiolo 2006 describes it as "Very pale and brick-hued. Cherry, tobacco, floral, violets. The tannin is high and proud, the fruit sophisticated and there is a perfume that persists across the whole palate." Sounds good enough to drink, doesn't it?

The Miolo Group of wineries is often mentioned as one of Brazil's quality producers, and two of their wines received strong reviews in Hemming's article. They are clearly ambitious, producing wines in many quality ranges, including a reportedly Parkeresque icon-level wine (unsurprising since Miolo is one of flying winemaker Michel Rolland's clients). World export markets are clearly in their plans. This is the next generation of Brazilian wine, but the Old World still lingers. I think this is a common characteristic of the BRICs today—one foot in the present, the other in the past, moving quickly toward the future.

RUSSIAN WINE: JUST SAY NYET!

The BRIC nations used to be characterized as "emerging" or "transition" economies, and in the case of Russian wine these terms still apply, but in a complicated way. Russia is an important wine country (the vineyards are down south, on the Black and Caspian Seas); it produced about 510 million liters of wine in 2009, which put it ahead of Greece and behind Portugal in the world wine league table. But the domestic industry today is just a shadow of what it was thirty years ago.

Mikhail Gorbachev's 1980s antialcohol campaign targeted wine along with spirits (but oddly not beer, which has only recently been considered an alcoholic beverage in Russia) and both production and consumption of wine declined dramatically. The *Global Wine Markets Statistical Compendium* indicates that per capita wine consumption in Russia more than doubled from 6.2 liters in the early 1960s to about 15 liters in 1970s (consumption of other forms of alcohol also rose—wine makes up less than 10 percent of Russia's total alcohol intake) then fell dramatically as Gorby's program gained traction. The Gorbachev crackdown and continuing antialcohol efforts pushed wine consumption down to just 3.7 liters per capita by the late 1990s. It has risen since then, up to about seven liters per capita today. Wine is only now reemerging and is still stained by its association with spirits and alcoholism.

I have not visited Russia nor sampled any of the wines on offer there, but the reports I've read make it sound like I am not missing too much. The good wines are certainly there. Jancis Robinson's tasting notes from her 2009 visit to Russia include some tempting wines. A Myskhako Organic Red Cabernet 2008 from Kuban, Russia's warmest wine-producing region, received sixteen-plus points out of twenty, with the descriptive note, "Sweet and very wild and direct. Different! Very lively. Really wild tasting. Explosive." Sounds like something I'd like to try. A Fanagoria Tsimlansky Black 2007 Kuban (sixteen points) is "Dusty, bone dry, rather interesting flavours with good round tannins and acidity and plenty of fruit weight on the palate. Very dry finish with good confidence." I'll have a glass of that, please!

Bad wines, and there are many of them, reflect Russia's sorry wine history. It seems like every country has experienced the stage where wines are simple, sweet alcohol. These bad wines still figure prominently in Russia. Wine for the masses sells for less than one dollar a liter in many cases, and it seems to be sourced in bulk from whoever in the world offers the least costly supply. Imported bulk wines from countries as varied as Spain, Ukraine, France, Argentina, Bulgaria, and Brazil are shipped to factories near Moscow and Saint Petersburg, where they are mixed with sugar (to appeal to local tastes) and water (to bring the alcohol level down to 10.5 percent), packaged, and sent to market.

Traditionally much of the wine came from Moldova and Georgia, but these countries were on the Russian government's political blacklist, and Moldovan wines were banned when this chapter was written, causing great hardship for a country that is very dependent upon wine for export earnings. Low quality is the official excuse—a Russian health official says of Moldovan wine "it should be used to paint fences"—but it is hard to see how Moldovan wines can be worse than the factory-made sugar-water wines I just described. I think it's politics.

There are also ugly wines—frauds—not even made from grapes in some cases. One report suggests that perhaps 30 percent of the bottled wine on offer in Russia is counterfeit. This is bad for consumers, of course, but particularly bad for legitimate producers, whose reputations suffer from unhappy experiences with fake wine.

Thinking of trying to sell your wines in Russia? Despite all that I've said, many people see great potential in the Russian market. Some are just interested in the "bad wine" bulk market, but others have grander plans. Russia is a BRIC, after all, one of the fastest-growing major economies in the world. Russia will host the 2014 Winter Olympics and the 2018 soccer World Cup; this international exposure may accelerate changing domestic tastes as many assume it will do in Brazil. Russia is already a major market for Champagne, with more than a million bottles purchased annually. As Russia's middle class expands, a larger market for quality wines can be expected to emerge. So it is not surprising that winemakers are testing the waters and negotiating joint ventures of various sorts.

There are reasons to be cautious, however. Alcoholism is still a major concern in Russia, and the expanding wine sector will have to swim against a prohibitionist tide. Tastes and social attitudes will change as better quality becomes available, but the transformation will not happen overnight. And then there's the "oil patch" problem. Petroleum is a major driver of the Russian economy, and this introduces an element of economic instability. Exporters will need to be able to ride out falling-oil-price effects in order to benefit from high-price periods. Finally, there is the Russian legal and administrative system, which makes it difficult to bring wines into the country and to ensure payment. The fact that some in the Russian government would prefer that the wines stay away—because of the alcoholism problem—probably contributes to this problem.

It is easy to be very pessimistic about wine in Russia given its current state and recent history, but I believe that cautious optimism is warranted for the long run. There are many cases of countries that have opened up their wine markets with positive results, and perhaps Russia will follow this path. In the meantime, it looks like a difficult project.

INDIA WINE: CAUGHT IN A CROSS FIRE

India's wine markets are full of surprises for anyone who hasn't been following them closely in recent years. Because most people don't associate wine with India, you might think that wine is quite new in India, but it is also very old. As in the other BRIC nations, wine in India is going through a dramatic transition today, but one that is quite distinct because of India's unique history, politics, and culture. Persian conquerors brought grapevines to India nearly twenty-five hundred years ago; wine consumption is first mentioned in a text on statecraft written about 300 BCE. Wine was a beverage for elites, not the masses (who apparently wanted stronger stuff), and lived a shadowy existence that continues today due to concerns about alcohol consumption. The influence of British colonizers contributed to the growth of Indian wine production in the nineteenth century, before the scourge of phylloxera hit India's vineyards in the 1890s with predictable results.

Table grapes are a major crop in India, and wine grapes are grown in several regions, generally at altitudes of two hundred meters to eight hundred meters, although vineyards at one thousand meters exist in Kashmir. Growing conditions are surprisingly good, using viticultural practices that take humidity and rainfall patterns into account (harvest must be complete before the monsoon). Two crops per year are common, as in Brazil. Indeed, India's vineyards are among the most productive in the world.

Since independence in 1947, wine has been caught in a cross fire in India. On one hand, it is a heavily controlled substance. Article 47 of the constitution makes it a function of the state to discourage alcohol consumption (Gandhi and some other early leaders were teetotalers), so wine imports have always been highly taxed, and advertising is forbidden. Individual state governments within India tax and regulate wine sales much as in the United States, creating a distributional crazy quilt. At the same time, however, some state governments promote viticulture and wine making as an economic development tool. It's a push-and-shove situation for wine.

The surprising state of wine in India today reflects this complicated condition. On one hand, wine is highly taxed, and the national market is fragmented by uncoordinated state-regulator regimes. At the same time, pro-development government policies seem to have led to an overexpansion of supply by encouraging new vineyard plantings. Wine consumption is growing rapidly as India's expanding middle class embraces the fruit of the vine, but for the moment at least there's a shakeout taking place among producers who find themselves out ahead of demand.

The Indian wine market has obvious potential that has attracted investors to the domestic industry and international firms seeking markets for their products. The US Wine Institute commissioned a 2008 study of the Indian wine industry,[3] which reports that only a very small percentage of India's total population has the right combination of religious views, legal age, location (in states where alcohol can legally be sold), disposable income, and exposure to wine to be considered potential customers. However this tiny percentage amounts to twenty-four million people, a considerable and growing potential market! "What is remarkable," wrote Jancis Robinson in a 2012 *Financial Times* column, "is the speed with which India has gone from a country where a tiny handful of the very rich drank nothing but the most famous names in wine to one in which thousands, and possibly tens of thousands, of young, well-travelled Indians are beginning to appreciate the nuances of a wide range of wines, both domestic and imported."[4] That's good news indeed, even if thousands or even tens of thousands is a very small number in the context of the vast Indian marketplace. Plenty of room to grow here.

It is pretty clear that good wine can be made in India and that a large and growing potential consumer market exists. A lot of work remains to realize India's potential. While there are many challenges to the development of the Indian wine industry, I suspect that the biggest obstacle will be reforming government policies that fragment the market and create counterproductive domestic incentives and barriers to foreign competition. After that, serious infrastructure limitations must still be addressed.

In the meantime, India rides the classic wine boom-bust cycle, which is modified and magnified by its own particular history and experience. The industry experienced a pronounced slump in the past few years after a period of very strong growth, and in 2012 one of the most important producers, Grover Vineyards, was forced to merge its operations with Vallée de Vin, which makes the Zampa wine brand. Grover Zampa is India's second-largest winery after the ambitious and innovative Sula Vineyards, which is a project of Stanford grad and Silicon Valley veteran Rajeev Samant that has been in production since 1997.[5]

THE CHINESE IDEA OF WINE

Many of my conversations with winemakers and wine sellers in recent years have looped back around to the question of China. China seems to be the Great Hope for people who see it as a vital future market and also a Great Mystery for those who haven't yet figured out how to uncork it. Uncertainty is the Grape Wall of China to those who wish to penetrate its market borders. The known knowns are few and the unknown unknowns many, or so I am told. Talk about asymmetric information inefficiencies! So everyone's interested in learning more about wine in China. Hence my interest in Li Zhengping's slender book *Chinese Wine*, part of Cambridge University Press's Introduction to Chinese Culture series.[6]

The term "wine" can easily be misunderstood in this context. Wine here in the US is grape wine for the most part, but wine in China is a much broader concept, including fermented fruits and grains. Grain wine, especially rice wine, is much more important than grape wine in this narrative. Why? The author explains that "Rice wine is easier to produce than grape wine. As grapes are seasonal and cannot retain their freshness for long compared to grain, grape wine-making technology was not adopted extensively in China." Whereas grape wine is made when the grapes are harvested, rice wine (like beer) can be made year-round from stored grain—a practical advantage. But grape wine was favored in times when it was necessary to conserve grain stocks.

The cultures and traditions associated with Chinese wine are superficially very different from ours. Wine is if anything much more important in China (if I have read this book correctly) than it is here, but the social rituals of wine drinking seem to be the point, not the beverage itself. Maybe this is not so different after all? *Chinese Wine* is making me reconsider what I thought I knew about grape wine's social function in the world of *vitis vinifera*.

Chinese Wine treats us to discussions of the origins of Chinese wine, the varieties of Chinese alcohol, rituals and traditions, legends (a very interesting group of tales), and finally, toward the end, a bit about imported wine and its growing popularity. Seriously, imported wine takes up just a couple of pages, if you don't count the photos, and the most important brand name mentioned is Gallo's Carlo Rossi red (which is credited with boldly entering the Chinese market in 1992).

Is that it? Is imported wine in China just an afterthought? No, although it is good to put things in perspective. It doesn't hurt to remember that wine exports to China do not enter a sort of market *tabula rasa*. Just because there are few European-style wine traditions in China doesn't mean there are no wine traditions at all. And the importance of grain wine should not be ignored.

THE JUDGMENT OF BEIJING

The conventional wisdom until very recently was that China was the wine market of the future for foreign wines (especially trophy wines from Bordeaux and Burgundy) but Chinese wines themselves were another matter. A combination of inexperienced and undiscriminating demand and inefficient supply was the problem, according to popular opinion, and the result was wines like one that I cited in *Wine Wars* for its pronounced aroma of ashtray, coffee grounds, and urinal crust. I blamed the tortured supply chain for many of the wines' faults. Wine grapes are typically grown by hundreds of small farmers, each of whom chooses what to plant, how to grow it, and when to harvest. Unsurprisingly, these family farms choose certainty over risk, so they grow for quantity more than quality and pick early rather than taking a chance that bad weather might ruin the crop while they wait for it to achieve perfect ripeness. The result is low-quality grapes that any winemaker would struggle to turn into high-quality wine. No wonder Chinese wines developed a dismal reputation.

So the results of the Decanter World Wine Awards of 2011 created quite a stir. A wine from Ningxia, a province in north-central China, earned one of the highest awards in the blind tasting competition. The Helan Qing Xue's Jia Bei Lan 2009 Cabernet blend won the international trophy for the best red Bordeaux varietal over ten British pounds—quite an honor! Much of the wine world greeted the news with a combination of shock and disbelief. Was the announcement a hoax? Was the wine itself real—or was it perhaps a completely unexpected fake (who would expect a Chinese faker to concoct a bogus Chinese wine when there's such good money in faking famous French labels)? But ten other Chinese wines also received awards, and the number of medals rose to eighteen in 2012. So maybe, just maybe, Chinese wine was changing.

This feeling was reinforced in December 2011 at an event that I call the Judgment of Beijing in honor of the 1976 "Judgment of Paris" that signaled California wine's emergence on the international scene (and that has spawned a number of similar events, including, in 2012, a "Judgment of Princeton" where wines from New Jersey reportedly bested both California and the French). The competition, judged by an equal number of Chinese and French experts, pitted five red wines from Ningxia against five Bordeaux reds selling for about the same price in China. Four Ningxia wines topped the table before the first Bordeaux appeared. Here are the top five wines:

1. Grace Vineyard Chairman's Reserve 2009
2. Silver Heights The Summit 2009
3. Helan Qing Xue Jia Bei Lan Cabernet Dry Red 2009
4. Grace Vineyard Deep Blue 2009
5. Barons de Rothschild Collection Saga Médoc 2009

The French judges ranked the Chairman's Reserve top while the Chinese judges favored The Summit, but both groups rated the Chinese wines from Ningxia over those from Bordeaux. Was the Judgment of Beijing a fair trial or was it a kangaroo court? Well, I agree with those who say that no tasting of this type can be conclusive, and the fact that the French wine prices reflected China's 48 percent import duty surely distorted the price-based comparison. But it seems to me that the fundamental point was clearly made. Chinese wines (or at least these wines from Ningxia) are no joke—they clearly can compete on the international stage.

THE CHINESE NAPA VALLEY?

So is Ningxia the new Napa Valley? No, my friends, I'm sure the status-conscious Chinese would rather call it in the new Bordeaux! But then it doesn't look much like either of these classic wine regions when you look at the satellite images on Google Maps. Ningxia is a mountainous region with narrow valleys where not much seems to thrive because of the harsh climate (even the hardy grapevines have to be buried in the fall and dug out each spring to keep them from freezing). It was perhaps the lack of better agricultural alternatives that prompted the Ningxia Agricultural Reclamation Management Bureau to experiment with grapevines in the late 1990s. Soon the one existing winery, Xi Xia King, was joined by several others, including projects involving French multinationals such as Möet & Chandon and Pernod Ricard.

What makes Ningxia so special? Well, we say that wine is grown in the vineyard, so certainly the local growing conditions are important. But an accommodating government is also a key factor. Wineries are able to negotiate leases for large vineyard areas that they can plant and harvest to their own specifications, an important solution to the small-farmer quality problem mentioned earlier. Labor is cheap (for now) and plentiful, too, because although Ningxia is remote, this is still China, and though the capital city of Yinchuan may be small by Chinese standards, it still boasts two million inhabitants. LVMH is building a 5,500-square-meter winery for its Chandon sparkling wines.

Chinese wine is wine, so there's a lot that can go wrong, but it seems as though many of problems that have plagued Chinese wine in the past are absent in Ningxia; perhaps this is the future of wine in China. China was last in O'Neill's BRIC "next-generation" acronym, but it has always been first on everyone's business hit list. Maybe Ningxia is the wine world's next generation as well. We'll know for sure if Yao Ming sets up a winery there!

THE NEW BRICS

The idea of the BRICs celebrated its tenth anniversary in 2011. I've spent the last few pages examining wine in each of these important markets and so, with China just finished, it seems like it is time to sum up. But just when I thought I was done with the BRICs, it turns out that there are more of them! According to the *Financial Times*, O'Neill has decided to expand the list to include Mexico, South Korea, Indonesia, and Turkey.[7] I think for now people are calling them "the New BRICs" since MSKIT, MITSK, SKIMT, or even TIMSK lacks the cool simplicity of BRIC. Maybe they should call them the Lego countries—they come in lots of styles and colors and you can put them together pretty much any way you like. You see, the New BRICs are a not a very coherent concept. They feel sort of cobbled together—like a kid's Lego project.

O'Neill's New BRICs are strange bedfellows, but that is not the end of the story. The original BRIC nations have decided that they are more than a figment of an investment banker's imagination; they actually work together on various global issues. And they recently decided to expand their membership. Apparently they didn't consult O'Neill, because their invitation list didn't include any of the MSKIT countries. The BRICs have invited South Africa to join their club.

NOT YOUR FATHER'S BALI HA'I

Indonesia, the world's most populous Muslim country, is an unlikely wine producer. And indeed, production is limited to relatively small amounts on the island of Bali, according to *The Oxford Companion to Wine*, which reported three wineries as of 2005. Hatten Wines (founded in 1994) was the largest and is a pretty ambitious project according to its website, with more than forty employees at the winery, distribution center, and 14.5-hectare vineyard.

Some of Bali's wine is produced from imported grape juice (the home winemaker's practice of making wine from rehydrated grape juice concentrate is surprisingly common in really extreme wine country), but several producers are going to the extreme of growing their own grapes and trying to build a wine tourism industry. Since Bali is so close to the equator, tropical viticultural practices apply—pergola-trained vines to cope with humidity, *vinifera* and hybrid grape varieties, and three crops a year (harvested every 120 days, according to Hatten's website). A recently released Shiraz breaks new ground for tropical wine making.

I found one tasting note on CellarTracker—written by a tourist happy to find a local alternative to expensive imported wines. He scored the Hatten AGA White eighty-six points. "The wine was very aromatic, with banana, honey, lemon, pineapple, and hints of peach and grass on the nose. On the palate, the wine showed banana, honey, lemon, kiwi and citrus. It was slightly off-dry, with medium-level acidity. The wine was much better than we expected. It lacked the structure to earn high-end scores, but it was extremely delicious and drank very well in the tropical climate. In addition, it paired extremely well with Indonesian cuisine."

There are obviously all sorts of challenges facing Bali's wine industry, so I was particularly pleased to hear that the large modern Sababay Winery opened its doors (overlooking Saba Bay) in 2012, its website going live at 7 a.m. on July 7 of that year (just for good luck). Sababay's owners hope to open a new chapter in the history of Bali wine, with wine made from locally grown grapes but to an international standard using sustainable practices. "A passionate taste from a new latitude" is their motto, and I wish them good luck with their "next-generation" venture. Bali wine today has little in common with the Bali Ha'i brand of tropical fruit-flavored California wine that Italian Swiss Colony introduced to the US market back in the 1960s!

South Korea is better known for producing table grapes than wine grapes. There is a tradition of fruit wines, including the blackberry wine that was featured in the television soap opera *Terroir* discussed earlier. It is strong (15 to 19 percent alcohol by volume) and good, I've read, for both your health in general and your sexual stamina in particular.[8]

The first grape wines were made in 1901 by missionary Father Antonio Combert for the members of his Korean Catholic church. Contemporary production dates to 1977, when the drinks company Doosan Baek Wha began production of Majuang wines, which dominate the domestic wine market. As in China, Korean wine is often a mix of domestic and imported products. None of the tasting notes I found on the Internet were very detailed. Doosan had 140 hectares of vineyards in 2005 and, while my research turned up substantial vine acreage beyond this, most of the fruit goes to the fresh grape market. Wine-grape production is also limited by climate concerns— although Korea is at about the same latitude as Napa Valley, its winters can be brutally harsh.

My guess is that Korea will be more important as a consumer of wine than as a producer. Perhaps Korean-born Jeannie Cho Lee, the first Asian master of wine, will lead the way. Indications are that wine sales have increased rapidly in recent years, so things are looking up. The US–Korea Free Trade Agreement that went into effect in March 2012 was not uncontroversial in either Korea or the United States, but its cause was surely helped by elimination of a 15 percent tariff on US wine.

TWO TAKES ON "OLDEST WINE"

What in the world do Turkey and Mexico have in common? It is easy to generate a list of differences, ranging from geography to history, language, and religion. Jim O'Neill probably included them on his list of the New BRICs because they both have relatively large populations (107 million in Mexico, 75 million in Turkey) and so substantial market potential as their middle classes expand. From a wine standpoint, Mexico and Turkey are linked by the term "oldest." Turkey may be the oldest Old World wine producer, with evidence of wine production going back more than six thousand years. You cannot get much more "Old World" in wine than Turkey, even if most people in the Old World never give Turkish wine a second thought.

Mexico is the oldest wine producer in the New World. Spanish soldiers and priests brought wine grapes with them. The first evidence of wine production dates from 1521 (I see a five-hundred-year anniversary celebration on the horizon). Conquistador Cortés ordered that new settlers plant grapevines (one thousand vines for every one hundred persons, according to *The Oxford Companion to Wine*), thus spreading Spain's wine culture throughout the New World empire. Wine production in Mexico grew so successful that King Felipe II of Spain ordered a stop to new production in 1699 in an effort to protect Spain's domestic wine industry.

It is ironic that we don't associate wine production with these two countries today, given their deep historical roots. Turkey? It's a Muslim country, of course, so we don't think of alcohol or, if we do, it is raki, the fiery anise-flavored drink. Mexico brings images of tequila (and wasting away in Margaritaville), beer, and perhaps Mexican brandy, the national liquor. Casa Pedro Domecq's Presidente brand is said to be the best-selling brandy in the world. Domecq is now part of the French drinks group Pernod Ricard.

Both Mexico and Turkey are important grape- and wine-producing nations today. Mexico produced a little over 44 million liters of wine in 2009. Turkey is the world's sixth-largest table-grape producer, surpassing Italy in this area, but only a small fraction of its grape output is made into wine. Turkey makes roughly the same amount of wine (23 million liters in 2009) as Israel. Wine production in Mexico has fallen by almost 50 percent since the 1980s, while Turkey's production levels have been more stable. Both Turkey and Mexico have the potential to rise up in the world wine rankings, but they each face particular challenges.

Turkish wines can be stunningly good. Jancis Robinson's tasting notes (from a 2009 research trip) find many peaks among wines made from international grape varieties. A Corvus Corpus 2004 received a rating of seventeen out of twenty, for example. "This right bank style wine is really quite rich and full, verging on overripe. Extremely opulent and velvety." A Robert Parker kinda wine, she said. Ron and Mary Thomas, my senior Turkish-wine correspondents, reported similar success on their 2010 tasting trip. "We found the wines of Turkey to be ubiquitous, great values, and extremely enjoyable," they wrote. Among the reds, they found the Syrah wines hard to beat: some of the best Syrahs they have tasted anywhere—high praise. But the highest peak came from an unexpected source, a white wine called Emir. "It had a light golden color and a very crisp finish," according the Thomases. "This was a favorite wine we would drink anytime. . . . Emir is king."

As one of the oldest of the Old World countries, Turkey has (along with Georgia) a rich treasury of native grape varieties. But who has heard of them, of King Emir and his court? Very few, I think, and this is problematic in a world where so many consumers are already confused by wine and have trouble mastering the basics. The domestic market for wine in Turkey is relatively small, and its international exports are limited. Belgium is its largest international customer, according to a government report (Belgium?) followed by Northern Cyprus, Germany, Britain, the United States, and Japan. A local search for Turkish wine uncovered a few bottles at a Mediterranean restaurant and a single bottle of minerally delicious King Emir at a local shop. As the report says, there is much work to do for Turkey to realize its great wine potential.

"Baja—the New California?" was the title of Jancis Robinson's review of Mexican wine after her visit to Baja California in 2010. "I am excited about the potential for wine in Mexico," she said. And indeed some of her tasting notes are enough to make anyone excited. Here's what she had to say about Union de Productores Textura 1 2007 (a blend of Tempranillo, Zinfandel, and Grenache): "Deep crimson. Very sweet and dusty and ripe berried. Very Mexican. Very rich. Sweet spicy then nice dry finish. There's a real beginning, middle and end to this wine. Good refreshing stuff on the finish." Very Mexican! I like that. Not a me-too wine. Not all the wines are big or sweet, of course, which is just as well. Lots of variety. Lots to look for and to like.

The biggest challenge? Climate, according to Jancis Robinson. Not enough rain. And, while I'm sure she is right in the long run, I think that infrastructure is probably an even bigger short-term problem. People who taste the wines of Mexico at wineries rave about their quality. But then when they order them in restaurants in the cities, they are sometimes puzzled. Is *this* the wine I liked so well? I wonder what's happened to it? they ask. The answer, in many cases, is that Mexico's system of poor roads and long rides in hot trucks has baked the freshness out of the wine and left just a hollow shell behind. Mexico can produce excellent wines, but it must also find ways to get them to market in good condition.

THE UNDISCOVERED BRIC

So now I turn at last to the overlooked BRIC: South Africa. With a relatively modest population (less than 50 million), it was probably too small to qualify for O'Neill's signature group in terms of market size. But South Africa punches above its weight in many fields and has great symbolic importance, too, which is one reason it was chosen to host the 2010 soccer World Cup.

If South Africa is too small to be a BRIC in gross domestic product terms, it towers over many of the other countries with respect to wine. South Africa was listed at number seven on the world wine league table for 2009 with total production of over 1,050 million liters, just ahead of Germany (950 million liters) and behind Australia (1,179 million liters). Among the BRICs, only China is in the same ballpark (964 million liters and growing rapidly), although it isn't clear that all Chinese wine is actually wine (the fraud problem) or really made in China (bulk wine imports are a common additive to inexpensive Chinese wine).

South Africa has a deep wine history. Cape Town was an important reprovisioning stop for the sea trade between Europe and the East Indies. Someone noticed that wine-drinking crews were not so plagued by scurvy, so vineyards were planted, and the first wine was pressed on April 6, 1652. The famous Groot Constantia wine estate was established overlooking False Bay just outside Cape Town in 1682. By the eighteenth century, its eponymous Muscat-based sticky wine was one of the three most-sought-after wines in the world.

South Africa's wine history has been filled with peaks and valleys, both the usual ones, such as phylloxera, and some that were more country-specific. Persistent surpluses early in the twentieth century led to the creation of cooperatives in South Africa, just as they did in most other parts of the wine world. But South Africa's solution was extreme. KWV—Kooperatieve Wijnbouwers Vereniging—essentially monopolized the wine industry, setting grape prices, allocating production quotas, and so forth. It may have succeeded in stabilizing the industry and grower incomes, but at the cost of suppressing the potential quality and distinctiveness of the wines. Apartheid further damaged the industry by effectively shutting off export markets and distorting domestic demand during the long period of isolation. The end of apartheid opened up the markets, creating an export boom. Surplus turned to a shortage that was met by importing grape-juice concentrate to supplement local grape supplies and the blending of cheap bulk wine imports with local production. The eventual stabilization of the industry was encouraged by the restructuring of KWV.

With the overwhelming shadow of the vast cooperative vat removed, South African winemakers have seemingly rediscovered a complex terroir mosaic that promises a rich wine future. In terms of simple geography, South

Africa is really a bit too close to the equator for quality wine production—it depends upon winds blowing inland off cold ocean currents to moderate temperatures. The necessarily uneven penetration of these cool blasts and the complex geology and geography of the region create a terroirist's playground that is only beginning to be fully appreciated. The Wine of Origin appellation system has been established to better identify the microterroir and promote the resulting wines.

What is South Africa's future? Like the rest of the wine world, South Africa has a history of boom and bust, and there is little chance that instability will ever completely disappear. But it does seem like the country is poised for growth. South Africa's beer industry has become a world-beater. The SAB in SABMiller plc—maker of eighty beer brands, including Miller Lite, Foster's, Peroni, Lion Lager, Castle Lager, and Pilsner Urquell—originally stood for South African Breweries. Why shouldn't South African wine also rise and regain in some measure the fame it had two hundred years ago?

LONG SHADOWS

Thanks for staying with me through this tour of wine in the "next-generation" BRICs and New BRICs. The journey has taken us to several extremes of geography and climate as well as politics, economics, and religion. I let Jim O'Neill do the driving and, although he wasn't looking for wine when he made up his lists, we managed to find it everywhere. What did we learn along the way?

For me, it's all about history and the long shadows cast by the past that shape or condition the world of wine today. And it's about the ingenuity of today's winemakers and the way they struggle to overcome obstacles to create the wine they love. You can see history and human persistence everywhere in the world of wine, I suppose, but they jump from the glass when you stare down at the rim. Especially when the wine you are drinking comes from a BRIC.

I think this tour has affirmed my belief in the extreme wine idea. Oh, it's true that the BRICs, new BRICs, and newest BRIC aren't all on the cutting edge of wine, but they are all changing, adapting, and transforming themselves. They are not the future of wine, because there is no single future that wine is heading toward. Rather they are some of the many futures of wine, and won't it be exciting to see how it, they, and we turn out as the future unfolds?

12

Extreme Wine Adventure

Cape Town, South Africa, isn't really at the opposite end of the earth from my home near Seattle. The antipode of Seattle or Tacoma is hundreds of miles to the southeast of Cape Town, far out in the ocean. Cape Town isn't the furthest extreme I could travel to, but it's pretty close—more than ten thousand miles away as the crow flies.[1]

I always planned to write about South Africa in *Extreme Wine*—it seemed like a perfect fit for the wine tourism chapter, since the Cape Winelands are so spectacularly beautiful and the wine tourist industry so varied, but I didn't think I'd be able to go in person—too far away, too extreme. But then a pair of invitations came to visit South Africa, and suddenly I found myself aboard a KLM flight headed to Amsterdam and then on to Cape Town. My mission was to attend Cape Wine 2012—South Africa's big biannual wine show— and give the keynote address at the Nederburg Wine Auction. Talking with winemakers and speaking about wine comes naturally to me by now, so I was looking forward to an interesting trip.

I wasn't disappointed. In fact, it was pretty extreme. So extreme (or encompassing so many extremes) that I thought I would tell you about it as a way of bringing *Extreme Wine* to a close. I invite you to come with me to Cape Town and see what I discovered there.

SOUTH AFRICA: OLD OR NEW?

The conventional wisdom classifies South Africa as part of the New World of wine, based mainly on geography. Europe is the Old World. Everything else is New. QED. Fine, if that's how you want to have it, but wine has been made in South Africa for more than 350 years and some of the vineyard estates (sensibly called "wine farms") have been in family hands for six or seven generations—longer than most Old World vineyards and far longer than anything you might find in California. So it's not entirely New, even if isn't officially Old.

The stronger case for the New World classification is that South Africa's modern wine history is less than twenty years old. When the period of isolation ended and the postapartheid era began, the South African wine industry was suddenly reconnected with a rapidly changing global wine market. Significantly, Chile, Argentina, Australia, and New Zealand all also reemerged on the international scene in the decade bracketing South Africa's opening, changing the face of global wine. It didn't all happen at the same time and certainly not for the same reasons, but looking back you can see that the seeds of today's New World of wine were being sown.

Each of the countries I've just mentioned has navigated the new ocean in a different way, finding markets, raising quality benchmarks, avoiding crisis (or not avoiding it), and trying to steer a clear course through uncharted seas. South Africa is New World wine in the sense that it has embarked on this voyage and is constantly changing, adjusting, and learning as the trip progresses. There's something new around every corner and inside every bottle. Visiting Cape Town and tasting the Cape wines was certainly an eye-opening experience for me.

But then there's the Old World angle. The New did not suddenly or magically appear, it grew or evolved out of the older wine industry—and this complicates things in South Africa, as elsewhere. Adjusting to the new external environment obviously also required considerable internal renegotiation, and it is understandable that this came as a shock.

What were those pre–global era (the "old" South Africa) wines like? Many of them were below the current international standard of course (as was true in the other New World countries and the Old World ones, too). But some of the wines were apparently spectacularly good, as a pair of older-wine seminars I attended at Cape Wine 2012 made clear. The first, organized by Michael Fridjhon and Simon Back, surveyed white wines from the early years of the new era and red wines from the sixties, seventies, and eighties. I am not an expert taster, but even I could appreciate the quality of these wines and, especially in the case of the reds, how time had transformed them into something very different and special. My spirits were lifted by this tasting. If the new South Africa is built upon a foundation that includes wine like this, I thought, it is in very good shape indeed.

The second seminar afforded a rare opportunity to taste older Pinotage, including a 1964 Lanzerac. Are you familiar with Pinotage? Everything about Pinotage is contested, I believe, and everyone seems to have an opinion. Pinotage is South Africa's distinctive red-grape variety. It was created in 1925 when University of Stellenbosch viticulturalist A. I. Perold crossed Pinot Noir with Cinsault. Most people called it Hermitage in the early days, but then the French got picky about the name (Hermitage is perhaps the most famous area in the North Rhône) and so a Pinotage compromise was revealed. It is the most-planted red-grape variety in South Africa (Chenin Blanc, known hereabouts as Steen, leads the white-grape ranks) and a source of almost patriotic pride in the local wine community.

But its reputation abroad and perhaps especially in the United States is quite different. I'm not sure what is to blame—poor wine making in the early days, poor viticulture that yielded unripe grapes, or maybe damage due to excessive heat during shipping—but a lot of faulty Pinotage reached American shores when South Africa reentered the international market, with the result that the first (and last!) taste of South African wine for many American drinkers was "peculiar Pinotage." How peculiar? I asked a friend—Daniel McKeown, a seasoned wine professional—about his experience with Pinotage, and he told me that "I once had a Pinotage that tasted like someone had soaked smoked meat in a barrel of wine. It was not pleasant. Honestly the worst wine I've ever tasted, unless you count that bottle of white that was a gift to everyone attending a wedding in Michigan. A non-vinifera white wine from Michigan . . . need I say more?" I can relate. I was at an "unusual varietal" blind tasting of world wines organized for wine bloggers. South African wines were not even on the agenda, but as the blind tasting progressed every unfamiliar or unpleasantly peculiar red wine was jokingly identified by someone in the crowd as Pinotage based on the poor reputation of that wine (formed years ago, I'll bet). Oh no, another Pinotage! And everyone would laugh. Really, it was as bad as that. Need I say more?

Pinotage today is a different animal, or at least the wines that I was served, made from the low-yield older bush vines, were excellent. If the question is whether Pinotage can age (as Old World wines are supposed to do), the answer, based on the seminar I attended, is very clearly yes, it can. These particular older vintages evolved into quite fascinating creatures—interesting enough to make a fan of old Burgundies stop and think. Another eye-opening experience. We were fortunate to have some of the old-timers in the room— the people who made these wines or were involved in significant ways in the process. As they talked about how the wines were made back in the day, I got the impression that the session was meant to be much more than nostalgic. I think there was a concern that today's wines might not age as well—that the adjustments necessary to compete in international markets came at a cost, and that cost was that these wonderful old wines were becoming (figuratively as well as literally) things of the past.

EXTREMELY NEW AND OLD AT THE SAME TIME

My interest in seeing what's new in South African wine provoked me to call on a number of wineries in the Cape Wine 2012 exhibition hall. One of them was De Toren Private Wine Cellar, a boutique winery started by Emil and Sonette Den Dulk in 1994 to make Bordeaux-style wines that showcase Cape wine terroir. Their very first wine, a 1999 vintage, was Fusion V, a Left Bank (Cab-centered) Bordeaux blend using all five (or V, if you will) traditional grape varieties. I tasted the current release of De Toren Fusion V as well as a Right Bank (Merlot-centered) blend called De Toren Z. Both were classic representations, noteworthy for their fine tannins and delicate balance. This part of the new South Africa is doing very well, I thought. And then things started to get extreme.

Emil reached behind the counter and pulled out a bottle labeled Book 17 XVII, the most extreme wine in the De Toren collection. It's extreme in several ways at once. First, its inspiration is pretty extreme. Pliny the Elder wrote about wine and viticulture in book 17 of his treatise on natural history, and De Toren sought to apply Pliny's farming principles to making a modern wine (Emil showed me the relevant passages from Pliny's text). Pliny's favorite wines were quite sturdy, potent, and age-worthy, but elegant, too, and that's what this project aimed to achieve.

Having started with an extremely old way of growing grapes, De Toren's winemaker Albie Koch then studied the most extreme contemporary wine-making techniques, focusing on American cult wines such as Screaming Eagle and Harlan Estate. Extremely low yields in the vineyard (just three hundred grams of grapes per vine). Hand destemming, foot stomping, hand punch-down, and 200 percent (not a misprint) French oak. I tasted from one of the extremely scarce 650 bottles that resulted. I don't have much experience tasting cult wines, and I admit to being a little frightened as I stared into the black hole at the bottom of the glass. Book 17 XVII was notably darker and more extracted than the other wines I had tasted. But in fact the wine was balanced and elegant, and while all the oak showed in the glass, it didn't knock me down with a two-by-four as might happen if it were made by less skilled hands.

Going to extremes without going over the edge is a tricky business, and you can see it in Neil Martin's *Wine Advocate* review of the wine (I think he was tasting from the barrel). On one hand, "It has a super-ripe crème de cassis, fruitcake and fig scented bouquet with a palate that is ostentatious to the point of vulgarity," which sounds like it's over-the-top. "However, this full-bodied turbo-charged wine is so damn silky smooth and seductive in a super-Tuscan kind of way, that its charms will be nigh impossible to resist."[2] Hmmm. Sounds a little like Lady Gaga.

Making cult wines must be a bit like the "chicken" game in *Rebel Without a Cause.* I think De Toren Book 17 XVII succeeds in mixing ancient inspirations with extreme techniques to make a very interesting wine. Martin was obviously seduced by the wine's elegance in the end (as was I), which pulled it back from the cliff edge at the last minute. Unlike the Z and Fusion V wines, I wouldn't want to drink XVII every day (which would be impossible in any case given cost and limited production). But I appreciate its potential to make wine enthusiasts reconsider the potential of South African wine.

WORLD'S OLDEST LIVING WINE?

I received many invitations to sniff, swirl, and chat while I was in South Africa, and I had to decline most of them because of my tight schedule. But I'm glad I made time for lunch with Cobus Joubert of Maison Joubert and his wine-making brothers. It was a most memorable extreme wine experience.

The agenda for the tapas lunch was mainly to talk about wine and South Africa (and for me to autograph a copy of *Wine Wars* that Cobus brought along for that purpose). Cobus and his winemaker brother Meyer opened several bottles of wine from the family wine farm, Joubert-Tradauw, which were excellent and paired well with the tasty food. But the simple tasting turned a bit competitive when brother Schalk-Willem Joubert, cellar master at Rupert and Rothschild Vignerons, pulled out some of *his* wines for comparison. Joubert-Tradauw and Rupert and Rothschild represent two faces of South African wine that, like the brothers, compete in a friendly way. The Joubert family history in South Africa goes back ten generations to 1688, when French Huguenot Pierre Joubert arrived in Cape Town. The current wines date from 1982, when vines were planted in Klein Karoo, and 1997, when the cellar was established.

Rupert and Rothschild, on the other hand, is a partnership between the Rupert family of South Africa and the late Baron Edmond de Rothschild. The Rupert family, whose wealth is measured in the billions, controls the Swiss luxury-goods multinational Richemont (brands include Cartier, Alfred Dunhill, Van Cleef & Arpels, Piaget, Sulka, Montblanc, and Baume and Mercier), as well as South African wine and spirits producers such as La Motte Wine Estates. Baron Benjamin de Rothschild, who continues his father's work in this project, is descended from the non–wine-making branch of the Rothschild family tree, but certainly the Rothschild name unlocks doors, in wine as in other things, especially in the growing China market. The R&R wines have South African roots to be sure, but global aspirations.

It was interesting to taste the brothers' wines at lunch. Sometimes Meyer's wine would shine a bit brighter, other times it was Schalk-Willem's wine that stood out. The wines were deliciously different, but not without a certain family resemblance, just like the brothers themselves. The brightest star of all came at the end of the meal, when Cobus brought out a small bottle of Jaubert Muscat d'Alexandrie—*vintage 1800!* Wow, what an experience it was to taste this wine. Here is Neal Martin's *Wine Advocate* tasting note:

> Just twelve 250-millilitre bottles of this incredibly rare and ancient Muscat d'Alexandrie are released from a 100-litre French oak barrel in Klein Karoo that is topped up each year. It has an iridescent clear amber hue with green tints on the rim. The nose is simply stellar: candied orange peel, toffee, apricot and almond

soar from the glass and fix you to the spot. The palate is perfectly balanced and fresher than some South African wines two centuries younger! . . . Very long and intense and yet somehow refined and elegant, this is an ethereal experience. Drink now—2100+.[3]

The brothers date the wine in their barrel to 1800 because that is the date that is given for the few similar lots of wine that are still around, but they think it could be older. The barrel has been in the family for many years, and in fact the house they grew up in was built around the barrel, so there is no way to get it out. They worried a bit (as brothers would about an aging uncle) that the oak barrel was getting old and might someday simply collapse. But they had no plans to try to fix it up—too risky. They maintain the wine—and share it!—through a sort of solera practice where, as the tasting note above explains, three liters of the wine are drawn off each year, replaced with new wine and a little bit of spirits. Is it the oldest living wine in the world, as some have said? That probably depends upon your point of view, but it is certainly the oldest wine that I have ever sampled. And one of the youngest and freshest, too.

One of my goals in visiting South Africa was to taste a wine as close as possible to the Vin de Constance that Napoleon famously requested on his deathbed. I did in fact get to taste a 2007 Klein Constantia Vin de Constance (made by Adam Mason, who was at the Joubert lunch) at a dinner party hosted by Mike Ratcliffe and it was great—hats off to Napoleon and special thanks to Mike and Adam. But the glass that Cobus put in my hand brought me as close as any human being can come to that two-hundred-year-old taste experience.

EXTREME WINE IN THREE ACTS

Since I'm writing about South Africa's extreme wines, I cannot neglect a wine so extreme that it took an act of congress (figuratively) to get it produced, and an act of will (literally) to initiate the tradition that can only be sustained when acts of nature permit. The wine also provoked the creation of a very special stage for extreme acts and actors. I'm talking Nederburg Edelkeur, one of South Africa's (and the world's) treasured extreme wines.

This is a personal story for me because my small cellar now contains two half bottles of Edelkeur from the 1977 and 1979 vintages. They were given to me by Carina Gous, Distell business director of wines, as a token of thanks for giving the 2012 keynote address at the Nederburg Auction. I'm looking forward to sharing these wines with Sue (and perhaps one or two special friends) on an appropriately special occasion. Edelkeur was the personal vision of an extreme wine person, Günter Brözel, one of South Africa's most honored winemakers, who was Nederburg's cellar master for thirty-three years until his retirement in 1989. Brözel's extreme idea was to create a Noble (made with botrytis-infected "noble rot" grapes) Late Harvest wine that would express the elegance and power of South African terroir in much the way that German Trockenbeer-enauslese, French Sauternes, and Hungarian Tokaji represent their respective wine-producing regions. The only things that stood in his way were mother nature and the South African wine law.

Mother nature is easy enough to understand. Late-harvest wines are tricky to produce because the grapes need to stay on the vines long after the usual harvest. They are at risk for damage from birds, mold, and disease. Making a Noble wine is even harder and requires both luck (in the vineyard) and lots of harvest labor. You can't count on making a Noble late-harvest wine every year, and indeed the first Edelkeur vintage, in 1969, was not followed by a second until 1972. So Edelkeur required an act of nature to make, but an act of congress? Well, not literally congress, but it's a fact that South African wine laws prior to the 1969 vintage did specifically forbid this kind of wine. The rules permitted (and protected) sweet fortified wines but outlawed the production of natural (unfortified) wines with more than 30 percent residual sugar. Tokaji Eszencia often has as much as 50 percent to 70 percent residual sugar (90 percent in the 2000 vintage!). Brözel was going for an extreme, and the law got in his way, so the law had to be changed. And it was. But not all the laws yielded to Nederburg's cellar master. The most reliable way to get late-harvest grapes (because mother nature's part is reduced) is to harvest them earlier and dry them on racks, concentrating the flavor. (Just as the most reliable way to make icewine is to pick unfrozen grapes and then . . . freeze them!) But nature's law prevailed here and so the grapes for Edelkeur are left to hang, exposed to and expressing wild nature before being finally picked and vinified.

Finally Brözel was able to make Nederburg Edelkeur, but that created another problem: how to distribute the tiny amount of this precious wine that law and nature permit. After some early trial and error, it was decided that a special stage was needed, and this became the now famous Nederburg Auction, where a juried selection of rare South African wines are offered up once a year to the international wine trade. Some of the 1972 vintage was sold at the first Nederburg Auction in 1975, and the link between the auction, Edelkeur, and the best of South African wine has been going ever since. The "first five" founding wineries—Nederburg, Delheim, Groot Constantia, Overgaauw, and Simonsig—are now joined by many others, the Auction Selection wines determined through rigorous blind-tasting panels. It's an honor just to be selected for the auction and to have your bottles wear the Nederburg Auction Selection ribbon. The auction today does much more than just allocate one extreme wine. It honors an extreme wine person's vision and draws international attention to South Africa's best wines.

So what does the wine taste like? Well, I'm not going to open my bottles for several years, but I was able to taste through several vintages of Edelkeur on the first day of the auction, and they were memorable and gave a hint of how this wine can develop over the years. I don't rate wines or write reviews, but I found this CellarTracker tasting note for the 1976 Edelkeur vintage that sums up my experience. "Brown with a bright yellow rim. Fabulous nose—intense citrus, caramel and leather with a very slight flor touch. Amazing attack. Citrussy sweetness. Amazing life. Huge depths of flavour. Great length. Excellent."[4]

One of the people I tasted with that day had this reaction: "They shouldn't sell these wines; they should hold them back." She didn't care about the money, she just knew that the wines would get better and better and that it was a sin to drink wines like the 1979 and the 1977 so young. She's right, I suppose, because certainly the wines will continue to develop for many years, but I think she's wrong, too. Yes, the wines will get better with age, which is why I'm not rushing to pull these corks, but putting some of them up for auction isn't really about the money or maybe even (just) about the wines themselves. There's something bigger going on here—defining the identity of South Africa and its wine and honoring the passion of the winemakers—and that's what makes it really extreme.

THE NEDERBURG AUCTION

This brings me to the Nederburg Auction, which was invented for the extreme purpose of releasing this precious wine to the world. I was invited to give the keynote address (which was in fact the only speech at the event) because of South Africa's difficulties in the US wine market. Europe and the UK are important export markets for Cape wine, but the continuing economic crisis made them a difficult market in 2012, a fact reflected in the auction hall, where European buyers were notably absent. So South Africans were turning their attention to other likely markets, including China (of course), India (naturally), and other African countries (like Nigeria, for example, where the growing middle class promises strong wine-market growth). And the United States, which is where I come into the picture. With the American wine market emerging from the recession at the moment that Europe was slipping back in, the US was on everyone's wine export radar.

My job was to talk about the challenges and opportunities that South Africa faced in America, and I wanted to put a positive spin on my remarks both because optimism is always appreciated (fewer pitchfork-wielding mobs that way) and also because I spoke just before the charity part of the auction, and no one wanted me to depress the bidders and hurt fund-raising for the children's charities. So naturally I started with a joke. I'm an economist, I told the packed hall, and economists always make predictions. So I logged onto the top-secret economist predictions website this morning and searched for a South African event to predict for today. I only found one, and here it is: Australia eighteen, South Africa twenty-one.

Eighteen to twenty-one. Do you know what it means, I asked? Everyone in the room knew *exactly* what it meant, because South Africa's national rugby team the Springboks were scheduled to play rival Australia in Pretoria later in the day. A victory prediction was exactly what they wanted to hear, even if it came from an unlikely source—an American wine economist! (No one complained when my prediction proved wrong. South Africa did win the game, but by a blowout score of 33 to 8.) It was an auspicious beginning. And so, once the applause died down, I went on.

I started by talking about globalization. Global markets present both opportunities and threats. They create opportunities for both suppliers, who benefit from access to global buyers, and consumers, who can choose from an astonishing selection of world wines. But globalization is also a threat because the global markets are highly competitive and the pressures to cut cost (and quality) or sacrifice diversity and integrity for market access can sometimes be quite strong. Consumers can find themselves overwhelmed by globalization and lack the confidence they need to choose among the hundreds or even thousands of options available. Sometimes it's a miracle that they buy any wine at all. A strong brand can help consumers by simplifying the choice. They don't have to know all about appellations, grape varieties, and vintages. They just have to find a brand they like and trust.

Brands are powerful weapons in the confidence game that is the US wine market today, I noted, but there's a problem that I call Einstein's Law. Albert Einstein said that everything should be as simple as possible—but no simpler. By this he meant that, while simplicity is useful, there comes a point where simplifying becomes oversimplifying and essential qualities are lost. Brands simplify in order to sell, but they can go too far. When wine becomes a choice between Bud Red and Bud White and the diversity and distinctiveness of wine is lost, we will have crossed the line.

What is to prevent this? Well, in *Wine Wars* I argue that "the Revenge of the Terroirists" will save the day. Terroirists worship (or at least honor) the idea of terroir—a sense of "somewhereness" (to use a term coined by Matt Kramer) that is so important to us in today's everywhere, anywhere, nowhere world. Wine, better than almost anything else, connects us to a particular time and place and is thus a fitting focus of terroirist zeal. Globalization has created the battlefield; the Wine Wars pit the forces that seek to oversimplify wine against the terroirists who strive to preserve its soul.

WINNING THE WINE WARS

Can South Africa win its wine war in the United States market? Yes, I told the audience, but it won't be easy. The US market is crowded, intensely competitive, and structurally difficult to penetrate. It will take "boots on the ground," sustained commitment, well-conceived strategy, opportunistic tactics, and a little bit of luck. If that sounds like the description of a military battle plan, you are starting to understand.

South Africa has long experience in dealing with globalization's two faces. I think that South Africa may understand globalization better than we do in the United States, I told the audience, because you have been through the shock of reentering hot global waters after long years of isolation, while we Americans have been swimming along as the waters have slowly heated up. And then there is the Revenge of the Terroirists. South African winemakers are terroirists—how could they not be with such wonderful terroir all around them—and, although most consumers in the United States don't yet understand the complexity of South Africa's terroir, the fact of the diverse Cape wine terroir is terribly useful.

So this brings us to brands and reputation. What does Brand South Africa look like in the United States? I asked. My industry informants tell me that when winery or distributor representatives are present to provide samples and information, South African wines fly out the door, but they need that personal connection. The key, one successful distributor of South African wines told me, is for the wines to stand on their own—sparkling against sparkling, Cabernet against Cabernet, and so on. Then their quality and value carry the day. Emphasize the "made in South Africa" element, he told me, and interest wanes. Why?

Well, part of it is the "peculiar Pinotage" effect. If your first taste of South African wine was back in the bad old days, then you might not risk a second sip. A friend of mine compares trying a new wine to going on a first date. You only get one first date, she said. And although we would like Brand South Africa to be defined by the great diversity of its wine, the fact is that the space currently available for South African wines on highly competitive US retail shelves and restaurant lists is very limited. South Africa has two feet to tell its story, a national wine distributor executive told me. And the story that is often told is defined not so much by the wines as by their labels. I told the audience that when I went to the local wine shop with the most comprehensive South African selection, I found that fifteen of the sixteen wines on offer were "critter wines"—wines with creatures on the label.

The paradox of critter wines is that while they can be hugely successful for the individual wineries that deploy them (think Yellow Tail in the US market), they can potentially undermine a region's reputation if they are so numerous and prominent that they become the de facto collective brand. So Brand South Africa could use an upgrade in the US if it wants to expand beyond the self-limiting critter category

So how *will* South Africa win the wine war for the US market? Well, the good news, given what I have said, is that Brand South Africa is actually something of a clean slate for many US wine consumers—especially the rising millennial generation, who are open to new wines from new places and show no particular reverence for conventional wisdom. They are refreshingly original in their thinking, bold in their actions, and willing to open their pocketbooks. These new wine drinkers and others like them around the world are high-value targets. How should they be approached?

Millennials are very independent. They are accustomed to writing their own narratives, and they embrace products and experiences that integrate into a lifestyle experience. They aren't just buying wine, they are building an identity. Millennials are not fundamentally different from earlier generations in this regard, simply more skilled, self-empowered, and interconnected. Reaching them, which requires more emphasis on storytelling, social media, and first-person wine experiences, is ultimately the task of South African wineries and their US distributor partners; there is also a role for Wines of South Africa in shaping perceptions.

I think that millennials and other "clean-slate" consumers are predisposed to respond to the Terroirists' Revenge message. They are seeking wine and a story about wine that connects them to the wine, to an engaging culture, to a rich and exciting lifestyle, and ultimately to each other. It's about the wine, but it's not *just* about the wine. South Africa's terroirists have a secret weapon in their beautiful land and inviting culture that gives them a critical Wine War storytelling advantage.

AN EXTREME SOLUTION

How can South Africa connect with the millennials? I asked the audience. "Well, don't look to me for answers," I said. "I've only been in South Africa for a week. You will have come up with the answers. Only you will know what there is in South African culture and society that will make the connection." I think this statement came as a surprise to the audience, who are probably used to outsiders telling them what to do. But I am sure I am right. I felt I had to make a contribution, so I took a chance. My first full day on South African soil was Monday, September 24, 2012—National Heritage Day, which is also National Braai Day. I had my first braai at a lunch at the beautiful Durbanville Hills winery. It reminded me of the barbecues we have back home, with delicious meats, salads, and wine. I particularly enjoyed the sausages.

The braai is a cherished South African institution—an opportunity for friends and family to gather and share food, wine, and fellowship. What could be better? Braai is so important in South African culture that it has a language of its own. *The* braai (noun) is the grill itself, usually but not always set up over a wood fire (braai masters endlessly debate the proper fire choice). The braai is also the act of communal gathering that the grill creates. *To* braai (verb) is the act of cooking on the grill. *Braai* may also be used as an adjective to describe the elements of the feast, as in braai meats or braai salads.

There are different braai traditions in different parts of the country—fish braai near the coast; lamb braai in the Karoo region; beef, pork, sausage, fowl, and veggies nearly everywhere; and even a type of braai that celebrates the Cape Malay cuisine. South Africa is an incredibly diverse country, and if there's one thing that unites all its peoples (besides sports), it is probably the braai. Water keeps people apart, I told the audience, but wine brings us together (repeating one of my favorite lines). And the braai seems to bring South Africans together, too. And so I proposed braai as South Africa's secret weapon.

Almost no one in the US knows what a braai is, but we all love the barbecue experience, and this is a good starting point. Any country that makes the braai its national food culture speaks to us in a language we can understand. But the braai, I have learned, is not merely a food, and this is its magic. It is an expression of generosity and hospitality. If you ask someone to share your braai, you are opening your heart and your hearth to them, whether you are preparing a gourmet meal or more humble fare. If South African wines are seen as an extension of that warmth and engagement, they might well strike a sympathetic chord among American wine enthusiasts. And happily there are many different cultures of the braai in South Africa—there are diverse braai terroirs, if you know what I mean—and each has its own story and each lends itself to a different kind and style of South African wine. Americans will love the unique experience of an Afrocentric winelands braai once they get to know it, and this can be the gateway to a fuller appreciation of South African culture and lifestyle and to the diverse wines that have evolved along with them.

"If you invite Americans to join with you and to celebrate your people, land and culture—to make every day National Braai Day," I said, "they will toast your success with your own wonderful wine. And that's how South Africa can win the Wine Wars. Thank you."

EXTREME WINE ADVENTURE

Wine Enthusiast reported that the crowd actually cheered when I finished (or perhaps they just cheered that I *finally did* finish!).[5] One local columnist said that I gave the assembled guests food for thought (unlike, he noted, most South African politicians). "Words drive the world. I heard a Formula One word driver last Saturday and I couldn't help comparing him to our own dilapidated jalopy jockeys."[6] Ouch!

So the reaction to my talk was extreme, like just about everything else in my South African adventure. South Africa encompasses many of the extremes that I've talked about in these pages and a few that I would never have thought of. It is probably only possible in South Africa to score a double "big five" in one day—to see the animal "big five"—lion, leopard, elephant, buffalo, and rhinoceros—and also taste wines made from the "big five" Bordeaux grape varieties—Cabernet Sauvignon, Merlot, Cabernet Franc, Petit Verdot, and Malbec.[7]

I can't connect South Africa to *all* the extreme wine types that I've examined here, but there are enough extreme elements to make it a fitting way to draw the book to a close. South Africa represents a geographical extreme, of course, and as we've seen it is at once extremely old and very new. It certainly has its share of extreme wine people and even a certain amount of celebrity wine (I spent an afternoon tasting local wines at professional golfer Ernie Els's beautiful winery in Stellenbosch). South African wine is both famous and forgotten, and the wine industry there has been through its own unique booms and busts. It is even in the running for the best (perhaps the Edelkeur), worst (the dreaded Pinotage of years past), and most unique (the Jouberts' two-hundred-year-old wine). I could keep going, citing one extreme after another, but I don't want to weaken my argument by stretching it too far. I don't think anyone will disagree with me if I say that South African wine is pretty extreme.

And where do we end up after exploring all these extremes? Well, if we take my address to the Nederburg Auction and generalize it a bit, we find that all the extremes lead us back to the heart of wine, to the giving and sharing that make wine a particularly important part of our lives. The extremes take wines in many directions, but I can't see that they truly change its essence. Wine is prone to boom and bust, to best and worst, to fame, infamy, and celebrity. Wine is driven by money, tainted by it, and rewarded with it. Wine has changed with the times, as it probably must to remain relevant, but its timeless value remains.

Or at least that's what I think if wine in the end brings us back together again, touching glasses and sharing emotions over something as simple but important as a smoky barbecue grill.

I guess wine really *is* like sports. The X Games are driven by money and fame, but at heart sports remain as they always were, physical and mental tests that engage, excite, and inspire. Wine stays the same, too, even as it changes. I think we should join the South Africans and fire up the braai, share some wine, and tell each other a few extreme wine stories. Cheers!

Acknowledgments

I didn't really go to the ends of the earth of gather information for *Extreme Wine*, but I came pretty close, and I want to acknowledge the all the help I received along the way.

Thanks to these wine industry professionals who made time to help me understand what they do and why: Annette Alvarez-Peters (Costco), Kym Anderson (University of Adelaide), Andrés Arena (Bodegas Salentein), Kevin Arnold (Waterford Estate), Ken Avedisian (Cordon Selections), Simon Back (Backsberg Estate), Annette Badenhorst (Wines of South Africa), Peter Baumgartner (Cantina Produttori Valle Isarco), Guillermo Banfi (Sur de los Andes), Aldo Biondolillo (Tempus Alba), Giuseppe Bologna (Braida), Stewart Boedecker and Athena Pappas (Boedecker Cellars), Jean-Charles Boisset (Boisset Family Estates), Laura Catena (Bodega Catena Zapata), Lorena Cepparo (Bodegas Salentein), Scott Chambers (Linfield College), Dr. Paul Cluver and his son Paul Cluver (Paul Cluver Wines), Philip Coates and Katrina Lange (21 Cellars), Katherine Cole (*The Oregonian*), Tyler Colman (Dr. Vino), Michael and Lauri Corliss (Corliss Estates), Rich Cushman (Viento Wines), Emil Den Dulk (De Toren Private Wine Cellar), Nat DiBuduo (Allied Grape Growers), Patrick Egan (Boisset Family Estates), Patrick Emmons (Metropolitan Market), Kirk Ermisch (Southern Wine Group), Ken Forrester (Ken Forrester Vineyards), Kelley Fox (Scott Paul Wines), Steve Fredricks (Turrentine Wine Brokerage), Jon Fredrikson

(Gomberg-Fredrikson), José Antonio Galante (Bodegas Salentein), Albert Gerber (Durbanville Hills), Rebecca Gibb (Wine-Searcher), Lesley Gikas (Nederburg Auction), Jamie Goode (Wine Anorak), Paul Gregutt (*Wine Enthusiast*), Tom Hedges (Hedges Family Estate), Steve Heimoff (*Wine Enthusiast*), Richard Hemmings (JancisRobinson.com), Charlie Hoppes (Fidelitas Wines), Dave Jefferson (Silkbush Winery), Cobus Joubert (Maison Joubert), Charles Karren (Terra de Promissio), Alois Lageder (Alois Lageder Winery), Jason Lett (The Eyrie Winery), Benjamin Lewin MW (author), Jim Lapsley (University of California–Davis), Bryan Maletis (Fat Cork), Adam Mason (Mulderbosch Wines), Tom Matthews (*Wine Spectator*), Daniel McKeown (Winebow), Mark Merrill (Pour at Four), Moe and Flora Momtazi (Maysara Winery), Martin Moore (Durbanville Hills), Amy Mumma (Central Washington University), Neil Pendock (*Pendock Uncorked*), Sky Pinnick (Rage Productions), Ksandek Podbielski (Anne Amie), Stephen Rannekleiv (Rabobank), Mike Ratcliffe (Vilafonte), Norma Ratcliffe (Warwick Estate), Chuck Reininger (Reininger Winery), Jancis Robinson (JancisRobinson.com), Andrés Rosberg (Association of Argentinean Sommeliers), David Rosenthal (Château Ste. Michelle), Hans Schattle (Yonsei University), Anabelle Sielecki (Mendel Wines), Jeremy Soine (Gallo), Dalene Steyn (Nederburg Auction), Karl Storchmann (American Association of Wine Economists), Sean Sullivan (*Washington Wine Report* and *Wine Enthusiast*), Liz Thach MW (Sonoma State University), George Taber (author), Allison Tonkin and Andras Nemeth (Alana-Tokaj), Nick Vink (Stellenbosch University), Mike and Karen Wade (Fielding Hills Winery), Nadine Weihgold (Braida), Amy Wesselman (International Pinot Noir Celebration), John Williams (Frog's Leap Winery), Scott Paul Wright (Scott Paul Wines), and Ron Zimmerman (The Herbfarm).

Special thanks to my crack team of "research assistants" (a.k.a. friends and colleagues who keep me supplied with breaking news, crazy ideas, and thoughtful observations):

Marina Balleria, Ken Bernsohn, Scott Hogman and Janice Brevik, Kevin Chambers, Ben Cohn, Lowell and Dorothy Daun, Valerio Franchi, Barry and Joyce Gehl, Ky Lewis, Pierre Ly and Cynthia Howson, Bonnie Main and Richard Pichler, George Matelich, Michael and Nancy Morrell, Jeni Oppenheimer, Allan Sapp, Holden Sapp, David and Anne Seago, Mary and Ron Thomas, Kristi Veseth, Kylor Williams, and Ken and Rosemary Willman.

This book did not make itself. I appreciate the expertise and support of the professionals at Rowman & Littlefield who have made it possible: editorial director Susan McEachern, production editor Jehanne Schweitzer, copyeditor Elizabeth Lund, cover designer Devin Watson, and proofreader Susan Barnett.

And finally the biggest thanks of all (and hugs and kisses, too) to my number-one research assistant, Sue Veseth.

Notes

1. X-WINES: *IN VINO VERITAS*?

1. My guide here is wine taster extraordinaire Michael Broadbent's book *Wine Tasting*, rev. ed. (New York: Simon and Schuster, 1990). There is more to the "sideways" analysis of wine than just an intense rim. Broadbent or any good wine guide will explain the factors to look for in different types of wines.

2. Jancis Robinson, ed., *The Oxford Companion to Wine*, 3rd ed. (Oxford: Oxford University Press, 2006). You can find the list on page 808.

3. John Schreiner, *The Wines of Canada* (London, UK: Mitchell Beazley, 2005).

4. See Jack Williams, "Standard Atmosphere Tables," *USAToday.com* http://www.usatoday.com/weather/wstdatmo.htm, accessed May 13, 2011.

5. See the "High Altitude Vineyards" discussion on the Bodega Colomé website, http://www.bodegacolome.com/bodega/vinedos-de-altura.php?lang=en, accessed December 1, 2012.

6. For a fuller description see Jacques Fanet, *Great Wine Terroirs*, trans. from the French by Florence Brutton (Berkeley: University of California Press, 2004), 226–27.

7. Matt Kramer, who now writes a column for *Wine Spectator*, is credited with characterizing terroir as "somewhereness."

8. Mike Veseth, *Wine Wars: The Curse of the Blue Nun, the Miracle of Two Buck Chuck, and the Revenge of the Terroirists* (Lanham, MD: Rowman & Littlefield, 2011).

9. Pam Belluck, "Cave Drops Hints to Earliest Glass of Red," *New York Times*, January 11, 2011, http://www.nytimes.com/2011/01/11/science/11wine.html?_r=1&scp=1&sq=oldest%20wine&st=cse, accessed April 21, 2011.

2. THE BEST AND THE WORST

1. James T. Lapsley, *Bottled Poetry: Napa Winemaking from Prohibition to the Modern Era* (Berkeley: University of California Press, 1996).

2. Benjamin Lewin, *Wine Myths and Reality* (Dover: Vendage Press, 2010).

3. Jamie Goode and Sam Harrop, *Authentic Wine: Toward Natural and Sustainable Winemaking* (Berkeley: University of California Press, 2011).

4. Goode and Harrop, *Authentic Wine*, 112.

5. Hugh Johnson, "The Wines of California," in *History in a Glass: Sixty Years of Wine Writing from* Gourmet, ed. Ruth Reichl (New York: Modern Library, 2006), 155–61.

6. See "Recommended Wines," http://www.wine-searcher.com/recommendations .lml, accessed May 9, 2011. The data at the time I checked the website were current roughly the 2010 review calendar.

7. Review found on the eRobertParker.com website, http://www.erobertparker.com /newSearch/th.aspx?th=106845&id=1, accessed May 9, 2011.

8. CellarTracker uses a "freemium" business model. Basic use is free, but certain premium functions such as cellar valuation come with the expectation (but not requirement) of a voluntary contribution.

9. See Goode and Harrop, *Authentic Wine*, for an excellent analysis and critique of the natural wine movement.

3. THE FAME GAME

1. Benjamin Lewin, *Wine Myths and Realities* (Dover: Vendage Press, 2010).

2. Lewin, *Wine Myths*, 512.

3. Robert H. Frank, *Luxury Fever: Why Money Fails to Satisfy in an Era of Excess* (New York: Free Press, 1999).

4. The Exposition Universelle was popular, too, with more than five million visitors, but was not a financial success. Apparently receipts covered only a tenth of the costs.

5. My favorite reference is Benjamin Lewin, *What Price Bordeaux* (Dover: Vendage Press, 2009.

6. Jamie Goode and Sam Harrop, *Authentic Wine: Toward Natural and Sustainable Winemaking* (Berkeley: University of California Press, 2011). This section of the chapter draws directly from this work.

7. See Goode and Harrop, 130.

8. Eric Asimov, "Vintner with Nothing to Hide Finds That Few Are Looking," *New York Times*, October 4, 2012, http://www.nytimes.com/2012/10/10/dining/bonny-doon-vineyards-labeling-policy-draws-little-attention.html?pagewanted=all&_r=0, accessed October 31, 2012.

9. Lewin, *Wine Myths and Realities*, 248–51.

10. The book is Benjamin Wallace, *The Billionaire's Vinegar: The Mystery of the World's Most Expensive Bottle* (New York: Crown, 2008). The film, still in the rumor stage when I wrote this, is said to star Brad Pitt.

11. Jancis Robinson, Julia Harding, and Jose Vouillamoz, *Wine Grapes: A Complete Guide to 1,368 Vine Varieties, Including their Origins and Flavours* (New York: Ecco, 2012).

4. THE INVISIBLE WINE

1. I've written quite a bit about globalization and McDonald's, and I actually think that we overstate the ubiquity and importance of the Big Mac. See chapter 4, "Golden Arches Globaloney," in my book *Globaloney 2.0* (Lanham, MD: Rowman & Littlefield, 2010).

2. See JancisRobinson.com.

3. Jancis Robinson, *Jancis Robinson's Guide to Wine Grapes* (New York: Oxford University Press, 1996).

4. Burton Anderson, *The Wine Atlas of Italy* (New York: Simon and Schuster, 1990).

5. MONEY WINE

1. This is not the same supermarket that I wrote about in *Wine Wars*.

2. Jancis Robinson, "Bordeaux 2009s: There's a Price to Pay," *Financial Times*, June 3, 2010, http://www.ft.com/intl/cms/s/2/a2db3f3a-8560-11df-aa2e-00144feabdc0 .html#axzz1xVsxP5sR, accessed June 11, 2012.

3. Lettie Teague, "Why I Hate Ordering Wine by the Glass," *Wall Street Journal*, September 10, 2010, http://online.wsj.com/article/SB10001424052748703466704575 489752958839806.html, accessed September 10, 2010.

4. Nicholas Lander, "Collector's Items," *Financial Times*, September 17, 2010, http://www.ft.com/intl/cms/s/2/14e8bb96-c1ea-11df-9d90-00144feab49a .html#axzz1xVsxP5sR, accessed June 12, 2012.

5. Dorothy J. Gaiter and John Brecher, "10 Ways to Save Money Ordering Wine at Restaurants," *Wall Street Journal*, March 7, 2009, http://online.wsj.com/article /SB123638925101858707.html?mod=djemtastings, accessed June 12, 2012.

6. Description taken from the Cameron Hughes website, http://store.chwine.com /lot-247-2009-napa-valley-cabernet-sauvignon-p627.aspx, accessed December 4, 2012.

7. *Shanken Daily News*, "Bordeaux Pricing Has U.S. Retailers Reassessing the Business," April 29, 2011, http://www.shankennewsdaily.com/index .php/2011/04/29/246/bordeaux-pricing-has-us-retailers-reassessing-the-business/, accessed June 11, 2012.

6. EXTREME WINE BOOMS AND BUSTS

1. Winemakers' Federation of Australia, *Directions 2025* (1996), http://www .winebiz.com.au/statistics/strategy2025/2025_1.asp, accessed May 23, 2012.

2. Winemakers' Federation of Australia, *Wine Restructuring Action Agenda* (November 10, 2009), http://www.wfa.org.au/WRAA.aspx, accessed May 23, 2012.

3. Kym Anderson, ed., *The World's Wine Markets: Globalization at Work* (Northampton, MA: Edward Elgar, 2004). See chapter 10, "Australia."

4. Kym Anderson and Robert Osmond, "How Long Will Australia's Wine Boom Last? Lessons From History," University of Adelaide Centre for International Economic Studies Wine Policy Brief 1, August 1998.

5. Figures are for 2007–2009. See table 1 in *Global Wine Markets 1961–2009: A Statistical Compendium*, edited by Kym Anderson and Signe Nelgen (University of Adelaide Press, 2011).

6. Everyone except the French, apparently, who don't seem to appreciate wine's place in French culture to the extent that foreigners do, according to recent surveys, which is probably both cause and effect of the plunging per capita wine consumption there.

7. See Thomas Pellechia, *Wine: The 8000-Year-Old Story of the Wine Trade* (New York: Thunder's Mouth Press, 2006), 56–57.

8. Robb Graham, *The Discovery of France: A Historical Geography from the Revolution to the First World War* (New York: W. W. Norton, 2007).

9. Jancis Robinson, ed., *The Oxford Companion to Wine*, 3rd ed. (New York: Oxford University Press, 2006).

10. James T. Lapsley, *Bottled Poetry: Napa Winemaking from Prohibition to the Modern Era* (Berkeley: University of California Press, 1996).

11. Lapsley, *Bottled Poetry*, 43.

12. Pinnick, Sky, *Boom Varietal: The Rise of Malbec* (Bend, OR: Rage Productions, 2011). DVD.

7. EXTREME WINE PEOPLE

1. I recommend Theise's book, *Reading between the Wines* (Berkeley: University of California Press, 2010).

2. Neal Rosenthal has also written a book about his experiences, *Reflections of a Wine Merchant* (New York: Farrar, Straus and Giroux, 2008).

3. Kermit Lynch has written two books. The first and more famous is *Adventures on the Wine Route* (New York: North Point Press, 1988). The second, a cult classic, collects notes from the newsletter. It is called *Inspiring Thirst* (Berkeley, CA: Ten Speed Press, 2004).

4. Katherine Cole, *Voodoo Vintners: Oregon's Astonishing Biodynamic Winegrowers* (Corvallis: Oregon University Press, 2011).

5. Laura Catena, *Vino Argentino: An Insider's Guide to the Wines and Wine Country of Argentina* (San Francisco: Chronicle Books, 2010).

6. Ian Mount, *The Vineyard at the End of the World* (New York: Norton, 2011).

7. Joseph Bastianich, *Grandi Vini: An Opinionated Tour of Italy's 89 Finest Wines* (New York: Clarkson Potter, 2010).

8. Matt Kramer, *Matt Kramer's Making Sense of Italian Wines* (Philadelphia: Running Press, 2006).

8. CELEBRITY WINE

1. I wrote about the changing world of Chinese wine in *Wine Wars*—see chapter 15, "The China Syndrome." Although I focus on the Chinese fascination with Bordeaux here, I understand that there is also a rising interest in Burgundy wines, probably for the reason that they are even rarer and perhaps soon for that reason will be more expensive.

2. This is the China price and includes a 27 percent import duty and a 17 percent sales tax. For a good report on the business elements of Yao's wine, see Jason Chow, "Yao Ming Courts China's Wine Boom," *Wall Street Journal*, November 28, 2011, http://online.wsj.com/article/SB10001424052970203764804577059394247295010 .html, accessed June 13, 2012. A press release I received in November 2012 indicated that some of the wine was being offered for sale in the US market at $175 for the standard wine and $625 for the reserve Cabernet.

3. Visit the Yao Family Wines website to learn more: http://www.yaofamilywines .com/our-story/, accessed June 14, 2012.

4. Here is a link to the Wikipedia "Celebrity Wine" page: http://en.wikipedia.org/ wiki/List_of_celebrities_who_own_wineries_and_vineyards, accessed June 14, 2012.

5. The article appeared in the November 10, 2008, issue of *People*.

6. "Nielsen: "Consumers Attracted to 'Glitz' of Celebrity Wines," press release, http://www.nielsen.com/us/en/insights/press-room/2008/nielsen__consumers.html, accessed June 14, 2012.

7. The Nielsen report was found at http://www.nielsen.com/us/en/insights/press room/2008/nielsen__consumers.html, accessed November 6, 2012.

8. By the way, the Silverado Winery in Stags Leap, Napa Valley, is owned by the Disney family—it's another of my celebrity wineries.

9. For the French original go to http://fr.wikipedia.org/wiki/Grenouille_d'hiver, accessed June 16, 2012.

10. A good summary of the Moscato phenomenon is Robert Haynes-Peterson, "Moscato Mosaic: Moscato Sales Have Skyrocketed Thanks to a Whole New Group of Wine Fans," Beverage Media Group, February 24, 2012, http://www.beveragemedia.com/index.php/2012/02/moscato-mosaic-moscato-sales-have-skyrocketed-thanks-to-a-whole-new-group-of-wine-fans/, accessed June 18, 2012.

11. The section on Jay-Z and Cristal Champagne is based on Ben Cohn's unpublished paper "Poppin' Bottles: Rap's Unwanted Relationship with Champagne," May 9, 2012. Ben was my student at the University of Puget Sound, and this paper was written for my Idea of Wine class.

9. EXTREME WINE AT THE MOVIES

1. My personal experience in wine films is unsurprisingly limited. As you already know if you read the chapter "Extreme Wine Booms and Busts," I appeared in a 2011 documentary called *Boom Varietal: The Rise of Argentine Malbec* by Sky Pinnick. You might have seen it if you frequent indie film festivals, where it has made the rounds and even won a few prizes. I have my fingers crossed that one of the food or travel cable channels will decide to show it one day, but it's impossible to be confident because only a few wine films have crossed over to the general-audience market.

2. Alexander Payne and Jim Taylor, *Sideways* screenplay, 2003 (based on the novel by Rex Pickett) http://www.imsdb.com/scripts/Sideways.html, accessed July 5, 2012.

3. For basic information about *The Winemakers* series see http://www.createtv.com/CreateProgram.nsf/vProgramsByNola/WIMA#, accessed July 9, 2012.

4. "A Rocky Road for Ross Outon," *Bacchus and Beery Wine Blog*, August 13, 2012, http://wine-blog.bacchusandbeery.com/wine-blog/winemaker-interview/ross-outon-winner-pbs-winemakers-season-1/, accessed November 18, 2012.

5. Information about *A Brief History of Wine* can be found at http://shop.history.com/a-brief-history-of-wine-dvd/detail.php?p=68244, accessed July 9, 2012.

6. For details about this television series, see http://www.imdb.com/title/tt0466506/, accessed July 9, 2012.

7. Read about Jancis Robinson's television series at http://www.jancisrobinson.com/articles/bookdvd.html, accessed July 9, 2012.

8. The Oz and James television franchise has its own Wikipedia page, http://en.wikipedia.org/wiki/Oz_and_James's_Big_Wine_Adventure, accessed July 9, 2012.

9. For details visit the Internet Movie Database page for this series. See http://www
.imdb.com/title/tt1360424/, accessed July 9, 2012.

10. For more information about this Korean television soap opera see http://www
.hancinema.net/korean_drama_Terroir.php, accessed July 9, 2012.

11. Thanks to Hans Schattle for helping with details about the wine.

12. You can still view past episodes of Gary V's show on the *Wine Library TV*
website. See http://tv.winelibrary.com/.

13. Visit CellarTracker at http://www.cellartracker.com/intro.asp.

14. See the film's Internet Movie Database page at http://www.imdb.com/title
/tt0053355/, accessed July 9, 2012.

15. For the record, my favorite books in this genre are James T. Lapsley's *Bottled
Poetry* (University of California Press, 1996) and Thomas Pinney's *A History of Wine
in America* (University of California Press, 2005).

10. EXTREME WINE TOURISM

1. You can download the full report, "The Economic Impact of Napa County's
Wine and Grapes," http://www.napavintners.com/downloads/napa_economic_
impact_2012.pdf, accessed December 8, 2012.

2. Jancis Robinson, ed., *The Oxford Companion to Wine*, 3rd ed. (Oxford: Oxford
University Press, 2006), 705–6.

3. *The Oxford Companion to Wine* is my source for Pliny's preferences.

4. George M. Taber, *In Search of Bacchus: Wanderings in the Wonderful World of
Wine Tourism* (New York: Scribner, 2006).

5. The text is available at the Online Library of Liberty, http://oll.libertyfund.
org/?option=com_staticxt&staticfile=show.php%3Ftitle=1726&chapter=81683&layo
ut=html&Itemid=27, accessed August 4, 2012.

6. Here's Locke's list of wine-grape varieties if you want to see what was on offer
to wine tourists in the South of France more than three hundred years ago: Epiran,
Espiran verdau, Tarret, Barbarous, Grumeau negre, Grumeau blanc, Grumeau
blanc muscat, Laugeby, L'ougré, Raisin de St, Jean, Marroquin, Marroquin gris,
Marroquin bleu, Clarette, Clarette rouge, Ovilla de negre, Ovilla de blanc, Covilla de
Gal, Ramounen, Unio negro, Unio blanquo, Corinth, Effouimu, Iragnou, Piquepoul,

Farret, Piquardan, Musquat negre, Musquat blanc, Musquat d'Espagne, Palofedo, Servan, Damas violet, Raison de la fon, Sadoulo boyyier, Sergousan, L'ambrusque, Rovergas, Coltort, Masquadassas, Crispata.

7. Beringer has changed hands several times since the 1971 sale, being acquired by a private equity group, then becoming part of the Foster's Group, and finally becoming a key element of Treasury Wine Estates, the wine group that emerged from Foster's division of its beer and wine assets. Beringer is said to be Napa Valley's oldest continuously operating winery, being one of the few to continue operation during Prohibition making sacramental wines.

8. Napa Wine Train information at http://winetrain.com/winery-tours, accessed November 12, 2012.

11. EXTREME WINE: THE NEXT GENERATION

1. Much of this chapter's analysis of wine in the BRIC and New BRIC nations is derived from articles I wrote on *The Wine Economist* for the tenth anniversary of the BRICs in 2011.

2. Production data in this chapter is from *Global Wine Markets 1961–2009: A Statistical Compendium*, unless otherwise noted.

3. "Comprehensive Study of the Indian Wine Market," JBC International, 2008. You can download a copy of the report at http://www.corecentre.co.in/Database /Docs/DocFiles/alcohal_study.pdf, accessed June 19, 2012.

4. Jancis Robinson, "Wine Arrives in India," *Financial Times*, November 17, 2012.

5. For information about trends in the Indian wine industry see Sarah Jacob, "India Wine Market to Touch 2.4 Million Cases by 2020," *India Times*, May 1, 2012, http:// articles.economictimes.indiatimes.com/2012-05-01/news/31528261_1_wine-market-indian-wine-wine-consumption, accessed November 14, 2012.

6. Li Zhengping, *Chinese Wine*, 3rd ed., trans. Shanghai Ego (Cambridge University Press, 2011).

7. Jennifer Hughes, "BRIC Creator Adds Newcomers to List," *Financial Times*, January 16, 2011, http://www.ft.com/intl/cms/s/0/f717c8e8-21be-11e0-9e3b-00144feab49a.html#axzz1jyLPwvN00, accessed June 20, 2012.

8. Special thanks to Hans Schattle for tracking down this wine for me.

12. EXTREME WINE ADVENTURE

1. You can calculate distances "as the crow flies" at tjpeiffer.com/crowflies.html.

2. Neal Martin tasting note for 2010 De Toren Book XVII, eRobert Parker.com 196, http://www.erobertparker.com/newSearch/th.aspx?th=186469&id=2&___ z=4OIeTJjV7Vh1nbaFG1JURg%3d%3d, accessed November 19, 2010.

3. Neal Martin tasting note for 1800 Jaubert Muscat d'Alexandrie, eRobertParker .com 196, August 2011, http://www.erobertparker.com/newSearch/ th.aspx?th=184903&id=2&___z=aC7Q%2bP2Es9wC6MGvHrLOaA%3d%3d, accessed November 19, 2012.

4. You can read the tasting note at http://www.cellartracker.com/wine .asp?iWine=277471, accessed November 19, 2012.

5. You can find the report at http://www.winemag.com/Wine-Enthusiast-Magazine /Web-2012/The-2012-Nederburg-Auction-Celebrates-its-38th-Year/, accessed November 19, 2012.

6. David Briggs, "SA Politicians Need Remedial Class in Public Speaking," *Cape Argus*, October 2, 2012, http://www.pressdisplay.com/pressdisplay/viewer.aspx?issue= 6256201210020000000001001&page=17&article=c6f6eb3c-7f79-4cdc-bd0a-1bce3a1 726a6&key=4FCikO8gcD4VcZe5FTG4Rg==&feed=rss, accessed November 19, 2012.

7. Carménère is also permitted in Bordeaux, making this technically a big six, but it is rarely used anymore. Carménère was not widely replanted in France after phylloxera.

Selected Bibliography

Anderson, Burton. *The Wine Atlas of Italy*. New York: Simon and Schuster, 1990.

Anderson, Kym, ed. *The World's Wine Markets: Globalization at Work*. Northampton, MA: Edward Elgar, 2004.

Anderson, Kym, and Signe Nelgen. *Global Wine Markets 1961–2009: A Statistical Compendium*. Adelaide: University of Adelaide Press, 2011.

Bastianich, Joseph. *Grandi Vini: An Opinionated Tour of Italy's 89 Finest Wines*. New York: Clarkson Potter, 2010.

Broadbent, Michael. *Wine Tasting*. Rev. ed. New York: Simon and Schuster, 1990.

Catena, Laura. *Vino Argentino: An Insider's Guide to the Wines and Wine Country of Argentina*. San Francisco: Chronicle Books, 2010.

Cole, Katherine. *Voodoo Vintners: Oregon's Astonishing Biodynamic Winegrowers*. Corvallis: Oregon University Press, 2011.

Frank, Robert H. *Luxury Fever: Why Money Fails to Satisfy in an Era of Excess*. New York: Free Press, 1999.

Gale, George. *Dying on the Vine: How Phylloxera Transformed Wine*. Berkeley: University of California Press, 2011.

Goode, Jamie, and Sam Harrop. *Authentic Wine: Toward Natural and Sustainable Winemaking*. Berkeley: University of California Press, 2011.

Kramer, Matt. *Matt Kramer's Making Sense of Italian Wines*. Philadelphia: Running Press, 2006.

Lapsley, James T. *Bottled Poetry: Napa Winemaking from Prohibition to the Modern Era*. Berkeley, CA: University of California Press, 1996.

Lewin, Benjamin. *What Price Bordeaux*. Dover, DE: Vendage Press, 2009.

———. *Wine Myths and Reality*. Dover, DE: Vendage Press, 2010.

Li Zhengping. *Chinese Wine*. 3rd ed. Translated by Shanghai Ego. Cambridge University Press, 2011.

Lynch, Kermit. *Adventures on the Wine Route*. New York: North Point Press, 1988.

Mount, Ian. *The Vineyard at the End of the World*. New York: Norton, 2011.

Nossiter, Jonathan. *Liquid Memory: Why Wine Matters*. New York: FSG, 2009.

Pellechia, Thomas. *Wine: The 8000-Year-Old Story of the Wine Trade*. New York: Thunder's Mouth Press, 2006

Pinney, Thomas. *A History of Wine in America*. Berkeley: University of California Press, 2005.

Robinson, Jancis, ed. *The Oxford Companion to Wine*. 3rd ed. Oxford: Oxford University Press, 2006.

Robinson, Jancis, Julia Harding, and Jose Vouillamoz. *Wine Grapes: A Complete Guide to 1,368 Vine Varieties, Including Their Origins and Flavours*. New York: Ecco, 2012.

Rosenthal, Neal. *Reflections of a Wine Merchant*. New York: Farrar, Straus and Giroux, 2008.

Schreiner, John. *The Wines of Canada*. London: Mitchell Beazley, 2005.

Simpson, James. *Creating Wine: The Emergence of a World Industry, 1840–1914*. Princeton, NJ: Princeton University Press, 2011.

Smith, Adam. *The Wealth of Nations*. New York: Modern Library, 1937. First published 1776.

Taber, George M. *Judgment of Paris: California vs. France and the Historic 1976 Paris Tasting that Revolutionized Wine*. New York: Scribner, 2005.

———. *In Search of Bacchus: Wanderings in the Wonderful World of Wine Tourism.* New York: Scribner, 2006.

Theise, Terry. *Reading between the Wines.* Berkeley: University of California Press, 2010.

Veseth, Mike. *The Wine Economist.* WineEconomist.com.

———. *Wine Wars: The Curse of the Blue Nun, the Miracle of Two Buck Chuck, and the Revenge of the Terroirists.* Lanham, MD: Rowman & Littlefield, 2011.

Wallace, Benjamin. *The Billionaire's Vinegar: The Mystery of the World's Most Expensive Bottle.* New York: Crown, 2008.

Index

About the Author

Mike Veseth is an economist who studies global wine markets. He is editor of the blog *The Wine Economist* and author of a dozen books, including *Wine Wars: The Curse of the Blue Nun, the Miracle of Two Buck Chuck, and the Revenge of the Terroirists* (Rowman & Littlefield, 2011), which was named a 2011 Wine Book of the Year by JancisRobinson.com. Mike is emeritus professor of international political economy at the University of Puget Sound in Tacoma, Washington. He's currently working on his next book, *Around the World in 80 Wines.*